THE
RIFLEMAN'S
BIBLE

THE RIFLEMAN'S BIBLE

Sam Fadala

Doubleday
New York
1987

Photographs by Nancy and Sam Fadala unless otherwise credited.

Library of Congress Cataloging-in-Publication Data
Fadala, Sam, 1939–
   The rifleman's bible.

   1. Rifles.   I. Title.
TS536.4.F296   1987   683.4′22   87-431
ISBN 0-385-23747-2

For Nick

Contents

Preface

CAMP was a board shack set against a purple rim-rock bluff, rich grass carpet all around, and oak trees standing as silent sentinels everywhere. A tiny stream poured like liquid crystal through the smooth boulders, drinking supply for the occupants of the cabin who mined the Sonoran backcountry, probing the earth for precious metals. The miners were also riflemen. A youthful shooter, I was privileged to admire from a ringside seat their unerring accuracy. Images of their marksmanship may be overly polished from rubbing in the pockets of my mind all these years, but I see in the cinema of memory those tin cans doing a rumba over the landscape, jumping crazily at the crack of each rifle. The men fired their 94 carbines with natural fluidness of motion, instinct, second nature, and honed reflexes, but the excellent handling was also backed by serious practice.

A rifle in their hands was a precision instrument. A rifle in the hands of many modern shooters is the same. Much of our national character has been shaped by riflemen, a character of self-reliance and confidence. This book is for and about riflemen. It is a practical guide, a reference for hands-on enhancement of shooting expertise. Most useful and romantic of all shooting instruments, the rifle is covered from precision 17-caliber air gun through 458 elephant-stopper, to the 22 rimfire, 22 centerfire, the mediums of 30-30 deer rifle fame, to the high-intensity, long-range wonders of energy and accuracy, and even the supremely interesting muzzle-loaders—which opened the country and faded into obscurity, only to be brought back again by today's rifleman.

The book travels along the paths of greatest interest to rifle shooters, picking the right rifle for the task at hand, the correct ammo, boosting individual marksmanship and rifle handling, understanding ballistics and trajectory, proper sights, sight picture and sight-in, creating professionally perfect handloads, target shooting and practice, maintenance, safety, accessories, hunting skills, and more.

THE
RIFLEMAN'S
BIBLE

1

The Sporting Rifle in America

THE KENTUCKY/PENNSYLVANIA LONG RIFLE is father of the modern sporting rifle, as well as a symbol of the American shooting tradition. Known simply as the Kentucky rifle to most shooters, she was born in Pennsylvania but conceived in Europe. Mark this—for a time, the Kentucky rifle was gauged as the finest firearm in the world. And it is labeled the first truly American rifle. The exact chronology of firearm invention has been lost to antiquity, with bits and pieces of knowledge floating on a vast sea of ignorance. Many of these bits and pieces have been retrieved by firearms historians who have fitted the chunks together to reveal at least a fair overall picture.

There are almost as many theories as experts, but most agree that the first truly accurate "rifles" were created in that section of Europe occupied by Germany and her neighbors. The smoothbore was a decent firearm for various uses. It loaded quickly and was cleaned more easily than later rifles with deep grooves, which caught and held the soot of black-powder residue. The smoothbore was all

right for up-close shooting. But when inventors applied those "squirrely-gigs" to the bore, the rifle was born. Rifling, grooves cut into the metal interior of the barrel, with raised lands resulting, may not have been designed to give spin to the projectile.

There is strong evidence that the first rifling was straight-cut, that it paralleled the barrel. Some feel that this application helped to reduce friction in the bore, even made cleanup of black-powder fouling easier. Gunpowder was for a very long time no more than a mechanical mixture of saltpeter, charcoal, and sulfur, and as much as 50 to 60 percent of this mixture failed to change from solid to gas at combustion. The remaining solids, mostly salts of one kind or another, clung to the bore as fouling. I doubt that straight-cut rifling did much to aid the cleanup of the bore, but proof is lacking.

Somebody, no one knows who for sure, got the idea of spiraling the rifling in the bore to impart a spin to the projectile. The spin would keep the bullet rotating on its axis instead of tumbling along,

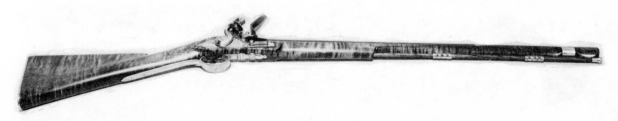

The early American rifle was usually a smoothbore similar to this replica of a 60-caliber trade rifle.

thereby giving it much greater precision to the target. The rifle was on its way to long-range accuracy with the advent of bullet spin and stabilization. But you still had to get the powder ignited in some way. At first, the shooter simply pulled a device which brought a slow-burning fuse in contact with the main charge of powder in the breech, something like touching a match to an old-fashioned cannon. In fact, the lock was called a matchlock.

A more complicated but very reliable device followed. It was a wheel lock and it created a shower of sparks that set off the powder charge. You wound this lock up like a little clock, and when the trigger was pulled, the whirling wheel created the sparks. A *snaphance* was another of the lock styles of days gone by. An old story suggests that snaphance translated to "hen snatchers" and that Dutch chicken thieves used the rifle. It was a pretty good lock, cheaper to produce than the wheel lock, and so the burning fuse was displaced. That snaphance had anything to do with chickens or chicken snatchers is doubtful. Most likely, the *hance* (or *haan,* since the lock was also known as the *snap haans)* meant cock, and cock had stood for "hammer" for a long time. The cock was eared back and it "pecked" forth and made fire.

Then came the flintlock. To say that the flinter was actually better than the wheel lock would be to exaggerate. But it certainly was simpler, cheaper to make, and faster to work with. The flinter was the heart of the firearm that would one day emerge as the Kentucky. Today, it's popular to think of the flintlock as a hit and miss proposition, the shooter simply hoping that when the trigger is pulled, the gun will go boom. Not so. That propaganda comes from writers who have never owned or mastered a

good flintlock, but who may have purchased a wall-hanger sold as a real shooting iron when its true duty was to rest on pegs.

The flintlock worked fine for a very long period of history, and Independence was earned by riflemen firing flintlocks. In fact, by 1804, when the Lewis and Clark Expedition began its trek westward, its members were armed with flintlocks. You might say that the East was opened with the flintlock and that the westward expansion was spearheaded by flintlock-carrying adventurers, too. Oh yes, there was even an air rifle along on the Lewis and Clark trip, but rest assured that the flintlock was the difference between starvation and survival, and kept the first tenants of the land at bay.

All the smoothbore muskets in the land were no match for the rifle that would be recognized as America's first, however. The Kentucky rifle began as another shooting tool, the German Jaeger rifle. The Jaeger dominated Europe between 1500 and 1700. For a short period in the early 1700s, the Jaeger underwent metamorphosis, which leads us up to the age of the Kentucky, 1725 to 1775. The Jaeger was a rifled firearm. Not all Kentucky rifles were actually rifles at first, because a few were of smoothbore style and some had the straight rifling pattern. The Jaeger wore barrels in the 30- to 36-inch range, generally; a few went into the 40s. These octagonal barrels were often bored 60 to 75 caliber.

Even though they might load a fairly decent charge of powder into such a bore, the great volume within meant very low pressures and consequently low velocity and high trajectory. In a word, you sure didn't shoot very far with a Jaeger if you wanted to register many hits. The big lead bullets

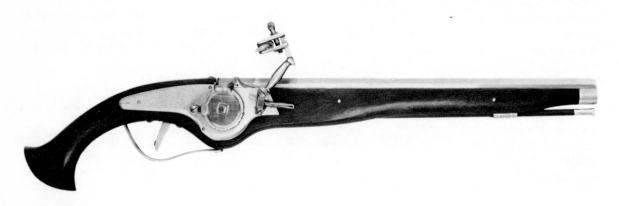

This replica wheel-lock design from the Navy Arms Company is a good example of a very early lock design which preceded the flintlock. *(Navy Arms).*

meant plenty of expenditure of metal, too, and if you wanted to carry a lot of ammo with you, your pockets had to be strong. The Jaeger was not right for American shooting conditions nor for American shooters. The gunsmiths went to work, and the result was the Kentucky rifle.

We credit the Pennsylvania smiths with the invention of the Kentucky. In fact, students of the Kentucky rifle have documented gunsmith names and places, and these sleuths have shown the various styles of Kentucky rifles, known as schools and named for counties in Pennsylvania in the 1700s. There was the famous Lancaster school, the Bedford, Jefferson, Clarion, Elk, and others. *Longrifles of Pennsylvania,* by Russell Harriger, treats Kentucky rifles of the last three counties.

The German, Dutch, and Austrian rifle makers who inhabited Pennsylvania handcrafted a magnificent long rifle for American riflemen. The best of the Kentuckys, and the majority, were not only rifled, but were very carefully fitted with lands and grooves to create fine accuracy. How accurate? In the hands of a good shot, these rifles would chew out the X-ring at 50 yards and often had the capability of one-inch groups center to center at 100 yards. Today, a few of these rifles have been tested with scope sights and they are on a par with our modern firearms in target grouping.

So accuracy was the byword. But there was more. The barrel had grown longer. Samples of 40- to 48-inch barrels are common. The long barrel aided in offhand shooting, for it was a steadying factor. Also, the sight radius—distance between front and rear sights—was increased and a sharper sight picture was possible, especially for older eyes whose ability to focus from rear sight to front sight to target was fading. Caliber had grown smaller as compared with the Jaeger. The range ran the gamut from sub-32 bore size to over 60 caliber, but there were many Kentuckys in the 38–45-caliber domain. With fine accuracy going for it, the Kentucky rifle was quite forceful, even against deer, because of accurate bullet placement.

Recoil was light. The smaller ball required a modest powder charge to propel it at reasonably good muzzle velocities. Many powder measures prove that enough black powder was used to give the ball 1,800- to 2,000-feet-per-second velocity. So trajectory, compared with the Jaeger, was flat. And you could carry plenty of ammo, for the light powder charge allowed quite a few shots for a small supply of fuel, and the smaller ball meant more

could be packed without undue weight. This was America's rifle for the times. The Kentucky was king.

Our riflemen were "raised on guns," and it was no trick for them to hit the mark with the accurate Kentucky. Also, shooting was a pastime as well as a serious business in early America. Many shooting matches took place. The good sights of the Kentucky allowed for "close holding," and small targets at modest range were whacked time and again. The rifle was making history. And it was, in its own way, building an American tradition for excellence. There was much competition among the gunmakers in a quiet sort of way, a competition that is still alive among modern arms manufacturers.

The Kentucky showed marksmen what they could really do with a fine tool. The Kentucky had ample power, plenty of accuracy, good ignition— yes, they did "go off" with sunrise/sunset reliability when properly loaded—and a rifleman armed with one was a formidable customer, be his antagonist a black bear or another man. But something did happen. The black bear turned into a grizzly, a far more powerful and dangerous customer. The deer became elk. And ranges got longer. A woods shot of 50 paces became a plains shot of 200 paces. The American rifleman had gone west. The fur trading era was on. Englishmen in London wanted fancy tophats ("beavers"), headgear made from the pelt of the flat-tailed animal.

Jefferson saw a good thing ahead for us. Out west, the lands were actually not American. Frenchmen roamed there. Englishmen likewise. Jefferson sent Lewis and Clark to get a good look at it, and John Colter, a member of the expedition, returned to the lands of the Far West, as it was known, discovering great waterways and high mountains—and beavers, lots of them. The smooth-bore muskets of Lewis and Clark were only fair on these grounds and no more than fair. The accurate Kentucky rifle was wonderful, but now it was a bit small. It had to change.

The Kentucky rifle gave way to the plains rifle, a different sort of firearm in many ways. The grace, charm, and absolute beauty of the Kentucky, with those wonderful patch boxes and carvings, full-length stocks of marvelously finished maple and other fine woods, those lithe and artistic pieces succumbed to one that was utilitarian. The barrel shortened. After all, these riflemen were often horsemen. You did not need a 40-inch barrel protruding at the side when mounted. And the caliber got bigger. So with barrels ranging from 32 to 36 inches in length, generally speaking, and calibers averaging around 53, the half-stock rifle was born.

It was powerful. You could shoot it one moment and wield it as a club the next, if you had to. And it gulped large doses of black powder. The patched ball was still the bullet used, but it was not an American invention at all, though often so credited. Patched projectiles are recorded back to Europe of the 1600s. So the shooting system was the same, in general—powder charge/patched ball. There were

flintlocks among the early half-stock plains rifles. But now there was something new. These plains rifles were mostly percussion models. They used the percussion cap, forerunner of the cartridge primer.

Some shooters altered Kentucky rifles during this era. In fact, thousands of Kentuckys underwent a little surgery called "drum and nipple" addition. The lock was removed. Where the touchhole had been in the side barrel flat, a drum was screwed into place. The drum had an attached nipple and onto that nipple the percussion cap was placed. So a flintlock rifle was now a percussion rifle. It was a

The plains rifle, exemplified here by a Browning Arms replica, dominated the Far West from the early to mid-nineteenth century.

The drum and nipple was used to transform thousands of flintlocks into percussion ignition systems.

good idea which worked well and which updated the Kentucky without much fuss. Kentucky rifles were commonly "freshed out" to larger bore.

The plains rifle, exemplified by the Hawken, a half-stock made by brothers Sam and Jake Hawken, in their St. Louis shop, was powerful and sturdy. It was just right for the westward expansion and for hunting western game. Was it as accurate as the Kentucky? That all depended upon individual rifles. The Hawken was rifled with a standard 1:48 rate of twist, certainly not correct for every caliber. The big bores would have done better with a much slower twist. The English gunmakers at that time knew this and gave a big bore a very slow rate of twist, sometimes as slow as a turn in 90 inches.

But the Hawken did all right. And as it progressed in manufacture, there were some positive changes. Some even wore peep sights, and a scope sight was not unknown on a Hawken, though it was rare. Workmanship, design, balance, materials— most arms lovers will give the nod to the Kentucky rifle. In fact, to this day no more beautiful or graceful firearm style has appeared. But the powerful Hawken was no doubt better for "out West." It served well until further improvements occurred: Somebody got the idea of putting the powder charge and the bullet into a container.

At first, it was no more than a paper affair. But before long, the metallic cartridge was on the scene, and with it rifles which could be loaded by merely slipping one into the chamber. By 1850 the rimfire cartridge was predominant. Flobert's BB Cap was invented by 1845. And a "central fire," or centerfire, round chambered in accurate, long-range, single-shot rifles proved to be a major factor in another segment of American history. The Congress of 1870 finally admitted, if not enthusiastically, that the Plains Indian was a very formidable opponent, and that on his own turf, he could be just about unbeatable. What to do? Perhaps the West was not worth fighting for after all, some said.

But another idea surfaced at that time. What single factor was most important in the life of the Plains Indians? What did they make their clothing from? What did they use for shelter? What constituted their major food supply? What, indeed, did their way of life revolve around? It seemed that the hub of their existence was the bison, commonly known as the buffalo. Get rid of the buffalo and the Plains Indian was in for a long winter indeed. Besides, once the West was won, the buffs would impede progress. They swarmed like giant gnats as they moved about the prairie, too numerous to be counted.

While it is romantic to conclude that the Indians' sense of conservation kept them from killing too many bison, their limited kills were more likely due to technology. The Indians stampeded herds over cliffs and took from the bottom of the hill what they wanted. They tried to collect buffalo in various ways, but lance and arrow were nothing compared with the new rifle that was to be seen on the plains,

a rifle in the hands of the "buffalo runner," as the breed preferred to be known. Now came the Sharps rifle and the Remington rolling-block and others similarly suited.

The Army would give you ammo for free if you would go forth to slaughter these great beasts. In fact, for a time you could get a dollar for each bison tongue you turned in, leaving the carcass with its meat and hide to rot on the plains. Few got wealthy shooting bison, but many took up the occupation. They adopted a carte blanche attitude toward the bison: If you saw one, shoot it down. In fact, the buffalo represented a paradox for hunters. He was not intrepid and certainly did not attack on sight. Yet the bison, largest four-footed game animal of all, bigger than a grizzly, bigger than a moose, could stomp you into prairie butter if he got his hooves on you.

The buff runners considered hunting shaggies a fairly safe endeavor, however, because of their excellent cartridge rifles. Calibers such as the 45-120-550 Sharps did the trick from very long range. Here was a 45-caliber cartridge using 120 grains of black powder and firing a long 550-grain bullet. There were many variations among rounds and loads, of course, and this cartridge is only *one* example of a buffalo hunter's ammunition.

Many of the buffalo hunter's rifles had telescopic sights. One famous old buff runner, Colonel Frank Mayer, lived into his nineties and was on the scene in modern times to tell much of the actual story. His favorite rifle was a 45-caliber Sharps topped off with a 20-power target scope using stadia wires for range judgment. The tradition had changed. Moving from the short-range Jaeger to the accurate and light-recoiling Kentucky to the stout and powerful Hawken-type rifle to the single-shot cartridge piece using a scope sight had enabled marksmen to

The Sharps 1874 model, especially in caliber 45-120-550, was a favorite with buffalo runners. This replica is from the C. Sharps Company of Big Timber, Montana.

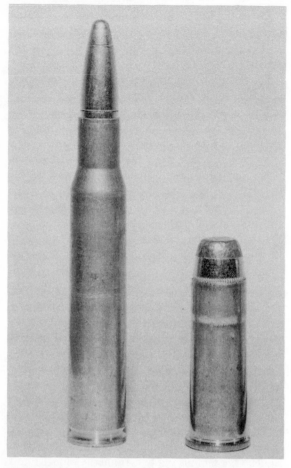

The cartridge replaced the muzzle-loader. One of the most popular and successful of the early cartridges was the 44-40 Winchester, right, which fired a 200-grain bullet at 1,200–1,300 fps MV with black powder, later at about 2,000 fps MV with smokeless powder loads. On the left is a 30-06 cartridge for comparison.

evolve. They could now hit rather small targets at very great distances, and the large targets presented by the bison were easy marks even at 400-plus yards for the practiced shooter.

Then the bison was gone. The Plains Indian was no longer a general threat. But there was still plenty of shooting in the Old West. The need for super long-range punch was displaced somewhat by a desire for repeated fire. Repeaters had been around, actually, for quite a while. Sam Colt had a repeater in the 1830s, a revolver with a long barrel. American riflemen soon had some pretty fine repeaters in hand, and sportsmen took to them, if not immediately. But soon the time to switch was obviously ripe.

The Volcanic, a repeating rifle, had appeared, but it was B. Tyler Henry's rifle which made the biggest splash in the pool of repeating-rifle invention. The Henry rifle fired fifteen times per one loading. The rounds were contained in a tubular magazine beneath the barrel of the rifle. Oliver Winchester hired Henry and before long the Winchester Model 1866 was a reality. It fired a 44-rimfire round. That round was not very powerful. Serious sportsmen stuck with the single-shots a while longer. Winchester answered with its Model 1873, fast, accurate, and loaded with the 44-caliber centerfire cartridge known as the 44 WCF (Winchester Center Fire) and later simply the 44-40, 44 caliber, 40 grains of black powder.

The 200-grain bullet of the 44-40—which traveled at a bit more than the speed of sound, around 1,200 to 1,250 feet per second—was all right up close for deer-sized game, not much for the bigger animals, and certainly nothing at long range. The old Sharps "buffalo rounds" could eat 44-40s for breakfast. The 45-120-550 Sharps propelled its 550-grain bullet at 1,400 feet per second or more. I personally chronographed one at 1,500 feet per second. With its 200-grain bullet at 1,200-feet-per-second muzzle velocity, the 44-40 earned a muzzle energy of 640 foot-pounds. The 45-120 Sharps, with a 550-grain bullet at 1,500 feet per second, achieved 2,749 foot-pounds of muzzle energy.

But rifle makers were hard at work. Soon, Marlins and Winchesters were chambered for some fairly powerful black-powder cartridges. The lever-action was now king. The American sportsman made known his needs and desires. Before too long there were 45-75s and 45-70s and even 45-90s, pretty good numbers even with black powder. The hunter took to these repeaters like a bird to wing. By the time the great Model 1886 Winchester was in the hands of sportsmen, there was a repeating firearm with power aplenty for any big game in North America.

In fact, the 1886 rifle remained popular into the 1900s. In caliber 33 Winchester, it was a very good 200-yard rifle for deer and similar game and it would drop an elk as well. The famous Ben Lilly, bear and lion hunter, used an 86 Winchester in 33 Winchester caliber. And when the rifle/cartridge combination did ride off into the sunset like a B-movie cowboy, it came riding right back at sunrise in an updated model. In 1936, the 86 became the Model 71 Winchester lever-action, repeating big-game rifle and the 33 Winchester cartridge was

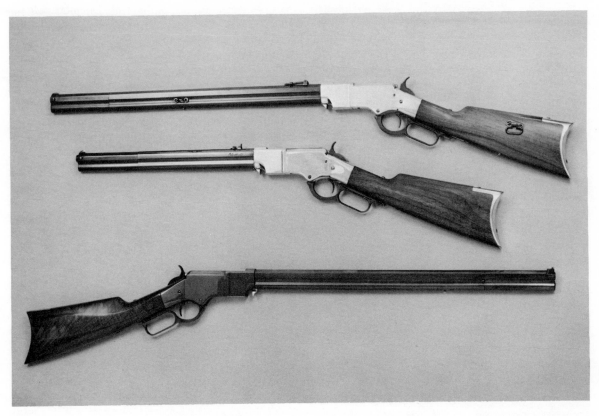

Versions of the Henry Rifle, one of the first reliable repeaters.

The Winchester Model 1886 rifle was famous well into this century. It was chambered for several powerful black-powder cartridges as well as the smokeless 33 Winchester round. This is Browning Arms's replica of the 1886. *(Browning Arms.)*

turned into the more powerful 348 Winchester round.

But even these fine repeaters of the black-powder-cartridge days were destined for the scrap pile with the next big change in sporting rifles. In 1894, a fine little flat-sided hunting rifle came off the drawing board, sprung from the fertile mind of John Browning, who sold the plan to Winchester. Appropriately, the little rifle was called the Model 1894 Winchester. It was a rifle, often with 26-inch barrel, but it was also a carbine with a 20-inch barrel, one of the handiest little firearms ever offered the American rifleman. The design included a flawless action. Of course, it was a repeater, lever-action, nine shots for the rifle's tubular magazine and seven for the carbine. Two black-powder rounds were offered, the fine 38-55 and the accurate 32-40.

easy-to-carry, easy-to-store, truly rugged, and totally reliable repeater. The Model 94 went on to become the most popular sporting rifle in the world. No single model has ever been able to take that claim away from it. In the hands of a good rifle shooter, the 30-30 is still an excellent round.

The sporting rifle was to undergo a few more changes, of course. The semiauto was perfected and there were several good ones available. The lever-action remained highly popular among big-game hunters. The single-shot was still around, too. But action for action, not even the fast-handling pump or slide could best the bolt model in the eyes of the modern rifleman. The bolt-action would handle the hottest of the hotshot rounds, the 220 Swift, the 270 Winchester, the 30-06, and many more. Scope-sighted, the bolt-action became the new king of

The Model 1894 Winchester, the first rifle to offer smokeless-powder cartridges for *sportsmen.*

But the Model 1894 was going to really shake the foundations of the shooting world. In 1895, a Model 1894 Winchester with a new nickel-steel barrel was offered. Why the stronger steel? Because this Winchester was going to be the first *sporting* rifle to be offered the shooting public in which smokeless powder cartridges were used. The cartridges were the 25 WCF and the 30 WCF, soon to be known as the 25-35 Winchester and 30-30 Winchester. Both were very good. The little 25 was offered with the fastest rate of twist to date, and it used a long 117-grain bullet.

But it was the 30-30 which would eclipse everything else. Smokeless powder had been used in at least two military rounds, one of them in America, the 30-40 Krag. But here was ample power and, for those times, fairly flat trajectory in a light-kicking,

long-range shooting. Many good models appeared from the major arms companies. It was not a total takeover, for the other rifle styles remained. But certainly things had changed.

Many books have been written on the transition from black-powder soot-burners to the modern firearm, and our *Bible* is not going to delve deeply into that history. But today's American rifleman should recognize that he lives in the richest period of sporting firearms. He has it all. Along the evolutionary path, the classics never became totally extinct. What about the great Kentucky rifle? Surely that has gone the way of the dodo bird.

Not on your life. In fact, some of the finest Kentucky rifles ever built are being made right now. Black-powder shooting, muzzle-loading, never did die. The craft of handbuilding these exquisite rifles

The bolt-action rifle has replaced all other action styles for big-game hunting. *(Remington Arms).*

was passed on from generation to generation. In one-room gun shops in many parts of the country, the skill lived on. *Foxfire 5,* fifth book in the popular series of texts on American craftsmanship and lifestyles, carries a complete section on modern Kentucky rifle building.

Of course, many of the rifles are also of the Hawken style, as well as other patterns. And the high interest that developed for the old muzzle-loader finally stimulated manufacturers to produce these old-time guns for today's riflemen. Several such companies exist, and a shooter can walk into a black-powder shop at this moment and buy a front-loader in many different calibers and designs. There are, some authorities say, as many as five million black-powder shooters, and most states have special black-powder-only hunting seasons for them. There are also clubs and organizations dedicated to the black-powder shooter. Shooting matches of old are recreated. Such rendezvous have become major events, where many riflemen replicate the old-time gatherings of the mountain men of the Far West who brought their furs to swap with traders, in wagons, waiting to exchange coffee and gunpowder and lead for beaver pelts.

All of the action styles live on as well. Those great single-shots are still with us, sometimes in bolt-action form, generally 22-rimfire caliber, but also in falling block and other styles. Our next chapter deals with such actions. The lever-action is ever popular, chambered in rounds from 22 rimfire to big-game, high-intensity powerhouses. The pump gun is still here, and not only in 22 rimfire, but also in stout rounds of the 30-06 league. The semiauto is appreciated by many modern riflemen. And the bolt-action is currently at its zenith in popularity.

Then what is the modern rifle? The matchlocks, wheel locks, and snaphances are mostly collectors' items, and are very rarely seen on any shooting range. The other muzzle-loader styles, however— flintlock and especially percussion—are very much with us and very much a part of the modern shooting scene. All the action designs, single-shot, double-barreled rifle, lever, pump, auto, and bolt, are widely represented. So it's the rifleman's choice. And he will have to choose from a vast array of fine rifles built in the traditions of accuracy, power, utility, and artistic design—a dilemma, but what a happy dilemma.

2

Choosing the Action

THE CARTRIDGE CASE arose as a miniature counterpart of the old muzzle-loader barrel—the muzzle-loader had a barrel into which a powder charge topped off with a bullet was fed. An avenue for an igniting spark was provided to set off the powder charge down in the breech section of the rifle barrel. The cartridge case was no more than a brass container holding a powder charge, gripping a bullet, and containing a source of ignition, priming compound around the rim of the case (rimfire), or a separate primer inserted into a "pocket" in the head of the case (centerfire). The cartridge case provided added strength and containment of expanding gases, allowing greater working pressure than the "open" muzzle-loader system.

However, some sort of device was now needed to contain the cartridge. Since it moved, this device was dubbed "the action," a mechanical system born of necessity. The action became the heart of the rifle and that heart dictated the entire character of the gun. Large action, large rifle. Small action, small

rifle. You did not have to follow the dictates of the action all the time—there were some ways to trim down a large-actioned rifle, or a big stout barrel could be fitted to a tiny action. But, all in all, the action did indeed suggest the complete rifle design. It also decided the handling characteristics of the rifle, and this is easily seen when comparing two very different action types, the single-shot and the semiauto.

THE SINGLE-SHOT

Single-shot designs were first to accept the new-fangled cartridge. A very early design was the Flobert Rolling Block. Flobert was responsible for the tiny 22 BB Cap which evolved into the 22-rimfire family of rounds. His little "parlor guns," made to fire the BB Cap, used this simple single-shot design. The hammer was eared back on the Flobert and a breech piece drawn rearward to allow

The bolt-action rifle is very popular in 22-rimfire caliber in single-shot, tubular magazine repeater, and clip-fed repeater. This Ruger Model 77-22 is a full-scale 22-rimfire, bolt-action rifle repeater, clip-fed. (Sturm, Ruger, and Co.)

entry to the breech itself. With the cartridge inserted, the breech was closed and the round was contained. The design was sufficiently strong for little rimfire rounds, but that was it. Remington made quite a few tiny 22s on this principle, as did Stevens.

The Standing Breech was another single-shot design of merit. A finger lever, which also formed the trigger guard, was dropped downward and the barrel itself hinged forward, allowing a full view of the breech. A round was then inserted directly into that breech and the system locked by snapping the barrel back in line. There were numerous variations, and this system could be made to work with rounds much more powerful than the 22-rimfire class.

A solid-frame Dropping Breech system was also a good single-shot design. A high-wall or low-wall variation was offered with this system, the high wall being the stronger because the receiver walls rose up level with the barrel, allowing for a lot of metal-to-metal contact. Some very accurate target rifles were built with this action style, especially using the high-wall dropping breech system. Again, many variations of the action were invented, but all were lever-action in principle. That is, they operated by tugging down on a lever which opened and closed the action. Sometimes the lever was also the trigger guard, but in other instances the lever was a separate unit.

The bolt-action design, when used without a magazine, became the bolt-action, single-shot rifle. We see 22-rimfire rifles in the single-shot, bolt-action class, but *any* of our cartridges can be contained by this action. The turning bolt system in single-shot form has been used with very accurate target/varmint rifles containing high-intensity, high-velocity rounds, and offers an inexpensive, but strong firearm.

Advantages of the Single-Shot

The first advantage of the single-shot is psychological. Having fired muzzle-loaders for a very long time, I know the feeling of having "one shot and one shot only." You simply have to make that shot count. And this can make a rifleman more careful with his aim. The single-shot action can be quite foolproof. One big advantage of the single-shot is its short action style. The overall length of a single-shot rifle can be very compact. Stand a bolt-action rifle with a 22-inch barrel next to a single-shot rifle with a 22-inch barrel and the latter is going to be shorter, "bullpup rifles" not withstanding.

Because of the action, a single-shot can be very lightweight. In takedown form, a single-shot package may be downright tiny, narrow as well as short. The action has strength aplenty for any cartridge, too, depending upon which single-shot action design is used. It can also be made up into a very handsome firearm. It's positive-loading. You certainly do not have to worry that the action may not pick up the next round from the magazine because there is no magazine. You feed the cartridge into the chamber with your fingers. The single-shot can be manufactured inexpensively or expensively. And its design makes it a sporty rifle.

Disadvantages of the Single-Shot

I taught myself to get off a fairly rapid second shot with an old Remington rolling-block 7mm Mauser I once owned, so I know the shooter is not limited to one shot under most circumstances. But with no magazine, you have no repeat fire of true rapidity. Some shooters proclaim that the single-shot design is not sufficiently accurate for long-range grouping on target, but this is so only with some rifles. I have witnessed benchrest accuracy of the highest order from the single-shot, even the older models, such as the Stevens Model 44½.

Not that long ago, it would have been impossible to locate a newly manufactured, big-game, single-shot rifle at your local gun shop. The great Sharps rifle was gone. The Remington rolling-block was of

The serious 22-rimfire target shooter most often uses a bolt-action rifle such as this Remington single-shot Target model. *(Remington Arms)*

A replica of the John Browning–designed Winchester 1885 single-shot. Although barrel length is 28 inches, overall length is only 43.5 inches. *(Browning Arms)*

Another modern single-shot is the Thompson/Center model, with multiple interchangeable barrel/caliber options.

the past. The fine Winchester Model 1885 was no longer made. However, now a shooter can enjoy a very fine single-shot big-game rifle. Browning offers its Model 1885, an extremely handsome rifle which is only 43.5 inches in overall length, with a barrel up to 28 inches long. Cartridges such as the 22-250, 270, and 7mm Remington Magnum make this rifle very up-to-date in range, and its 45-70 chambering offers big power for up-close shooting. The H&R Model 158 single-shot is an inexpensive rifle in 22 Hornet or 30-30 calibers. Ruger's Number 1 is offered in many different calibers and barrel lengths, as well as styles. The International is a full-stock single-shot in calibers 243, 30-06, 270, and 7×57. The Tropical version of the Model 1 is offered in 375 H&H Magnum or 458 Winchester Magnum. Thompson/Center has a whole system with their single-shot rifle, for interchangeable barrels allow calibers from 22 Hornet through 7mm Magnum all on one stock.

The single-shot, bolt-action 22 rimfire is strongly evident today, especially in boy's models, very tiny rifles with miniature dimensions for the smaller shooter. All in all, the single-shot design is well represented today. And I see no reason for its success to fade.

THE DOUBLE RIFLE

You can think of the double rifle as a couple of single-shots "glued" together, with barrels side by side or one on top of the other. Sometimes there may be more than two barrels, as the "drillings" may provide a combo of a couple of rifle barrels and a shotgun barrel or a couple of shotgun tubes and a rifle barrel—in many variations. There are various styles of double-barrel design, but the double gun is not used much these days, not even in Europe where many fine doubles originated. However, for those who like the double design, some of the most beautiful and functional rifles ever devised were double-barreled.

Advantages of the Double Rifle

Hunting dangerous game in thick cover with the double can mean two fast shots, thereby keeping some beast from romping all over your body. When hunting in Zimbabwe, I discussed doubles with a couple of professional hunters and each agreed that, for the fellow who could afford one, there was nothing like a two-barreled rifle in the bushveld or jungle. One of our trackers had been struck by a

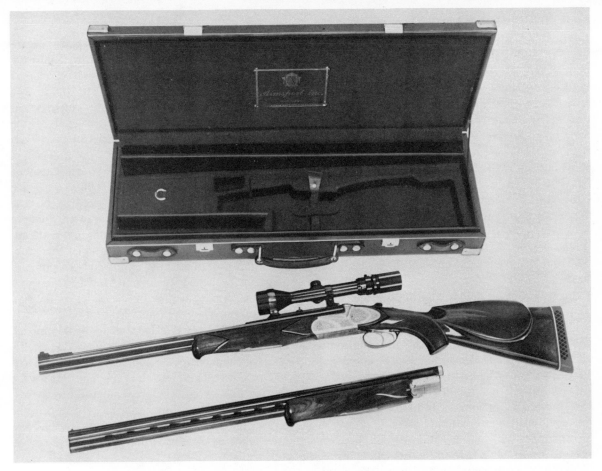

The double-barreled rifle is not common in North America today and is seen less in African game fields as well; however, the style is still available and preferred by a few riflemen. This Armsport double rifle has interchangeable shotgun barrels as well. *(Armsport)*

rampaging Cape buffalo and only luck kept him alive. The buff charges, head low. It likes to hook you with one of those lovely horns—owned by both males and females—toss your body into the air, whirl around, and come back to do a tap dance all over your hide with sharp hooves and maybe 1,500 or more pounds of heft.

The tracker was hooked and he was tossed in the air, but he was lucky in his landing. He landed in a thorn tree and stuck there like a rag doll. The bewildered buff turned around and found nothing to trample. Disappointed, it left. Now what about that charge? Here comes the buff, head low, eyes on you. If you drive a bullet up the snout that bullet may well lodge in the brain. End of buff. But if you miss that shot, a second opportunity is as welcome as a check in the mail you didn't know you had coming. The double gun gives you that fast second shot.

What's more, the double points. That is, it tends to line itself up as you bring it to shoulder, much as a good shotgun points. Of course, doubles can weigh well over a dozen pounds and they are nothing like an upland-bird shotgun. Also, the double rifle is short. It's easy to manage in close quarters because of its short length. And, contrary to what I've read, the double is also quite rapidly reloaded. You flip the barrels forward, pluck two rounds from your cartridge loops—you do have cartridge loops on your safari jacket, don't you?—and pop these rounds right up the spout.

Disadvantages of the Double Rifle

Good double rifles are not to be found at a garage sale. Even used models cost a pretty penny. Also, it's not every double which puts bullets from both barrels where they belong, in a neat group. When the two barrels are shooting to the same point of impact, that's called "regulation," and not every gunmaker can regulate a double rifle. Also, the double is oftentimes, but not always, quite heavy.

However, there are many doubles available today, a few in the "reasonable" price range. Armsport offers its Emperor double rifle, Model 4010, in many calibers—243, 270, 284, even 7mm Remington Magnum, as well as 338 Winchester and 375 Magnum. Prepare to part at about $13,000 for this baby. And if you prefer the same rifle in a fancier Model 4000, then unload your wallet to the tune of about 16,500 bucks. Beretta's Express double in 30-06, 9.3mm, 375, or 458 is a fine rifle at only $2,300 to $2,500, unless you want the fancier grade at about $7,500.

Browning has a double gun in 20 gauge by 20 gauge with a 30-06 by 30-06 interchangeable barrel set. Browning also has an Express rifle in 270 or 30-06. Colt's Sauer is another shotgun/rifle combo offered as a drilling. Heym has several fine double guns, too, and Winchester's Double Xpress is another beauty. If you want a double rifle, don't hesitate, but be sure of your needs first. And if you like the combo rifle but don't have a few thousand superfluous dollars lying around, then don't forget the Savage Model 24 O/U (over/under). Here, for less than $200 to not quite $300, you can have a 22 Long Rifle rimfire over a 410- or 20-gauge shotgun barrel, or a 22 Magnum over 20 gauge, or 22 Hornet, 222 Remington, 30-30, 223 or 357 Maximum coupled with a shotgun tube.

THE LEVER-ACTION

A lever-action rifle, the Model 94 Winchester, still lays claim to being the most popular single sporting rifle in the world, and that title is going to hold up for a while longer because well over six million 94s have been made. A lever-action design is seemingly simple, yet one look at its interior mechanics proves the genius of its developers.

In a single down-up stroke of the finger lever, several functions are accomplished. The fired cartridge case is extracted from the chamber as well as ejected from the rifle. Up from the carrier, a new round is lined up for pickup by the breech bolt. The new round is then slammed forward by the breech bolt into the chamber. The downstroke unlocked the action. The upstroke now relocks the action,

putting the locking bolt or bolts in place. Meanwhile, the hammer has been forced back into the cocked position when the breech bolt was in its rearward thrust.

All of this was accomplished with a mere down-up stroke of a single lever, and the fingers of the hand were already naturally placed in that lever, which functions as trigger guard as well as action activator. The magazine of the lever-action may be tubular, box style, or rotary. The tubular magazine rules out the use of pointed bullets because the nose of one bullet could set off the primer of the round in front of it during the recoil stage. Actually, the tubular magazine would not have to suffer this problem if designed differently, as proved by the tubular magazine of the old Remington Model 141, a spiral affair which put the nose of one bullet on the rim, not the primer, of the round in front of it.

The finger lever is a loop affair on this model, and it can be designed in various ways. Generally, it's large enough to accommodate a gloved hand. The breech bolt contains the firing pin. But it's the locking bolt or bolts which hold the breech bolt shut, at least in the Winchester models. In fact, the lever-action has remained popular for various reasons, some of them listed in the advantage section

The author firing the handsome and ruggedly constructed Winchester Model 71 in 348 Winchester caliber.

below, but one of the reasons is an intangible. The very style of the lever-action says "deer rifle," "Old West," and "cowboy." But mostly the lever-action has stayed "hot" because it works and works extremely well.

Advantages of the Lever-Action

The Model 94 and many of its counterparts, such as the Marlin 336 and similar styles, offer flat contours. This feature allows for easy access to saddle scabbards as well as easy storage and carrying. These little lever-actions are truly a joy to pack when you are in difficult terrain, especially in the thickets and riverbottoms. There is little to snag on brush, and I have returned heavily to the Model 94 whenever I want the added challenge (as compared with the high-power, scope-sighted bolt-rifle) and portability.

The lever-action models are also very fast. Anybody can train himself to rapidly place shot after shot on the mark with this style of firearm. The rifle handles well and carries quite a bit of ammo. Some of the earlier lever-action rifles were noted for large-capacity magazines. Today's 94 carbine loads six in its tubular magazine and is a seven-shot with one in the chamber. As for calibers, there have been thousands of fine 22-rimfire, lever-action rifles made, but the idea that this style cannot chamber "hotter" rounds is false.

When the Model 1886 Winchester lever-action was king, and the rifle was made from 1886 all the way up to 1936, its caliber 405 Winchester was as powerful a round as offered by any American gunmaker. Furthermore, the Model 1895 Winchester was offered in 30-06, a fact sometimes forgotten when detractors of the lever-action talk about action weakness. All in all, the lever-action design has served well, and the reason for its continued popularity is service.

Disadvantages of the Lever-Action

While the lever-action design can be strong, not all levers offer the strength of action necessary for high-intensity rounds. For example, the earlier Model 94s were good for about 40,000 psi (pounds per square inch) breech pressure before things got sticky and extraction problems set in. Today's Angle-Eject Model 94 is, however, another story. Its 307 Winchester and 356 Winchester rounds tread closely on the heels of the fine 308 and 358 rounds.

The Model 1899 Savage rifle, forerunner of the famous Model 99 Savage, is displayed here by author's son, Bill Fadala.

Counterpart of the Model 94 Winchester big-game rifle is this Winchester Model 9422 chambered for 22 rimfire.

All the same, the camming power of the lever-action is not as forceful as the bolt-action and you won't see target rifles built on lever-action systems. Furthermore, the lever-action does not lend itself that well to some of the longer rounds. Even the strong Browning BLR lever-action rifle stays away from the 270, 30-06, and 7mm Remington Magnum. But, all in all, trying to come up with an arm-long list of detriments for the lever-action is no easy chore.

The old 30-30 94s are also doing just fine and, in the hands of the practiced rifleman, are more than adequate for medium-range big-game hunting. The aforementioned Browning is offered in calibers 222, 223, 243, 257 Roberts, 7mm-08, 308 Winchester, and 358 Winchester. You really can't ask for much more. Modern manufacturers are turning out lever-action rifles suitable for everything from varmints up to moose and bear.

How about that old Model 1895 Winchester? It's gone, though many thousands are still used. And at the same time, it's back, for Browning has recently remanufactured the 95, in 30-06 and 30-40 Krag rounds. And what about that famous 1886 Winchester? Same thing. Today, a Browning 1886 is available, caliber 45-70. Browning has also revived the famous Model 92, calibers 357 Magnum and 44 Magnum, an eleven-shot rifle weighing only 5.5 pounds. Navy Arms offers replicas of old lever-action rifles, too. And Marlin continues its fine line of levers, including calibers 30-30, 35 Remington, 444 Marlin, and 45-70, to name only a few.

The fabulous Model 99 Savage lever-action rifle, with its rotary magazine allowing the use of pointed projectiles, is in strong demand today with 243 and 308 chamberings. This lever-action rifle, based on the Model 1895 Savage and then the Model 1899 Savage, really put power in the lever-action, for it featured the great 300 Savage round, with ballistics quite similar to the original authority of the 30-06.

Of course, the latter round was updated with hotter loads, but the 300 Savage was and still is a winner.

THE SLIDE-ACTION

Another uniquely American system is the slide, also known as the pump, or trombone action. Again, there is a mere two-stroke movement to work the action. After firing, the pump handle is pulled rearward. This unlocks the breech bolt, extracts the spent case, and ejects it, while also cocking the gun. Meanwhile, a new round is brought up on the carrier and chambered into the locked breech. The slide-action is well liked by some big-game riflemen because of an overall love of the pump shotgun. Pump shotguns are certainly big in this country.

Advantages of the Slide-Action

The slide-action is smooth and fast. You can fire it repeatedly without taking it down from the shoulder. While any action can be so operated, many shooters find it awkward to do this with the bolt gun or even the lever. But these riflemen have no trouble shooting the pump dry without lowering the rifle. Sturdy, too, and flat of receiver, the pump is a hunter's rifle, handy in the brush.

Also, it's been chambered for very powerful rounds for a very long time. When Remington moved away from its fine and famous Model 141 to its Model 760, the 30-06 was one of the new rounds for the new rifle. The pump is very fast, too. One time I had a contest with a fellow shooter. He owned a 22 semiauto rifle and he bragged about how rapidly he could empty ten shots from it, though surely there's nothing admirable about shooting fast. I told him my Model 61 Winchester

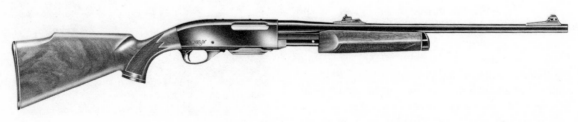

The stylish Remington Model Six is a slide-action big-game rifle chambered for a host of high-intensity cartridges. *(Remington Arms)*

The Marlin Model 9 is an extremely reliable semiautomatic rifle, chambered for the 9mm Luger round. The short clip holds twelve 9mm cartridges, the long holds twenty. Also available as the Model 45, chambered for the 45 ACP cartridge.

pump gun was faster than his semiauto, at which point a friendly bet ensued. I had ten shots out of that 61 before my buddy had *seven* out of his auto. With the 61, you could hold the trigger back and work the handle, and rounds spewed out like fireworks.

Disadvantages of the Slide-Action

Shooters who don't like lever-actions often claim that their accuracy is poor. The same is said of the pump gun. Is it true? Hunting-wise, a slide-action rifle is plenty accurate, but if you intend to enter benchrest competition, leave the slide-action at home. The two-piece stock does not lend itself to the best accuracy possible.

And what about camming power? As with the levers, the pumps are not going to give bolt-action efficiency in action lockup. Cartridge cases do stretch a bit more when fired in the pump rifle and the reloader must remember to full-length resize at all times, which I always do. He should also insure that the ammo is clean, as the extracting thrust of the pump is not quite as powerful as in some bolt-actions, especially those bolts with a claw-type extractor. Overall, however, the negative features of the pump gun are no deterrent to anyone who simply likes the style.

Remington's Model Six and Model 7600, as well as the Remington 76 Sportsman, keep slide-action big-game hunters happy. Calibers of 6mm, 243, 270, 308, and 30-06 fill the bill for today's slide-action fans. In the rimfire field, there are numerous pump-style rifles, all very fine, all totally reliable. One of my all-time favorite 22s is the pump-action,

and I own a Model 12 Remington pump gun and Winchester Model 62A, neither made today, but both enjoyable to shoot. The pump-action is a good one, not too popular among big-game hunters, yet in powerful demand by those outdoorsmen who appreciate its style and function.

THE SEMIAUTO

True automatic firearms are military guns. Sporting rifles are really semiautos or self-loading. However, since these semiautos are popularly called autos, we will stick with that term here. Naturally, the only force which can work the action of the auto is the power exerted by the cartridge itself. There are basically three kinds of semiauto action, though there are many variations of these types. There are gas-operated, blowback, and recoil-operated autos.

The gas-operated rifle bleeds off a small volume of the gas which is expanding behind the bullet in the bore. This gas is channeled into a special auxiliary chamber that contains a piston. Admittedly, there have been systems without the piston, but the piston-operated auto is prevalent. The forces exerted operate a "recoil spring," which then collapses to close and relock the action. So bled-off gas pushes the breechblock back, which extracts and ejects the sent case and recocks the action. Then the recoil spring forces the bolt back to close and lock the action. Naturally, a fresh round is also chambered.

The blowback action is the simplest of the semiautos and the cheapest to produce. A heavy breechblock is free-moving in the system. The rearward motion of the cartridge case forces the head of that case against the breechblock. This extracts and ejects the case, recocking the action. A spring similar to the recoil spring forces the floating breechblock back into position, which feeds another round into the chamber. Timing is important, but a phenomenon known as "case cling" helps out. When the gases expand, they do so in all directions simultaneously. Therefore, the walls of the case are pushed out against the chamber—clinging there, as it were. This allows the brief delay in activation of the breechblock which keeps the cartridge case in the chamber until the bullet is long gone from the muzzle.

The recoil-operated system employs Newton's Third Principle of Motion, every action has an opposite and equal reaction. Recoil forces the breechblock rearward. This force naturally withdraws and expels the spent case, cocks the rifle, and, on the spring-operated return, feeds a new round home.

Advantages of the Semiauto

Speed of fire is a key point here. Some shooters also feel that the lack of having to actually hand-operate the action leaves full concentration for aiming—maybe so; I can't prove or disprove the point. But there is certainly no lack of quite forceful testimony by many hunters that they can put a second and third bullet into big game amazingly fast when they have to, since the semiauto requires only aiming and trigger pull. Also, the semiauto is trim and flat-sided, and it can be a handsome rifle.

Disadvantages of the Semiauto

The semiauto system can be rough on cartridge cases. Reloaders sometimes complain that case life is short in big-game, semiauto rifles. However, full-length resizing will help, and the semiauto fan is not always bent on hunting with handloaded ammo anyway. Also, some shooters consider the semiauto less accurate than other rifle-action styles. In comparing a big-game semiauto with a bolt, this claim may stand up to a degree. But I note plenty of hunting accuracy with the auto. As for the semiauto 22 rimfire, some of the more accurate 22s I have tested were of the semiauto variety. Also, my tests have shone that loss in muzzle velocity in semiautos, as compared with other systems, is mostly theoretical.

Thousands of 22-rimfire semiautos are in use today. The popularity of the semiauto among big-game hunters is somewhat less dramatic, however. Remington's Model 4 and Model 74 semiautos are both available in many calibers, such as the 243, 6mm, 270, 280, 308, and 30-06. The Ruger Carbine in 44 Magnum is also quite popular. Browning's good-looking Auto Rifle is offered in some truly powerful rounds, not only 30-06, but also 300 Winchester Magnum and 7mm Remington Magnum.

Semiautos are very reliable, a feature which we sometimes attribute to other actions but deny when talking about these self-loaders. I tested a Marlin Model 9 Camp Gun, firing several brands of ammo from its clip, all mixed and interchanged. I even held the rifle at odd angles. And I intentionally allowed a few hundred rounds to be fired without ever touching a cleaning rod to the gun or wip-

This closeup of the strong Weatherby action reveals trigger housing, magazine, recoil lug, and the exclusive multiple locking lugs of this system.

ing away powder residue from the action. After several *hundred* shots, the rifle was still functioning perfectly.

THE BOLT-ACTION

When I was growing up in the West, none of my adult hunting partners owned a bolt-action rifle. Even in the late 1950s, the lever-action was king. But the many postwar Mausers and Springfields floating around helped, I think, promote the excellent commercial bolt-action rifle. Last hunting season, I conducted an informal survey where I live in the West and found the reverse of believed rifle popularity to be true. Most hunters were packing bolt-action rifles with telescopic sights. So the pattern goes among big-game hunters of the open West. Back East, the camps are still replete with lever-actions and pumps and semiautos. But even around eastern campfires one will see a fair number of bolt guns.

The bolt-action is a simple style. It has a receiver and a bolt that rides on rails. This "turn bolt" wears locking lugs and the lugs lock up tighter than an ax blade stuck in a stump. Lift that bolt handle and the rifle is cocked (usually). The lifting also rotates the locking lugs in the receiver, allowing the bolt to be withdrawn along the rails. Extraction of spent case and ejection take place, and with a push forward, a fresh round is picked up from the follower and chambered. The bolt handle is moved downward and the action is again locked.

Advantages of the Bolt-Action

Reliable and rugged, yes, but so are the other styles. The bolt shines because it offers tremendous lockup. There's nothing else like it. Yes, the brass case still stretches, but with reasonably modest powder charges, cases can be reloaded many times for the bolt-action. The one-piece stock offers rigidness of support for the action, and you can fully bed or float the barrel as necessary for best accuracy. Tune-up with the bolt-action rifle is quite simple as compared with other styles. Action strength is excellent. Whereas some systems have a 40,000 to 50,000 psi limitation for safety, the bolt-action is much stronger. Cartridge-case-strength limits compel us to keep load pressures down, of course, even in a strong bolt-action rifle. But some bolt-actions

will tolerate over 100,000 psi and more before letting go.

Disadvantages of the Bolt-Action

The bolt-action rifle is slower in getting off that second shot as compared with lever-action, pump, or auto models. Also, the bolt protrudes and though bolt-action rifles carry well, even in a saddle scabbard, they do not slide in and out as readily as a flat-receivered rifle does. Though there are some wonderfully fine-handling bolt-action rifles, there are also many bolt-action models which do not flow to the shoulder as a lever-action or pump gun may.

Also, the bolt is truly overkill in a 22-rimfire chambering. Yet, I own a couple of bolt-action 22 rifles I would not trade for anything, one being an H&R Targeteer, which may be my all-around most useful 22-rimfire rifle. The bolt-action remains popular, even in rimfire rifles, and especially in big-bore rifles. While there is no reason to trade a fine-handling brush rifle for a bolt-action model, the hunter has clearly stated his position today—the bolt-action rifle is rapidly becoming the most popular action style. It has already clearly taken over west of the Mississippi River.

CHOOSING YOUR ACTION

Consider first the function of the rifle in question. If you want a little 22 rimfire for tin can rolling, perhaps the semiauto action would be just right. If your interest is long-range marksmanship and varmint control, the bolt-action is going to be correct, for it will chamber those hot-rock, flat-shooting rounds. Brushland deer harvesting could call for a fast-action rifle, maybe a semiauto, perhaps a lever-action. And if you just happen to have a pump-action shotgun you get along well with, and you want to duplicate that action in a rifle, by all means do it. All of the actions are good, all reliable, all sturdy. But applications can guide you to one over another.

After thinking about function, decide which action fits you best as a shooter. Most of us get along fine with all of these actions. But I'd be first to admit that I have seen some shooters who took to the bolt-action like a cat to a bathtub full of water. These marksmen preferred a lever or pump and they knew it. But if you can manage the actions equally well, simply enjoy the fact and look at the rifle's function.

Don't forget your eye. That is, don't leave out visual appeal. It may seem off key to suggest art here when we are talking about rifle actions, but shooting is more than putting bullets downrange. If you find a sleek semiauto you like, buy it. Most of all, remember that you can mold yourself to a rifle, as well as fitting the rifle to you. A shooter's ability to adapt to a rifle will come up again when I talk about stock fit. So if you like that action, but if it first seems foreign to your shooting style, give it some time and practice before deciding to give up on it.

3

Sporting-Rifle Ammunition

FOUR BILLION of anything is an impressive number, be it four billion billiard balls, bottlecaps, buttercups or . . . cartridges. U.S. Department of Commerce records show that American ammo factories supplied American sportsmen with that many rounds in 1982. Today the output is higher. Of the four billion cartridges, about three billion were 22 rimfires. Today, it's not outlandish to assume that we may be seeing about 4.5 billion rounds of ammo flowing from the cornucopia of sporting-ammo producers. One major plant recently revealed that it turned out about three million 22 Long Rifle rounds in one workday. Numbers alone are not the impressive factor here—quality, too, is high.

Along with the vast offering of factory-loaded ammo, these companies also supply components for reloaders. But this chapter is about the shooting materials you buy over the counter at a gun shop. It also includes mention of some fine ammunition which is *not* made in this country. But first, what is a cartridge? The elements of the cartridge are the *case,* the *propellant* (powder), the *primer,* and, of course, the projectile or *bullet.* The cartridge case is a metallic container. Imagine an empty cartridge case resting on a flat surface in front of you. The very top of the case, where the bullet goes in, is the *mouth.* Right after the mouth of the case is the *neck.* The bullet is secured by the neck of the round. If it is a bottleneck case, there will be a *shoulder* next. This is the sloping part of the case and the slope or angle is measured in degrees.

The next part of the case is the *body.* This is the part of the case which forms the actual powder container. At the lower end of the case, we have the *head,* which seems a bit backward since the mouth is at the other end, but that's the way it is. The head is composed of thicker brass than the rest of the case, and this head section may be *rimmed* or *rimless.* The rimmed case, such as the 30-30, has a platform, a flanged section, while the rimless case's head does not extend beyond the line created by the body of the case. Instead, there is an *extractor groove* cut into the head of the rimless case. Next, you have to have a place for the primer to fit. That receptacle is called the *primer pocket,* logically enough. A much smaller hole in front of the primer pocket allows the flame from the primer to reach the powder in the case. This little avenue is the *flash hole.* The metal between the body and the head of the case, which separates the powder charge from the primer, is the *web.*

A wonderful thing, the cartridge, for it allowed three major components of the old muzzle-loader to be packaged in one, that is, the bullet, the powder charge, and the source of ignition. Going into detail as to who, exactly, came up with the idea of the cartridge case is a little like trying to determine who invented the first nutcracker. Proof is hard to come by. However, it's safe to say that Flobert's BB Cap was an early metallic case, that Smith & Wesson helped to improve that case a bit, and that B. Tyler Henry improved the case further. The first cartridges, of course, used black powder. And the cases were not as strong as our modern brass. Furthermore, the "balloon head" style made a thinner

The cartridge consists of the case, powder, and bullet. This case is *rimmed*. The case is composed of the head (the portion upon which the case is resting), body, neck and shoulder, a mouth at the end of the neck, and a primer pocket with flash hole leading from the head into the body of the case.

product, so those shooters reloading very old cases should watch out for weakness and a possible rupture.

A succession of improvements followed the first metallic rounds. Eventually, black powder gave way to smokeless. Smokeless powder was a much more efficient fuel, producing a lot of pressure from a much smaller amount of powder. That meant case size could drop while power went up. The weaker rimfire case gave rise to a stronger centerfire case. Smokeless powder was very clean-burning as compared with black, so you did not have to scrub cases with solvent or soap and water before reloading them. But primers were corrosive, so there was still quite a bit of chemical wear in the system.

Then that problem was solved with noncorrosive primers. Lead bullets were very good indeed and still are, but even with an alloy—adding tin or antimony to the lead to make the product harder—you could only get so much velocity before bore leading occurred. Even the metal cap on the base of the lead bullet, called a *gas check*, would not allow for a really high-speed projectile. But the metal-cased bullet did. So jacketed bullets allowed for a higher

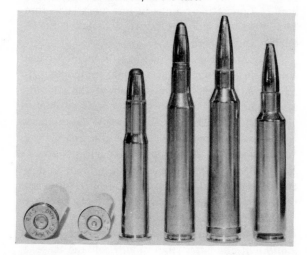

Cartridge-case style varies. On the far left is a Remington 7mm Magnum round and next to it a 30-30 case, both of centerfire design. Standing cartridges are, from the left, 30-30 Winchester, of *rimmed* design, 270 Winchester, with *rimless* head, 7mm Remington Magnum, rimless, but *belted* head, and 284 Winchester, with *rebated* rimless head.

The jacketed bullet allowed higher velocity than the lead projectile could withstand. On the right is a modern cast projectile.

There was the 45-120-3¼, too: 45 caliber, 120 grains of powder, and a case 3¼ inches long. Of course, you can't expect things to stay constant. That would be too simple. The 44-40, for example, did use 40 grains of black powder, but if you miked the bullet (measured it with a micrometer) you would find it to be closer to 43 caliber than to 44.

When the great 30-30 came along, it confused people, because they felt that this nomenclature belonged to the era of the black-powder round. So some experts claimed that the 30-30 was really a black-powder round to start with: 30 caliber, 30 grains of black powder. Not so. But it probably used about 30 grains of smokeless powder when it first appeared, hence the 30-30 nomenclature. In fact, the 30-40 Krag was also smokeless from the start, and it certainly never used 40 grains of black powder as a factory load. The 30-06 was 30 caliber, while the 06 meant the year it was invented, just like the 30-03 before it.

The 270 Winchester wasn't 27 caliber, but 270 sure sounded nice. It fired a bullet .277 of an inch, which was a perfect 7mm bullet, but 7mm bullets were not .277 of an inch because they had already been established at a .284-inch diameter. And when the 250-3000 Savage hit the streets, its inventor was surprised because it was probably destined to be a 250 Savage; however, the Savage people knew the value of high speed in 1915, when the round appeared. So the 250-3000 fired an 87-grain bullet at 3,000 fps MV (feet-per-second muzzle velocity). We could go on and on, with 22 Jets, 22 Hornets, 218 Bees, 219 Zippers, 22-250s, 257 Roberts, 256 Winchesters, the 25-06, 6.5mm Remington Magnum, 264 Winchester Magnum, and more.

The modern rifleman owes it to himself to have some knowledge of how today's ammunition evolved. By the late 1700s, paper cartridges were well established and in vogue. The bullet and charge were rolled up together in the paper, the paper usually greased to make it moistureproof. The shooter ripped the paper apart and poured the powder down the bore of his muzzle-loader, saving a bit of fuel to prime the pan of his flintlock. Then the bullet was rammed home.

The paper cartridge survived for quite a while. By the 1840s and until the last year of the Civil War, some paper cartridges used flammable paper, a "combustible envelope cartridge," according to Johnson and Haven in their fine 1943 book, *Ammunition* (currently out of print, but possibly available in libraries). Breechloaders came along, and you

velocity and smokeless powder was there to give it. With further powder improvements (and they are still occurring today), the day of 3,000 feet per second, even 4,000 and more, was here.

The naming of cartridges proved to be an interesting aspect of their invention and dissemination. Early nomenclature was fairly clear. A 45-70 was a 45-caliber round, a bullet of about .457-inch diameter, propelled by 70 grains of black powder. If you had a 45-70-500, it was a 45-caliber cartridge using 70 grains of black powder and firing a bullet weighing 500 grains (7,000 grains equal one pound).

could stuff a paper round into the chamber of some of these, close the action, and the action itself sliced the tip off the paper round, exposing the powder charge. A percussion cap ignited the powder, the flame directed through a channel from nipple to chamber.

Even as early as 1812, a real metallic round was on hand. M. Pauli, a Swiss inventor, offered this marvellous product to one Napoleon, who turned up his nose at it. Poor Napoleon. He may have carried his conquest even further had he the foresight to realize what Pauli held in his hand. There was even a bolt-action rifle to go with the round. By the 1850s we see Flobert's often-mentioned parlor guns using the BB Cap, a folded-head cartridge case. And by the way, though the rimfire may be a 22-caliber affair today, it was certainly a lot more in days gone by. Winchester's 1896 ammo catalog shows listings for the 32 Short, 32 Long, 32 Extra Long, 38 Short, 38 Long, and 38 Extra Long, all rimfires.

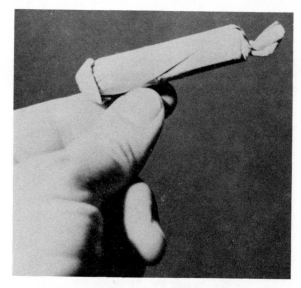

This original American Civil War paper cartridge preceded the metal case.

Two popular black-powder cartridges, the 44-40 and 38-40 (flanked by 06 rounds for comparison). Both are factory-loaded today with smokeless powder.

The same catalog offered the shooter a little 41-rimfire round for the many sidearms available in that caliber during the period. The 41 Swiss was another rimfire, this one a rifle round for the Swiss military. It used a bullet of 310 grains' weight pushed by 55 grains of black powder. And don't forget the 44 Flat rimfire for the Model 1866 Winchester. There was also a 56-46 rimfire, this one adapted to the Spencer rifle, 45 grains of powder, 330-grain bullet. The rimfire round was very popular. And everybody knows that it lives on today as the most fired round in the world, the 22 rimfire.

The middle 1800s saw no really good centerfire round. During the Civil War period, there were a few centerfire revolver rounds in trial run, but nothing exciting emerged from these dabblings. A folded-head centerfire was tried, with a case much like a rimfire design and a priming affair in the center, but it wasn't the answer. However, by the 1870s, the shooter did have a handful of good rounds, a big handful at that, which were of the "central fire" design, as centerfires were first called. The Winchester catalog of 1878 shows many of military design, but used by sportsmen in sporting rifles. Among these were the 40-70, 40-49, 43 Peabody, 43 Spanish, 43 Egyptian, 44-60, 44-90, 45-100 Sharps, 45 Government (the 45-70), 45-75 Winchester, 50-70, 58 Musket, and many more.

Good "central fires" were on hand in the 1890s. And a boatload of them to boot. Taking a look at the Winchester catalog for 1896, there were at least one hundred loads available, probably more than one hundred ten. These ranged from the 236 Navy (smokeless powder) through a 58 Roberts. Remember, the smokeless 25-35, 30-30, 30-40 Krag (called the 30 U.S. Army then) were all on hand in the late 1800s. The sportsman had a tremendous variety of rounds to select from. Smokeless powder was poised for a takeover. In 1886, the French military had its famous 8mm Lebel cartridge. This round of highly tapered body was fitted with a metal-jacketed bullet. The metal-jacketed bullet arose in Switzerland in 1880, according to Johnson and Haven, and Vielle of France had invented a viable smokeless powder. So, the 8mm Lebel was the first smokeless-powder round, and its 200-grain bullet left the muzzle at about 2,000 feet per second.

The sportsmen of the world not only had a cartridge, but also a jacketed bullet and smokeless powder. The chore of bore cleanup was diminished greatly, and noncorrosive ammo was freeing shooters to shoot instead of swab barrels. I want to inject that these advances were highly welcomed, but not every shooter took to cartridges and smokeless powder with cheers and adulation. Some diehards still had muzzle-loaders on hand and used them well. And to this very day, the relaxation and challenge of the smokepole lives on. But happy is the shooter who can grab a box of factory ammo and head to range or field knowing it will be accurate, dependable, and clean-shooting.

Modern ammo-crafting is automated. Winchester makes some of its own gunpowder at its plant, but also buys propellants from other companies. Raw materials are trucked or railed to the plant and Winchester-Olin makes brass on the spot. When the shape of the case is right, the head is pierced for the flash hole and the cartridge case is ready for its job as container of bullet and powder. Winchester also produces many bullets, of various designs, at the rate of several hundred per minute.

In order to produce quality ammo, quality control is the byword. Everything is constantly checked and statistical analyses are made along the way. Bullets are gauge-checked. They must be close to perfect. The bullets are tested not only by measurement, but also by shooting samples. The samples are randomly selected from the batch and if

The 8mm Lebel, left, was the first smokeless-powder cartridge to be widely used. It was France's military round. Note that it is a rimmed case. The 30-06 Springfield is on the right.

From the left, Speer 100-grain Plinker half-jacket, Hornady 110-grain RN, Sierra 125-grain HP, Speer 130-grain FP, Speer 150-grain Mag-Tip, Hornady 165-grain BTSP, Nosler 165-grain Ballistic Tip, Sierra 170-grain FN, Nosler 180-grain Protected Point, Nosler 200-grain Partition, and the Winchester 220-grain Silvertip.

these samples are not superb, the batch is checked further.

Primers are also made at the plant. Remember that a primer is composed of the cup, its housing, the compound which makes the flash, plus a metal anvil which acts as a sort of detonator of the primer, all perfectly fitted together.

With over five hundred rounds per minute spewing out of the machinery, it's rather astonishing that such high precision is the result, but it is. Actually, the operation is fully automated, with only a few steps requiring human intervention. As the cases are loaded with powder, everything is constantly policed by ever-watchful instruments and should a spark originate anywhere, even the slightest spark, it is instantly doused by a deluge. The finished ammo is even automatically packaged. Finally, there is inspection, and it's white-glove rigid. So much as a mere blemish means that the round is culled. Every company operates under the same code, and that is why our ammunition is so perfect.

In my lifetime of shooting, I have experienced one centerfire round which did not go off. That misfire happened to be with a 7mm Mauser cartridge, factory-loaded, and not terribly old, though it was not new either. That is, the cartridge was not from a brand-new box of fodder. I've had a few misfires with 22 ammo, but only with long-stored boxes, and ill stored at that. I once located a garage-sale batch of 22 Long Rifle ammo which was loose and which had been subjected to oil. The rounds all had to be wiped down before loading. Of the batch, maybe 10 percent failed to fire.

So factory ammunition is a marvel and that statement is provable on the range, not only in accuracy tests but in precision of dimensions and in reliability.

Ammunition should not be left in high-humidity environments, in spite of the good sealing which factory rounds undergo. I think this is more true of rimfire than centerfire rounds. Keep the ammo dry and boxed up. Those military-type ammunition boxes made of metal and provided with a rubber seal are superior for storing ammo. And a lock can be rigged on the box.

The range of factory-loaded calibers is wide for many different cartridges and deep in variation of loads. And don't forget that we riflemen not only have the wonderful ammunition created on our shores, but also a supply of fine shootables from across the waves and over the borders. Good ammo is made in Canada. Good ammo is made in Mexico and South America. Good ammo comes from Europe as well. I currently have in my ammo lineup 22-rimfire ammunition made in Mexico—some from Navy Arms Company, some from Sovereign. I have some good 22 fodder from Argentina, too, under the Charles Daly brand name. And I have some wonderful ammunition from RWS, from BB Cap to 375 H&H full metal jacket.

TODAY'S RIFLE AMMUNITION

22-Caliber Rimfire

The 22-caliber rimfire is well represented, from

the BB Cap all the way up to the powerful 22 Winchester Magnum Rimfire, or 22 WMR, as it is known. The 22 Long Rifle (22 LR) is most fired by far, of course, and of the three to three and one-half billion rounds of 22-rimfire ammo sent from the muzzle of 22 firearms in our country, most of it is 22 LR configuration. There was a very good 20-caliber-rimfire round available for a while, but it faded out.

17-Caliber Centerfires

The only factory-loaded 17-caliber cartridge now is the 17 Remington. Its factory load consists of a 25-grain bullet, .1725-inch diameter, zipped out at a MV of 4,040 fps. This flat-shooter is fun to fire and useful in varmint control. Coyote hunters also found that the bullet did modest hide damage to valuable furs. Beautiful, petite custom rifles can be made up on this small caliber.

22-Caliber Centerfires

From 22 Hornet, with a 45-grain bullet in the 2,600 to 2,700 fps range, the centerfire 22s move all the way to the still-hot Swift, throwing a 50-grain bullet at over 4,000 fps MV. These fast 22s are flat-shooting and they serve the long-range rifleman well.

6mm-Caliber Centerfires

The 6mm-243 group is represented by several very good 24-caliber cartridges. The 243 Winchester, 6mm Remington, and 240 Weatherby all make excellent long-range deer/antelope rounds. The 6mm caliber is not exactly new in America. The 6mm Lee Navy round was offered in the nineteenth century.

25-Caliber Centerfires

Believe it or not, the little 25-20 is still loaded. This fine little pest and small-game number was dropped by gunmakers, but enough rifles existed in 25-20 to keep it going at the ammo factory. The 25-caliber rifle runs the range from the 25-20 and 256 Winchester, all the way to the hottest 25 of the day, the 257 Weatherby Magnum, firing a 100-grain bullet at over 3,500 fps MV, even up to 3,600+ in handloads, with middle-of-the-roaders such as the 250 Savage and 257 Roberts still holding onto a very good following.

6.5mm-Caliber Centerfires

American shooters have never swooned over the

The extremely popular 30-30 is on the far left, then the famous 30-06, the big 8mm Remington Magnum, the 358 Winchester next, with the tiny 17 Remington with its 25-grain bullet on the far right.

6.5mm or .264-inch caliber, but it's a good one and our own 6.5 Remington Magnum and 264 Winchester Magnum are examples of its value. Today, these are the only 6.5s commercially loaded in the U.S., but Norma and RWS companies list several European rounds in their lineup.

270-Caliber Centerfires

It's a surprise that we don't have a bucketful of 270s around. The 270 Winchester cartridge, no more than a 30-06 necked down to shoot bullets of .277-inch diameter, has been amazingly popular. But as these words go to press, only the 270 Winchester and 270 Weatherby Magnum, a heated-up 270, are readily available.

7mm-Caliber Centerfires

A standard of the Europeans for years, the 7mms served even as elephant-takers in the hands of at least one famous ivory hunter, W. D. M. Bell. Our new and sensible 7mm-08, a 7mm based on the 308 Winchester case, shows that our interest is not lacking in this caliber. Furthermore, I believe that the 7mm Remington Magnum, or any round of the

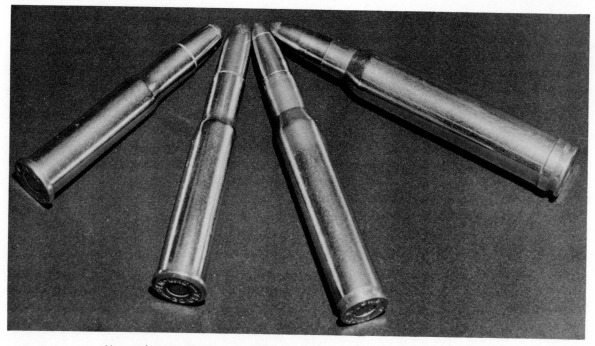

Here are four 30-caliber cartridges: the most popular 30 caliber of all, the 30-30 Winchester, on the left. Next, the 30-40 Krag, first smokeless round used widely in this country when it was called the 30 Army, then the 30-06, most popular round in the West today, and finally the powerful 300 Winchester Magnum.

same ballistics, is the finest all-around cartridge loaded in the world today. The late Warren Page supported the cartridge and was instrumental in increasing its popularity. The old 7mm Mauser is still loaded, too. Norma loads for the 7 × 64 Brenneke, a round resembling a 7mm-06 wildcat, and RWS offers factory ammo for the 7 × 64, too. Seven millimeter bullets are, in fact, .284 inch in diameter.

30-Caliber Centerfires

This caliber has most caught the eye of the American big-bore shooter over the years. Today, the little 30 Carbine is loaded for sporting use, as is the big 300 Winchester Magnum, 300 Weatherby Magnum, and 308 Norma Magnum. Naturally, the little 30-30 is still snorting around, and the newer 307 Winchester is offered in the Model 94 carbine for those who want more punch in a little 30-caliber rifle. The range of 30s runs broad indeed, and the 30-06 is still regarded by many as the best. The old 300 Savage is still with us; the 308 Winchester is widely used overseas as well as here; the old 30-40 Krag is still loaded; and the venerable 303 Savage, too. The 30 is well represented.

31-Caliber Centerfires

This little group includes the 303 British round, which is still used widely by sportsmen. The 303 British fires a bullet in the .309 to .317 range, very slightly larger than the .308-inch bullet standard for the 30 calibers. Of course, our own 303 Savage was a 31 caliber at first, being loaded with bullets in the .311-inch domain, but today the bullet for it, namely the 190-grain Silvertip, is indeed .308 inch. The old 32-20 Winchester is still loaded. It was supposed to be a varmint round with deer also in the picture. Never was a real deer slayer, but it made a lot of folks happy, including this shooter, and it's still loaded with its 31-caliber bullets (despite its 32-20 designation, it's a 31 caliber).

32-Caliber Centerfires

Represented by the old 32-40 Winchester, the 32 Winchester Special, and the 32 Remington these days, the 32s are not very popular. A few 32-40s were factory-loaded by Winchester not too long ago, but don't look to the gun shops for 32-40s today. It's unlikely that your dealer has any. The 32 Remington has also disappeared. It was a ballistic copy of the 32 Special, which is still loaded because so many Model 94s were chambered for it.

8mm-Caliber Centerfires

The German service cartridge, the 8×57, or 8mm Mauser, was brought into use in this country and is still loaded today by sportsmen. The newer 8mm Remington Magnum is a long-cased cartridge firing a 185-grain bullet at almost 3,100 fps MV and a 220-grain bullet at over 2,800 fps MV, a real powerhouse, but not terribly popular at the moment.

33-Caliber Centerfires

At one time, the 33 Winchester was a very popular round. In fact, it was the most modern round used in the famous 1886 rifle. But it's gone in factory form now. However, the 338 Winchester and 340 Weatherby Magnum are strongly favored by hunters of big game, so caliber 33 is still alive and well, and some hunters want a factory 33 based on the 30-06 case, though their pleas are presently falling on ears filled with cotton.

34-Caliber Centerfires

The only 34-caliber round loaded today is the 348 Winchester. It fires a 200-grain bullet at about 2,500 fps MV. It used to be loaded with 150- and 250-grain bullets as well, but today the 200 is it. It always was, still is, a powerful timber round for big game.

35-Caliber Centerfires

The 351 Winchester is still loaded. So is the fine 35 Remington. The powerful 358 Winchester is still used, and a new 356 with somewhat similar ballistics was recently chambered in the Model 94 lever-action rifle. The 350 Remington Magnum is loaded, too. Ammo for the powerful 350 Norma Magnum is pretty hard to locate at the moment.

375-Caliber Centerfires

The 38-55 Winchester is a 375 (shooting bullets of .375-inch diameter). And you can still buy 38-55 ammo today. The newer 375 Winchester is an update of the 38-55, though the two are *not* interchangeable, and the great 375 H&H round is loaded in this country, though its actual need here is limited. Weatherby has a hotter 375 in its 378 Weatherby chambering, too. It shoots a 270-grain bullet at almost 3,200 fps MV. The little 38-40 deer round is still loaded, too.

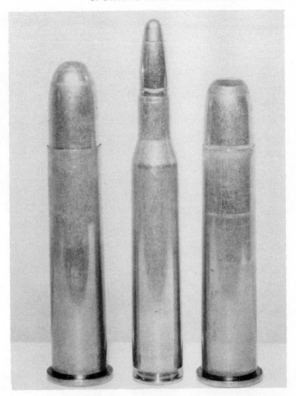

The U.S. Army adopted the 45-70 Government cartridge in 1873. It is still factory-loaded. The 270 Winchester is in the center. The 45-70 round loaded with a 500-grain bullet on the left, and with a 405-grain bullet on the right.

44-Caliber Centerfires

The famous 44-40 is presently loaded. The 44 Remington Magnum handgun round is very much a rifle round these days. And Marlin's 444 is available with a 240-grain bullet with about 2,350 fps MV. So the 44 is still bought in factory chamberings for sporting rifles.

45-Caliber Centerfires

This is about as large as American shooters care to go, though in muzzle-loader days 54s, 58s, even 60s to 75s were not uncommon. A holdover from the Civil War is the 45-70, or 45-70 Government, if you prefer the full title. This great old round is still a puncher, even in its factory form, which is loaded considerably lighter than the round's potential due to the old Trap Door Springfield 45-70 being fired to this day. However, there are also new loads with a 300-grain bullet at close to 1,900 fps, and the handloader can really make the old 45-70 rumble if his rifle will take it.

Using a plastic sabot, the 30-30 Accelerator fires a 55-grain, 22-caliber bullet at 3,400 fps MV.

A big surprise is the 458 Winchester, a wonderful African round loaded by Winchester since 1956. This is a powerful cartridge of 30-06 length. It is loaded with a 500-grain bullet, soft-point of full metal jacket (FMJ), and goes about 2,100 fps. It's considered adequate for elephants, and yet American shooters buy enough of this ammo to keep it going strong. If you want a more powerful 45-caliber rifle yet, Weatherby has its 460. The 460 Weatherby tosses a 500-grain bullet at 2,700 fps MV and its energy level is close to 6,500 foot-pounds.

Accelerators

It's hard to find a niche for a cartridge that exists as two calibers at once, so the Accelerators were held over for their own section. The 30-30, 308 Winchester, and 30-06 are offered as Accelerator rounds at the moment. A sabot (pronounced sah-bow) of plastic is used to contain a 22-caliber bullet, allowing this 22-caliber bullet to be fired from these 30-caliber cartridges. Actually, Accelerators work quite well, and my own chronograph tests showed the 30-30 Accelerator pushing its 22-caliber, 55-grain bullet at 3,400 fps MV. The 308 drives the same bullet at about 3,770 fps, and the 30-06 shoots the 55-grain, 22-caliber bullet at about 4,080 fps MV. The sabot idea is really quite old, but it still works.

We can have confidence in factory-loaded ammo because the companies, not only here but abroad, have earned that confidence. In fact, the ammunition of the hour is the best ever produced in the history of firearms. And yet, it is produced faster and in greater quantity for sportsmen than ever before. The American rifleman can walk into any sporting goods store in the country and he's likely to find his brand of shooting fodder, for ammo is well distributed. I don't know what more we could ask for.

Modern Cartridge Ballistics

CALIBERS	BULLET			VELOCITY FEET PER SECOND					
	Wt.-Grs.	Style	Primer No.	Muzzle	100 Yds.	200 Yds.	300 Yds.	400 Yds.	500 Yds.
17 Rem.	25	Hollow Point Power-Lokt®	7½	4040	3284	2644	2086	1606	1235
22 Hornet	45	Pointed Soft Point	6½	2690	2042	1502	1128	948	840
	45	Hollow Point	6½	2690	2042	1502	1128	948	840
222 Rem.	50	Pointed Soft Point	7½	3140	2602	2123	1700	1350	1107
	50	Hollow Point Power-Lokt	7½	3140	2635	2182	1777	1432	1172
	55	Metal Case	7½	3020	2562	2147	1773	1451	1201
222 Rem. Mag.	55	Pointed Soft Point	7½	3240	2748	2305	1906	1556	1272
	55	Hollow Point Power-Lokt	7½	3240	2773	2352	1969	1627	1341
223 Rem.	55	Pointed Soft Point	7½	3240	2747	2304	1905	1554	1270
	55	Hollow Point Power-Lokt	·7½	3240	2773	2352	1969	1627	1341
	55	Metal Case	7½	3240	2759	2326	1933	1587	1301
22-250 Rem.	55	Pointed Soft Point	9½	3680	3137	2656	2222	1832	1493
	55	Hollow Point Power-Lokt	9½	3680	3209	2785	2400	2046	1725
243 Win.	80	Pointed Soft Point	9½	3350	2955	2593	2259	1951	1670
	80	Hollow Point Power-Lokt	9½	3350	2955	2593	2259	1951	1670
	100	Pointed Soft Point Core-Lokt	9½	2960	2697	2449	2215	1993	1786
6mm Rem.	80	Pointed Soft Point	9½	3470	3064	2694	2352	2036	1747
	80	Hollow Point Power-Lokt	9½	3470	3064	2694	2352	2036	1747
	100	Pointed Soft Point Core-Lokt	9½	3100	2829	2573	2332	2104	1889
25-20 Win.	86	Soft Point	6½	1460	1194	1030	931	858	797
250 Sav.	100	Pointed Soft Point	9½	2820	2504	2210	1936	1684	1461
257 Roberts	117	Soft Point Core-Lokt	9½	2650	2291	1961	1663	1404	1199
25-06 Rem.	87	Hollow Point Power-Lokt	9½	3440	2995	2591	2222	1884	1583
	100	Pointed Soft Point Core-Lokt	9½	3230	2893	2580	2287	2014	1762
	120	Pointed Soft Point Core-Lokt	9½	2990	2730	2484	2252	2032	1825
6.5mm. Rem. Mag.	120	Pointed Soft Point Core-Lokt	9½M	3210	2905	2621	2353	2102	1867
264 Win. Mag.	140	Pointed Soft Point Core-Lokt	9½M	3030	2782	2548	2326	2114	1914
270 Win.	100	Pointed Soft Point	9½	3430	3021	2649	2305	1988	1699
	130	Pointed Soft Point Core-Lokt	9½	3060	2776	2510	2259	2022	1801
	130	Bronze Point	9½	3060	2802	2559	2329	2110	1904
	150	Soft Point Core-Lokt	9½	2850	2504	2183	1886	1618	1385
7mm Mauser	140	Pointed Soft Point	9½	2660	2435	2221	2018	1827	1648
7mm-08 Rem.	140	Pointed Soft Point	9½	2860	2625	2402	2189	1988	1798
280 Rem.	140	Pointed Soft Point	9½	3000	2758	2528	2309	2102	1905
	150	Pointed Soft Point Core-Lokt	9½	2890	2624	2373	2135	1912	1705
	165	Soft Point Core-Lokt	9½	2820	2510	2220	1950	1701	1479
7mm Rem. Mag.	150	Pointed Soft Point Core-Lokt	9½M	3110	2830	2568	2320	2085	1866
	175	Pointed Soft Point Core-Lokt	9½M	2860	2645	2440	2244	2057	1879
30 Carbine	110	Soft Point	6½	1990	1567	1236	1035	923	842
30 Rem.	170	Soft Point Core-Lokt	9½	2120	1822	1555	1328	1153	1036
30-30 Win. "Accelerator"	55	Soft Point	9½	3400	2693	2085	1570	1187	986
30-30 Win.	150	Soft Point Core-Lokt	9½	2390	1973	1605	1303	1095	974
	170	Soft Point Core-Lokt	9½	2200	1895	1619	1381	1191	1061
	170	Hollow Point Core-Lokt	9½	2200	1895	1619	1381	1191	1061

Remington Arms

TRAJECTORY† 0.0 Indicates yardage at which rifle was sighted in.

ENERGY FOOT-POUNDS						SHORT RANGE — Bullet does not rise more than one inch above line of sight from muzzle to sighting-in range.						LONG RANGE — Bullet does not rise more than three inches above line of sight from muzzle to sighting-in range.							BARREL LENGTH
Muzzle	100 Yds.	200 Yds.	300 Yds.	400 Yds.	500 Yds.	50 Yds.	100 Yds.	150 Yds.	200 Yds.	250 Yds.	300 Yds.	100 Yds.	150 Yds.	200 Yds.	250 Yds.	300 Yds.	400 Yds.	500 Yds.	
906	599	388	242	143	85	0.1	0.5	0.0	−1.5	−4.2	−8.5	2.1	2.5	1.9	0.0	−3.4	−17.0	−44.3	24″
723	417	225	127	90	70	0.3	0.0	−2.4	−7.7	−16.9	−31.3	1.6	0.0	−4.5	−12.8	−26.4	−75.6	−163.4	24″
723	417	225	127	90	70	0.3	0.0	−2.4	−7.7	−16.9	−31.3	1.6	0.0	−4.5	−12.8	−26.4	−75.6	−163.4	
1094	752	500	321	202	136	0.5	0.9	0.0	−2.5	−6.9	−13.7	2.2	1.9	0.0	−3.8	−10.0	−32.3	−73.8	
1094	771	529	351	228	152	0.5	0.9	0.0	−2.4	−6.6	−13.1	2.1	1.8	0.0	−3.6	−9.5	−30.2	−68.1	24″
1114	801	563	384	257	176	0.6	1.0	0.0	−2.5	−7.0	−13.7	2.2	1.9	0.0	−3.8	−9.9	−31.0	−68.7	
1282	922	649	444	296	198	0.4	0.8	0.0	−2.2	−6.0	−11.8	1.9	1.6	0.0	−3.3	−8.5	−26.7	−59.5	24″
1282	939	675	473	323	220	0.4	0.8	0.0	−2.1	−5.8	−11.4	1.8	1.6	0.0	−3.2	−8.2	−25.5	−56.0	
1282	921	648	443	295	197	0.4	0.8	0.0	−2.2	−6.0	−11.8	1.9	1.6	0.0	−3.3	−8.5	−26.7	−59.6	
1282	939	675	473	323	220	0.4	0.8	0.0	−2.1	−5.8	−11.4	1.8	1.6	0.0	−3.2	−8.2	−25.5	−56.0	24″
1282	929	660	456	307	207	0.4	0.8	0.0	−2.1	−5.9	−11.6	1.9	1.6	0.0	−3.2	−8.4	−26.2	−57.9	
1654	1201	861	603	410	272	0.2	0.5	0.0	−1.6	−4.4	−8.7	2.3	2.6	1.9	0.0	−3.4	−15.9	−38.9	24″
1654	1257	947	703	511	363	0.2	0.5	0.0	−1.5	−4.1	−8.0	2.1	2.5	1.8	0.0	−3.1	−14.1	−33.4	
1993	1551	1194	906	676	495	0.3	0.7	0.0	−1.8	−4.9	−9.4	2.6	2.9	2.1	0.0	−3.6	−16.2	−37.9	
1993	1551	1194	906	676	495	0.3	0.7	0.0	−1.8	−4.9	−9.4	2.6	2.9	2.1	0.0	−3.6	−16.2	−37.9	24″
1945	1615	1332	1089	882	708	0.5	0.9	0.0	−2.2	−5.8	−11.0	1.9	1.6	0.0	−3.1	−7.8	−22.6	−46.3	
2139	1667	1289	982	736	542	0.3	0.6	0.0	−1.6	−4.5	−8.7	2.4	2.7	1.9	0.0	−3.3	−14.9	−35.0	
2139	1667	1289	982	736	542	0.3	0.6	0.0	−1.6	−4.5	−8.7	2.4	2.7	1.9	0.0	−3.3	−14.9	−35.0	
2133	1777	1470	1207	983	792	0.4	0.8	0.0	−1.9	−5.2	−9.9	1.7	1.5	0.0	−2.8	−7.0	−20.4	−41.7	24″
407	272	203	165	141	121	0.0	−4.1	−14.4	−31.8	−57.3	−92.0	0.0	−8.2	−23.5	−47.0	−79.6	−175.9	−319.4	24″
1765	1392	1084	832	630	474	0.2	0.0	−1.6	−4.7	−9.6	−16.5	2.3	2.0	0.0	−3.7	−9.5	−28.3	−59.5	24″
1824	1363	999	718	512	373	0.3	0.0	−1.9	−5.8	−11.9	−20.7	2.9	2.4	0.0	−4.7	−12.0	−36.7	−79.2	24″
2286	1733	1297	954	686	484	0.3	0.6	0.0	−1.7	−4.8	−9.3	2.5	2.9	2.1	0.0	−3.6	−16.4	−39.1	
2316	1858	1478	1161	901	689	0.4	0.7	0.0	−1.9	−5.0	−9.7	1.6	1.4	0.0	−2.7	−6.9	−20.5	−42.7	24″
2382	1985	1644	1351	1100	887	0.5	0.8	0.0	−2.1	−5.6	−10.7	1.9	1.6	0.0	−3.0	−7.5	−22.0	−44.8	
2745	2248	1830	1475	1177	929	0.4	0.7	0.0	−1.8	−4.9	−9.5	2.7	3.0	2.1	0.0	−3.5	−15.5	−35.3	24″
2854	2406	2018	1682	1389	1139	0.5	0.8	0.0	−2.0	−5.4	−10.2	1.8	1.5	0.0	−2.9	−7.2	−20.8	−42.2	24″
2612	2027	1557	1179	877	641	0.3	0.6	0.0	−1.7	−4.6	−9.0	2.5	2.8	2.0	0.0	−3.4	−15.5	−36.4	
2702	2225	1818	1472	1180	936	0.5	0.8	0.0	−2.0	−5.5	−10.4	1.8	1.5	0.0	−2.9	−7.4	−21.6	−44.3	
2702	2267	1890	1565	1285	1046	0.4	0.8	0.0	−2.0	−5.3	−10.1	1.8	1.5	0.0	−2.8	−7.1	−20.6	−42.0	24″
2705	2087	1587	1185	872	639	0.7	1.0	0.0	−2.6	−7.1	−13.6	2.3	2.0	0.0	−3.8	−9.7	−29.2	−62.2	
2199	1843	1533	1266	1037	844	0.2	0.0	−1.7	−5.0	−10.0	−17.0	2.5	2.0	0.0	−3.8	−9.6	−27.7	−56.3	24″
2542	2142	1793	1490	1228	1005	0.6	0.9	0.0	−2.3	−6.1	−11.6	2.1	1.7	0.0	−3.2	−8.1	−23.5	−47.7	24″
2797	2363	1986	1657	1373	1128	0.5	0.8	0.0	−2.1	−5.5	−10.4	1.8	1.5	0.0	−2.9	−7.3	−21.1	−42.9	
2781	2293	1875	1518	1217	968	0.6	0.9	0.0	−2.3	−6.2	−11.8	2.1	1.7	0.0	−3.3	−8.3	−24.2	−49.7	24″
2913	2308	1805	1393	1060	801	0.2	0.0	−1.5	−4.6	−9.5	−16.4	2.3	1.9	0.0	−3.7	−9.4	−28.1	−58.8	
3221	2667	2196	1792	1448	1160	0.4	0.8	0.0	−1.9	−5.2	−9.9	1.7	1.5	0.0	−2.8	−7.0	−20.5	−42.1	24″
3178	2718	2313	1956	1644	1372	0.6	0.9	0.0	−2.3	−6.0	−11.3	2.0	1.7	0.0	−3.2	−7.9	−22.7	−45.8	
967	600	373	262	208	173	0.9	0.0	−4.5	−13.5	−28.3	−49.9	0.0	−4.5	−13.5	−28.3	−49.9	−118.6	−228.2	20″
1696	1253	913	666	502	405	0.7	0.0	−3.3	−9.7	−19.6	−33.8	2.2	0.0	−5.3	−14.1	−27.2	−69.0	−136.9	24″
1412	886	521	301	172	119	0.4	0.8	0.0	−2.4	−6.7	−13.8	2.0	1.8	0.0	−3.8	−10.2	−35.0	−84.4	24″
1902	1296	858	565	399	316	0.5	0.0	−2.7	−8.2	−17.0	−30.0	1.8	0.0	−4.6	−12.5	−24.6	−65.3	−134.9	
1827	1355	989	720	535	425	0.6	0.0	−3.0	−8.9	−18.0	−31.1	2.0	0.0	−4.8	−13.0	−25.1	−63.6	−126.7	24″
1827	1355	989	720	535	425	0.6	0.0	−3.0	−8.9	−18.0	−31.1	2.0	0.0	−4.8	−13.0	−25.1	−63.6	−126.7	

Remington Arms

Modern Cartridge Ballistics

CALIBERS	BULLET Wt.-Grs.	BULLET Style	Primer No.	VELOCITY FEET PER SECOND Muzzle	100 Yds.	200 Yds.	300 Yds.	400 Yds.	500 Yds.
300 Savage	180	Soft Point Core-Lokt	9½	2350	2025	1728	1467	1252	1098
	180	Pointed Soft Point Core-Lokt	9½	2350	2137	1935	1745	1570	1413
30-40 Krag	180	Pointed Soft Point Core-Lokt	9½	2430	2213	2007	1813	1632	1468
308 Win. "Accelerator"	55	Pointed Soft Point	9½	3770	3215	2726	2286	1888	1541
308 Win.	150	Pointed Soft Point Core-Lokt	9½	2820	2533	2263	2009	1774	1560
	165	Pointed Soft Point Core-Lokt	9½	2700	2440	2194	1963	1748	1551
	180	Soft Point Core-Lokt	9½	2620	2274	1955	1666	1414	1212
	180	Pointed Soft Point Core-Lokt	9½	2620	2393	2178	1974	1782	1604
30-06 "Accelerator"	55	Pointed Soft Point	9½	4080	3485	2965	2502	2083	1709
30-06 Springfield	125	Pointed Soft Point	9½	3140	2780	2447	2138	1853	1595
	150	Pointed Soft Point Core-Lokt	9½	2910	2617	2342	2083	1843	1622
	150	Bronze Point	9½	2910	2656	2416	2189	1974	1773
	165	Pointed Soft Point Core-Lokt	9½	2800	2534	2283	2047	1825	1621
	180	Soft Point Core-Lokt	9½	2700	2348	2023	1727	1466	1251
	180	Pointed Soft Point Core-Lokt	9½	2700	2469	2250	2042	1846	1663
	180	Bronze Point	9½	2700	2485	2280	2084	1899	1725
	220	Soft Point Core-Lokt	9½	2410	2130	1870	1632	1422	1246
300 H. & H. Mag.	180	Pointed Soft Point Core-Lokt	9½M	2880	2640	2412	2196	1990	1798
300 Win. Mag.	150	Pointed Soft Point Core-Lokt	9½M	3290	2951	2636	2342	2068	1813
	180	Pointed Soft Point Core-Lokt	9½M	2960	2745	2540	2344	2157	1979
303 British	180	Soft Point Core-Lokt	9½	2460	2124	1817	1542	1311	1137
32-20 Win.	100	Lead	6½	1210	1021	913	834	769	712
	100	Soft Point	6½	1210	1021	913	834	769	712
32 Win. Special	170	Soft Point Core-Lokt	9½	2250	1921	1626	1372	1175	1044
8mm Mauser	170	Soft Point Core-Lokt	9½	2360	1969	1622	1333	1123	997
8mm Rem. Mag.	185	Pointed Soft Point Core-Lokt	9½M	3080	2761	2464	2186	1927	1688
	220	Pointed Soft Point Core-Lokt	9½M	2830	2581	2346	2123	1913	1716
35 Rem.	150	Pointed Soft Point Core-Lokt	9½	2300	1874	1506	1218	1039	934
	200	Soft Point Core-Lokt	9½	2080	1698	1376	1140	1001	911
350 Rem. Mag.	200	Pointed Soft Point Core-Lokt	9½M	2710	2410	2130	1870	1631	1421
375 H. & H. Mag.	270	Soft Point	9½M	2690	2420	2166	1928	1707	1507
	300	Metal Case	9½M	2530	2171	1843	1551	1307	1126
44-40 Win.	200	Soft Point	2½	1190	1006	900	822	756	699
44 Rem. Mag.	240	Soft Point	2½	1760	1380	1114	970	878	806
	240	Semi-Jacketed Hollow Point	2½	1760	1380	1114	970	878	806
444 Mar.	240	Soft Point	9½	2350	1815	1377	1087	941	846
	265	Soft Point	9½	2120	1733	1405	1160	1012	920
45-70 Government	405	Soft Point	9½	1330	1168	1055	977	918	869
458 Win. Mag.	500	Metal Case	9½M	2040	1823	1623	1442	1237	1161
	500	Soft Point	9½M	2040	1770	1527	1319	1157	1046

TRAJECTORY† 0.0 Indicates yardage at which rifle was sighted in.

ENERGY FOOT-POUNDS						SHORT RANGE Bullet does not rise more than one inch above line of sight from muzzle to sighting-in range.						LONG RANGE Bullet does not rise more than three inches above line of sight from muzzle to sighting-in range.							BARREL LENGTH
Muzzle	100 Yds.	200 Yds.	300 Yds.	400 Yds.	500 Yds.	50 Yds.	100 Yds.	150 Yds.	200 Yds.	250 Yds.	300 Yds.	100 Yds.	150 Yds.	200 Yds.	250 Yds.	300 Yds.	400 Yds.	500 Yds.	
2207	1639	1193	860	626	482	0.5	0.0	−2.6	−7.7	−15.6	−27.1	1.7	0.0	−4.2	−11.3	−21.9	−55.8	−112.0	24″
2207	1825	1496	1217	985	798	0.4	0.0	−2.3	−6.7	−13.5	−22.8	1.5	0.0	−3.6	−9.6	−18.2	−44.1	−84.2	24″
2360	1957	1610	1314	1064	861	0.4	0.0	−2.1	−6.2	−12.5	−21.1	1.4	0.0	−3.4	−8.9	−16.8	−40.9	−78.1	24″
1735	1262	907	638	435	290	0.2	0.5	0.0	−1.5	−4.2	−8.2	2.2	2.5	1.8	0.0	−3.2	−15.0	−36.7	24″
2648	2137	1705	1344	1048	810	0.2	0.0	−1.5	−4.5	−9.3	−15.9	2.3	1.9	0.0	−3.6	−9.1	−26.9	−55.7	
2670	2180	1763	1411	1119	881	0.2	0.0	−1.7	−5.0	−10.1	−17.2	2.5	2.1	0.0	−3.9	−9.7	−28.5	−58.8	24″
2743	2066	1527	1109	799	587	0.3	0.0	−2.0	−5.9	−12.1	−20.9	2.9	2.4	0.0	−4.7	−12.1	−36.9	−79.1	
2743	2288	1896	1557	1269	1028	0.2	0.0	−1.8	−5.2	−10.4	−17.7	2.6	2.1	0.0	−4.0	−9.9	−28.9	−58.8	
2033	1483	1074	764	530	356	0.4	1.0	0.9	0.0	−1.9	−5.0	1.8	2.1	1.5	0.0	−2.7	−12.5	−30.5	24″
2736	2145	1662	1269	953	706	0.4	0.8	0.0	−2.1	−5.6	−10.7	1.8	1.5	0.0	−3.0	−7.7	−23.0	−48.5	
2820	2281	1827	1445	1131	876	0.6	0.9	0.0	−2.3	−6.3	−12.0	2.1	1.8	0.0	−3.3	−8.5	−25.0	−51.8	
2820	2349	1944	1596	1298	1047	0.6	0.9	0.0	−2.2	−6.0	−11.4	2.0	1.7	0.0	−3.2	−8.0	−23.3	−47.5	
2872	2352	1909	1534	1220	963	0.7	1.0	0.0	−2.5	−6.7	−12.7	2.3	1.9	0.0	−3.6	−9.0	−26.3	−54.1	
2913	2203	1635	1192	859	625	0.2	0.0	−1.8	−5.5	−11.2	−19.5	2.7	2.3	0.0	−4.4	−11.3	−34.4	−73.7	24″
2913	2436	2023	1666	1362	1105	0.2	0.0	−1.6	−4.8	−9.7	−16.5	2.4	2.0	0.0	−3.7	−9.3	−27.0	−54.9	
2913	2468	2077	1736	1441	1189	0.2	0.0	−1.6	−4.7	−9.6	−16.2	2.4	2.0	0.0	−3.6	−9.1	−26.2	−53.0	
2837	2216	1708	1301	988	758	0.4	0.0	−2.3	−6.8	−13.8	−23.6	1.5	0.0	−3.7	−9.9	−19.0	−47.4	−93.1	
3315	2785	2325	1927	1583	1292	0.6	0.9	0.0	−2.3	−6.0	−11.5	2.1	1.7	0.0	−3.2	−8.0	−23.3	−47.4	24″
3605	2900	2314	1827	1424	1095	0.3	0.7	0.0	−1.8	−4.8	−9.3	2.6	2.9	2.1	0.0	−3.5	−15.4	−35.5	24″
3501	3011	2578	2196	1859	1565	0.5	0.8	0.0	−2.1	−5.5	−10.4	1.9	1.6	0.0	−2.9	−7.3	−20.9	−41.9	
2418	1803	1319	950	687	517	0.4	0.0	−2.3	−6.9	−14.1	−24.4	1.5	0.0	−3.8	−10.2	−19.8	−50.5	−101.5	24″
325	231	185	154	131	113	0.0	−6.3	−20.9	−44.9	−79.3	−125.1	0.0	−11.5	−32.3	−63.8	−106.3	−230.3	−413.3	
325	231	185	154	131	113	0.0	−6.3	−20.9	−44.9	−79.3	−125.1	0.0	−11.5	−32.3	−63.6	−106.3	−230.3	−413.3	24″
1911	1393	998	710	521	411	0.6	0.0	−2.9	−8.6	−17.6	−30.5	1.9	0.0	−4.7	−12.7	−24.7	−63.2	−126.9	24″
2102	1463	993	671	476	375	0.5	0.0	−2.7	−8.2	−17.0	−29.8	1.8	0.0	−4.5	−12.4	−24.3	−63.8	−130.7	24″
3896	3131	2494	1963	1525	1170	0.5	0.8	0.0	−2.1	−5.6	−10.7	1.8	1.6	0.0	−3.0	−7.6	−22.5	−46.8	
3912	3254	2688	2201	1787	1438	0.6	1.0	0.0	−2.4	−6.4	−12.1	2.2	1.8	0.0	−3.4	−8.5	−24.7	−50.5	24″
1762	1169	755	494	359	291	0.6	0.0	−3.0	−9.2	−19.1	−33.9	2.0	0.0	−5.1	−14.1	−27.8	−74.0	−152.3	
1921	1280	841	577	445	369	0.8	0.0	−3.8	−11.3	−23.5	−41.2	2.5	0.0	−6.3	−17.1	−33.6	−87.7	−176.4	24″
3261	2579	2014	1553	1181	897	0.2	0.0	−1.7	−5.1	−10.4	−17.9	2.6	2.1	0.0	−4.0	−10.3	−30.5	−64.0	20″
4337	3510	2812	2228	1747	1361	0.2	0.0	−1.7	−5.1	−10.3	−17.6	2.5	2.1	0.0	−3.9	−10.0	−29.4	−60.7	
4263	3139	2262	1602	1138	844	0.3	0.0	−2.2	−6.5	−13.5	−23.4	1.5	0.0	−3.6	−9.8	−19.1	−49.1	−99.5	24″
629	449	360	300	254	217	0.0	−6.5	−21.6	−46.3	−81.8	−129.1	0.0	−11.8	−33.3	−65.5	−109.5	−237.4	−426.2	24″
1650	1015	661	501	411	346	0.0	−2.7	−10.0	−23.0	−43.0	−71.2	0.0	−5.9	−17.6	−36.3	−63.1	−145.5	−273.0	
1650	1015	661	501	411	346	0.0	−2.7	−10.0	−23.0	−43.0	−71.2	0.0	−5.9	−17.6	−36.3	−63.1	−145.5	−273.0	20″
2942	1755	1010	630	472	381	0.6	0.0	−3.2	−9.9	−21.3	−38.5	2.1	0.0	−5.6	−15.9	−32.1	−87.8	−182.7	
2644	1768	1162	791	603	498	0.7	0.0	−3.6	−10.8	−22.5	−39.5	2.4	0.0	−6.0	−16.4	−32.2	−84.3	−170.2	24″
1590	1227	1001	858	758	679	0.0	−4.7	−15.8	−34.0	−60.0	−94.5	0.0	−8.7	−24.6	−48.2	−80.3	−172.4	−305.9	24″
4620	3689	2924	2308	1839	1469	0.7	0.0	−3.3	−9.6	−19.2	−32.5	2.2	0.0	−5.2	−13.6	−25.8	−63.2	−121.7	
4712	3547	2640	1970	1516	1239	0.8	0.0	−3.5	−10.3	−20.8	−35.6	2.4	0.0	−5.6	−14.9	−28.5	−71.5	−140.4	24″

	Remington Order No.	Wt. Grs.	Bullet		Velocity— Foot-Pounds		Energy— Foot-Pounds		Mid-Range Trajectory
			Style		Muzzle	100 Yds.	Muzzle	100 Yds.	100 Yds. inches
HYPER VELOCITY 22 CARTRIDGES									
22 Long Rifle "Viper"	1922	36	Truncated Cone, Solid		1410	1056	159	89	3.1
22 Long Rifle "Yellow Jacket"	1722	33	Truncated Cone, Hollow Point		1500	1075	165	85	2.8
"HIGH VELOCITY" 22 CARTRIDGES									
22 Long Rifle	1522 1500†	40	Lead		1255	1017	140	92	3.6
	1622 1600†	36	Hollow Point		1280	1010	131	82	3.5
22 Long	1322	29	Lead		1240	962	99	60	3.9
22 Short	1022	29	Lead		1095	903	77	52	4.5
	1122	27	Hollow Point		1120	904	75	49	4.4
"TARGET" STANDARD VELOCITY 22 CARTRIDGES									
22 Long Rifle	6122 6100†	40	Lead		1150	976	117	85	4.0
22 Short	5522	29	Lead		1045	872	70	49	4.8

† 100-pack. All others packed 50 per box.

4

Picking Your Cartridge

A CHICKEN AND EGG problem exists. Which comes first, cartridge selection or choice of rifle? Do you pick a rifle because it chambers the round you really want, or do you select the rifle of your dreams first, even though it may not carry the exact cartridge you decided on as correct for the task at hand? I think that either avenue of choice can work. But all in all, the heart of that rifle is the cartridge. In other words, though I would far rather pack along a neat saddle gun on a high mountain elk hunt, I'd prefer a bolt-action, long-range powerhouse round, so my little saddle gun stays home.

The trouble with choosing a caliber—and that word is being used in its everyday connotation here—is knowing exactly what you want to do with the sporting rifle that chambers it. My suggestion is first sort out the performances you expect from a round, and then look for the specific cartridge which fills the bill for you. When you do this, you eventually end up with a group of rifles suited for several different tasks. That's called a battery of rifles. And it takes a battery, albeit a small one sometimes, to do the range of work required of the modern sporting rifle.

TRAINING

If you've never owned a rifle, what will you buy as your first one? Or if you are looking to supply a youth with a rifle, which round will it be chambered for? I'm an advocate of air power for a starter rifle. Further, let the rifle be a 17 caliber. You need no larger. Were I to begin a training program with a young shooter, I'd latch onto a very accurate, 17-caliber air rifle of the precision class. Today, there are many of these from various companies. I like the spring-piston design very much and will go into that and other styles in the air-rifle chapter. Much has changed over the years. For the older shooter who remembers the "pellet gun" as an underpowered tin can roller, take note that today's hotshot air rifles can knock a fox out at thirty paces.

Graduation to powder-burning means the 22 rimfire. After teaching the basics of safety and marksmanship with the 17-caliber air rifle, a 22 rimfire would enter the scene, along with plenty of standard-velocity, 22 Long Rifle ammo. Today, there are good bargains on 22-rimfire ammo of the standard-velocity class and a "brick" of 500 rounds will often set you back less than $10.

Finally, there are plenty of reasons for looking to the muzzle-loader as an early training rifle. The muzzle-loader requires hands-on loading techniques. Essentially, each round fired is prepared by the shooter and loaded in the breech by him. (Safety precautions for frontloaders vary from those of the modern rifle in some aspects. See the chapter on safety before starting out with a smoke-and-fire longarm.) But there are advantages other than the first mentioned—for example, the familiarity one gets by seeing the round go downbore first-hand.

There is also a strict responsibility in maintaining

a one-pound can of powder. Patches? You can buy enough pillow ticking to make a shoe-box full of little 32-caliber-sized patches for a buck. All that is left is the percussion cap. If you really want to save, you can make your own caps, too, using the Tap-O-Cap tool from Forster Products. This tool turns aluminum beverage cans and toy caps into percussion caps that work.

Training means laying out the ground rules, especially those of safety, but it also means practice. And these rifles allow for practice without much noise, recoil, or expense.

PLINKING

Some called it plunking for a while. Happily, that term faded out with the Hula-Hoop and 3-D movie glasses, and plinking was left in our shooting vocabulary. Even Honest Abe Lincoln was known to plink a bit. It is a wonderful pastime. When Dave Andrews of CCI, the ammo company, was asked where in the world all of that annually produced ammo went to—upwards of four billion rounds—

Most beginning shooters start with a 22-rimfire rifle, such as this scaled-down Chipmunk model, a single-shot designed to fit the small frame of a youngster. Though this young marksman is not ready to shoot on her own, she's gaining familiarity and learning the safety rules of the sport by examining the rifle that will one day be her own.

the muzzle-loader. You don't shoot, wipe down with an oily rag, and stuff her back in the closet. The bore must be swabbed with solvent and patches and preserving oil introduced in order to preserve the piece. This part of muzzle-loader shooting helps to instill responsibility, too, as does the load-it-yourself aspect. Another good feature of the front-loader as a training piece is cost. If you are willing to do some of the work yourself, there is nothing cheaper to fire than a muzzle-loader. Pick caliber 32 as a starter rifle. It gets the work done and it's the least expensive to shoot. If no 32s are available in the rifle you want, the 36 is a good second choice. And there are plenty of rifles in that caliber.

Think about it—if you scrounge the lead, or even buy it, about one hundred fifty 32-caliber, 45-grain round balls can be home-cast from a single pound of metal for very little cost. Buy a mold. Learn how to *safely* cast your own projectiles, the way our forebears did, and you can create your own bullets for just pennies. As for powder, a mere 10 grains will propel the 45-grain, 32-caliber round ball at pretty close to 22 Long Rifle muzzle velocities. That 10-grain charge gives seven hundred shots for

This little Mowrey 32-caliber Squirrel Rifle can be fired more cheaply than a 22-rimfire rifle.

The Forster Tap-O-Cap tool turns strips of aluminum from beverage cans into percussion caps. Toy caps provide the spark for ignition. Such homemade percussion caps are a part of the muzzle-loader shooting economy plan.

he said, "Most of it goes into dirt banks." And Dave was right. Plinking, informal shooting at tin cans and similar targets, certainly does account for a great quantity of ammo each year.

Of course you can plink with any caliber. I use a 17-caliber air rifle frequently in plinking because of the obvious low cost of projectiles. A few bucks buys five hundred shots. But plinking is mostly a 22-rimfire game. The 22 rimfire offers a "real" firearm for the plinker who has a nice sand hill backstop, and for a buck or two he can spend some very enjoyable time shooting just for the fun of shooting.

I use whatever ammo I can buy at sale prices. The 22 BB Cap, CB Cap, Short Mini-Cap, Short, Long, Long Rifle—all of it works great for plinking. It usually works out that standard-velocity 22 Long Rifle ammo is the easiest to come by, and often the least expensive. Plinkers are inventors of sorts, too. We have invented at least a dozen plinking games, shooting tin cans out of a circle scratched in the dirt in front of a safety bank, drawing pictures on cardboard cutouts using bullet holes

for "crayons," even lighting matches at close range.

Finally, plinking with muzzle-loaders is also a good way to get in a lot of shooting inexpensively. Everything said about the 32- and 36-caliber frontloaders a few breaths ago pertains here. In fact, bullet casters know that they can press their big-game rifles into service at a reasonable rate of cost by making their own projectiles and underloading them appropriately.

INFORMAL TARGET PRACTICE

The idea here is to emulate a later match shoot where the stakes are high. Naturally, cartridge selection here is based on accuracy and appropriateness. When I want to truly chew the center of the bull out, I have a few fine rifles made for the job. In fact, the first is a match-grade, 17-caliber RWS air rifle. Within its own range limitations, basically the 10- to 20-yard domain, it will produce a ragged hole for ten shots.

There are a number of 22-rimfire rifles which do quite well, too, in eating up the bull's-eye, and if you want to see some of the same at longer range, give the 222 Remington and similar rounds a try. I once had a 222 Remington chambered in a heavy-barreled Sako rifle and many times ten shots clustered into a half-inch center-to-center group from the bench at the 100-yard range. Black-powder shooters do a lot of informal target work, too, and with many calibers. But the 40s and up are a bit better in the wind than the smaller numbers. So we often see 45s, even 50s and larger calibers for target work.

MATCH SHOOTING

All sorts of matches exist, from Olympic competition right down to the local gun-club shoot. Naturally, cartridge selection depends on rules. Although neither air-rifle ammo nor black-powder ammo is in cartridge form, both are being considered in this chapter because of their usefulness to riflemen. And again, both fit into some very important matches. There are Olympic-type shoots for both air-powered and black-powder-powered rifles.

The 22 rimfire is used in many highly competitive matches. And, of course, there are big-bore competitions of all sorts, from 100-yard offhand skill-testing to grouping those bullets at a full 1,000 yards from the muzzle. There is also the silhouette match, based on the original *silueta* shoots which came out of Mexico. These matches, in which big bores are used against metallic-cutout targets at very long ranges, require high accuracy in offhand shooting style.

The silhouette shoot has, happily, invaded all of the branches of rifles, from air to big bore. Little silhouette cutouts of chickens and wild turkeys and wild pigs and mountain sheep are clanked on by pellets—Crosman offers a fine set of these targets with official rules for their use. The 22 rimfire is a silhouette rifle, and there is widespread production of special silhouette ammunition for these matches. In big bore, the 7mm-08 is a good choice, as are the 308 Winchester and similar rounds. The rifles are usually customs with very good triggers and special scope sights, appropriate when the targets may be 500 meters away and you have to shoot at them offhand with rifles in the eight-pound class.

LONG-RANGE VARMINT

Now cartridge selection is actually simpler because the choices are narrower. You can shoot long-range at varmints with anything you please, but if you think it's going to be fun banging away all day with a 7mm Magnum, then I hope you have a cast-iron shoulder. I have, to be sure, tested some big-game rifles by helping to control varmints of the prairie dog type on local ranches. When these "dogs" reach certain numbers, their towns are often poisoned, for the tunnels they build cripple livestock and sometimes destroy the range. Therefore, judicious control with long-range artillery is wise. But you can't call a big bore a long-range varmint rifle no matter how ballistically good it is, and the 22-rimfire class is useful on varmints, but only up close. The muzzle-loader is also a short-range tool.

This leaves the 17-caliber Remington, a host of hotshot 22 centerfires and a few 6mm cartridges. Any of them will work. For real long-range shooting, I prefer the 17 Remington up to 300 yards and the 222 Remington for about the same distance. Ballistics of the 220 Swift/22-250 group are good for 400 yards and even a bit more. It is a matter of trajectory, of course, but also a matter of delivered

Match shooting is a very specialized form of marksmanship, often requiring a very special rifle, such as this Remington Model 40-XC National Match Course Rifle in 7.62 Nato caliber (308 Winchester). *(Remington Arms)*

The 220 Swift. Its MV of over 4,000 fps continues to lead the field. *(Norma)*

energy. The 220 Swift or 22-250, as well as several others in this category, deliver over 400 foot-pounds of energy out to 500 yards. The 22 Long Rifle with a 40-grain bullet, starting at 1,300 fps MV, has an energy, an inch from the barrel, of about 150 foot-pounds.

The 6mm family is good, too, for long-range varmint work because of relatively light recoil—no 6mm will kick you out from under your hat—and yet these 24s have flat trajectory. The 6mm Remington will shove a 75-grain bullet from the muzzle at 3,600 fps. Remaining energy at 500 yards from the muzzle is still over 500 foot-pounds. The fine 240 Weatherby will throw an 87-grain bullet at that same 3,600 velocity for even greater performance. Noisier, with a little more recoil (a bit more than the 22 hotrocks), the 6s are my second choice for long-range work unless the wind is blowing; then they are my first selection.

THE HANDMATE CALIBERS

There are still many of us who set forth into the outback with rifle tagging along, sometimes in a pickup truck rack or even stuffed in a saddle scabbard. Then the idea is to carry a rugged little rifle that won't be in the way, one which will jump into your hand and deliver the goods when a varmint appears. In fact, there are times when you have a deer tag in your pocket and you aren't really deer hunting, but that buck just shows up. Then the handmate rifle has to go to work.

There are many rifles which qualify here. For me, the handmate rifle is a Model 94 that will fit just about anywhere, and the old 30-30 is my cartridge

choice. My handloads make the little 30 quite versatile.

Today, there are also a host of handgun calibers which have gone to work in the rifle. Because these little rounds take up small space in the action or the magazine, trim rifles are possible with rather high-capacity payloads. For example, my Marlin Model 9 is a twelve-shot rifle with one clip or a twenty-shot rifle with another clip. Caliber is 9mm Luger, plenty of power for up-close work on varmints and good to have along in the lonely places.

Browning's Model 92 is offered in 357 Magnum and 44 Magnum. The old 44-40 rifle/handgun round is found in a couple of short rifles from Navy Arms, lever-actions of the 1866 design. The 357 Maximum is chambered in the H&R Model 158 single-shot rifle. Marlin's Model 45, counterpart of their Model 9, is the same rifle, but chambered for the 45 ACP (Automatic Colt Pistol) round. And the 45 Colt (often referred to as the 45 Long Colt, though actually that's not its proper title) is a Model 94 Winchester chambering in the short-barrel Trapper model.

The list is long and growing longer. Shooters like the idea of having a rifle and a handgun firing the same ammo, though the actual benefits somewhat escape me for today's firearm work. The handgun rounds do deliver workhorse ballistics in the rifle and these chamberings are useful. The little 32 H&R Magnum, I think, will find its way into a rifle someday. The 9mm Luger already has. The 38 Special will fit rifles chambered for the 357 Magnum. The 357 Magnum and its bigger brother, the 357 Maximum, both work well in the long arm. So does the 41 Magnum. The 44-40 and 44 Remington Magnum are both good close-range deer takers, and the 45 ACP and 45 Colt are also worthwhile handgun rounds serving in rifles.

BIG-GAME CALIBERS

Brush Rifles

Since my personal favorite in the brush is a lever-action rifle, and since that rifle happens to be a 30-30, that round is the one I have used to harvest a number of deer up close. Any of the 30s or larger make good rounds for timber work when the game is deer or black bear. A 35 Remington, 358 Winchester, the new 356—any of them serve well. In this instance, I'm more prone to look first at the firearm, its handling and aiming qualities, and carrying dimensions, leaving the caliber choice second. In fact, there is no such thing as a perfect brush cartridge. Any bullet will deflect if enough brush is encountered. My informal tests, even with 45-70s well loaded, have proved this to my satisfaction. Learn to aim through the holes in the brush. Do not depend on any cartridge, even those driving heavy bullets at modest velocity, to break through dense cover and drop game.

The Plains

Antelope, and sometimes mule deer, may demand long-range shooting on the plains. Any of the high-velocity cartridges with flat trajectories and reasonably decent remaining energy can be used to bag big game in the open spaces. Calibers in the 243–6mm class serve well here, as do the 25s with bullets in the 100–120-grain class leaving the muzzle at velocities in the 3,000-fps domain. Larger bores, 270–7mm, are excellent, too, for plains shooting, as are the high-velocity, 30-caliber loadings. I own a Dean Zollinger 257 Weatherby Magnum custom rifle which drives a 100-grain bullet at over 3,600 fps MV. Sighted dead on at 300 yards, the bullet only rises 3 inches at 100 yards and it falls 7 inches low at 400. For plains shooting, it is hard to beat such flat trajectory.

The Mountains

Rugged ranges in the Rocky Mountains can present very long shots at big game. A range I roam in Idaho is built like giant dragon teeth. At the bottom of some of these serrations you could toss a pine cone across and hit the other side. But ridge-to-ridge shooting in many mountain settings means 200- and 300-yard shots, too. Brush and trees on your side of the canyon hide game. Often, the only shot is *across* the canyon where game can be seen.

Chambered in the Model 1894 Winchester as early as 1894, the 32-40 round was always considered very accurate, and it still has a small following.

The Marlin Model 9 is easy to manage in 9mm Luger caliber. It's another example of a rifle chambered for a handgun round.

The Browning Model 92 is another rifle which serves well for brushland conditions. In caliber 357 Magnum, especially with handloads, it has sufficient potency for close-range deer hunting. The Model 92 is also available in 44 Magnum caliber, another handgun round. *(Browning Arms)*

Here is where the more powerful rounds come to the fore—the 270 Winchester, 280 Remington, 30-06, 7mm Magnum, and similar numbers. My personal favorite here is the 7mm Magnum, Remington or Weatherby version. In it, I use a handload firing a 162-grain bullet at more than 3,150 fps MV, or the factory RWS load with a 162-grain bullet chronographed at close to the same velocity. Although the 7mm Magnum is my personal favorite for such mountain hunting, other rounds are also excellent, including the 264 Winchester Magnum, and any of the 300 Magnums. All shoot flat. All have tremendous remaining energies at long range for big mountain mule deer, elk, sheep, and similar game.

Larger-than-Deer Game

Most of us won't do much on moose and elk annually, though where I live the latter are open-tag every year. However, when you do want a cartridge for the larger-than-deer game animals, you may wish to look into the 300 Magnums and upward. I am well aware that the 30-30 has decked more moose than all of the Magnums put together, and in the hands of a careful shot who is willing to get close to his game, that round will still do the

trick. The 7mm Mauser and its ballistic counterparts have also knocked off all kinds of moose and elk.

But just to keep things in perspective, let's look at the class of round going upward of the 30s—33s, 34s, and 35s. In caliber 33 we have the great 338 Winchester, with bullets of 225 grains traveling at 3,000 fps MV. Energy rating here is almost 4,500 foot-pounds. A 30-06, with a 180-grain bullet at 2,800 fps MV (a healthy handload), gains a bit over 3,100 foot-pounds. The 8mm Remington Magnum, with a 220-grain bullet at about 2,900 fps MV, another good handload, will produce close to 4,000 foot-pounds of energy at the muzzle. No, you don't need rounds like these for elk or moose, but they do exist for those who want the added punch.

Big American Bears

Two friends of mine who guide for a living in Alaska have had run-ins with big bears. Both carry 338s as a matter of course, but one of these men, Harold Schetzle, was happy to have a 375 H&H Magnum along when a mad bear tried to make a movable feast of his client and him. The 300-grain bullets from Harold's and his client's 375s decided the argument in their favor, but by the time the last

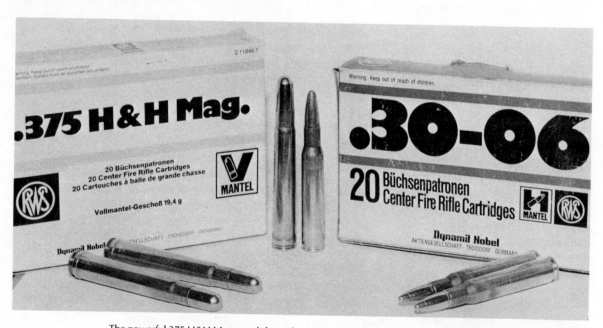

The powerful 375 H&H Magnum, left, made its reputation in Africa, but is often preferred by grizzly bear hunters in North America. The 30-06 is considered one of the all-around rounds, capable of harvesting all of our big game. These factory loads are from RWS of West Germany.

shot was fired, they could reach out and touch the nose of the bear with their rifle barrels.

Any of the larger-than-deer rounds make pretty good bear takers when the grizzly or polar is the bear. The old 348 Winchester, with a 200-grain to 250-grain bullet, is a good bear stomper at close range. The 338, 8mm Remington, and the 340 Weatherby likewise. That big 350 Norma Magnum, the same. And the largest of this particular class is the 375 H&H Magnum, or an "improved" version of it. Guides in the alders along the coast of Alaska have also been known to carry life insurance in the form of a Winchester 458 Magnum—and other 45s, even top-loaded 45-70s and custom 45 Alaskans (348 blown out and fitted with 45 caliber bullets).

Dangerous Game

Quite a few American sportsmen have found themselves in Africa cutting the spoor of dangerous game, such as the Cape buffalo or elephant. You learn a lot on an African safari. You find out that there are many dwellers of the dark continent that can mash you into the ground in a few seconds of charge- and stomp-time. There are a few American-loaded rounds which are designed for stopping the plans of these fellows. The 458 Winchester is the most common of these rounds. The 460 Weatherby is another. The 375 H&H is considered a medium in Africa, and having seen one perform on a Cape buff I would agree that that is the niche for this otherwise fine round. Were I to again head for the land of beasts big enough to bowl us over, I'd go with a 458 Winchester or similar as my shooting iron. Or, I'd at least want something on that order as backup if I were using a lesser round.

THE ALL-AROUND CARTRIDGE

There are dozens of rounds which qualify as all-around in ballistic qualities. It all depends upon the criteria you want to apply. A little 7mm-08 will do a great many things. With the Hornady 139-grain, flat-point bullet, it will serve for deer at close range. Load up with a 120-grain bullet, 3,100 fps MV, and you have an antelope rifle. The same will do well for mule deer in the open lands. Or how about a 140-grain bullet at about 2,850 fps MV? Plenty for mule deer, too. A 150-grain bullet will buzz off at about 2,700 fps MV. And a 160-grain will leave at about 2,650 fps MV. A long 175-grain bullet from

this little case (the 308 Winchester necked down) will do close to 2,550 fps from the muzzle.

That set of ballistics constitutes the all-around round. A 7×57 will do the same. So will a 284. A 280 Remington will, too. And the one round which is king of the all-arounders in most shooters' minds is the fabulous 30-06. It will shove a 150-grain bullet at about 3,100 fps MV, with trajectory patterns very much like the 270. But unlike the 270, the 06 will push a 180-grain pill at 2,800 fps. Or you can even go up to a 220-grain bullet at very close to 2,600 fps.

If I were saddled with any of these rounds, from 7mm-08 up to 300 Magnum, I could hunt everything from squirrels (with special handloads) to elk and bears. However, at the risk of attracting a lynch mob, I say the greatest all-around cartridge is the 7mm Magnum. A day on the range recently affirmed that choice. I was using an Oehler Skyscreen chronograph. The large shooting area of its special screen design permitted me to test actual remaining velocities at 300 yards.

The 300 Winchester Magnum and 7mm Remington Magnum were tested, the former firing a 180-grain Spitzer bullet starting at 3,100 fps MV and arriving at 300 yards with a remaining velocity of 2,450 fps and an energy just short of 2,400 foot-pounds. That's more energy than a 30-30 has at the muzzle. However, the 7mm Magnum firing a 175-grain boattail Spitzer proved even more dramatic.

The long, 175-grain, 7mm bullet arrived at 300 yards with a shade over 2,625 fps remaining velocity for an energy of 2,678 foot-pounds. I reported my findings to gunmaker Dean Zollinger, who repeated the tests with his own chronograph, finding the same results. In this particular test, with chronographed velocities at 300 yards, the 7mm Magnum was delivering more energy than a 300 Magnum.

A 139-grain bullet departed the muzzle at just shy of 3,400 fps MV with one maximum load, making the 7mm Magnum one of the flattest-shooting big-game rounds on the street. The most accurate bullet in our tests proved to be a 162-grain boattail, which achieved a MV of over 3,150 fps. In a custom rifle with Douglas air-gauged barrel, witnessed groups of under an inch at 200 yards were registered. A Sierra 170-grain round nose was then underloaded purposely as a brush load for deer. It duplicated, at the muzzle, the power of a 30-30. A 120-grain bullet with maximum powder charge achieved 3,500 fps MV, a varmint load. The problem, of course, is that the all-around cartridge is not perfect for everything. The 120-grain bullet, above, is flat-shooting and accurate, but noisy, and it develops more recoil than true varmint rounds. I'd rather use a 22 centerfire for varminting.

In the woods, the 7mm's underloaded 170-grain round nose would serve for deer, but I'd prefer my more compact 30-30. Antelope hunting with the fast 139-grain bullet would prove nearly ideal, but the lighter recoiling 25-06 would be even more ideal for pronghorns. Given an opportunity for a bull elk across a high mountain canyon, the 7mm Magnum would serve well with a 160–175-grain missile. But, ballistically speaking, there are better elk rounds.

CARTRIDGES WE DON'T HAVE

We lack few rounds in modern rifle shooting. However, I would like to see the return of the 22 WRF (Winchester Rim Fire), a cartridge which falls between the 22 Long Rifle and 22 WMR (Winchester Magnum Rimfire) in power and range. The 22 WRF will chamber in 22 Winchester Magnum rifles. Its 45-grain bullet, at about 1,400 fps, is good for small game when the 22 WMR is often too powerful. The use of the 22 WRF in the 22 WMR would give the latter greater latitude.

Furthermore, there are many fine old rifles chambered for the 22 WRF which can no longer be used because there is no ammunition available. When shooters do find 22 WRF ammo nowadays, it's often priced at collector rates. So I would like to see the 22 WRF back in the cartridge lineup, not only in limited offering, but as a standard. I would also like to see a comeback of the old 32 rimfire. It was an excellent wild turkey cartridge, with enough power for the big birds, without meat-ruining explosiveness. A 32 rimfire with a 100-grain bullet would be a useful small-game round, as well as turkey taker.

Practice ammunition from factories—we used to have it. A shooter could waltz into his gun shop and pick up a box of 30-30 ammo loaded with a lead projectile at modest velocity. The mild-mannered load, using a 117-grain cast bullet, was good for small-game hunting as well as practice, and it was priced lower than big-game ammunition. I enjoy reloading and I make my own practice loads for big-game rifles. But it would be convenient to purchase practice ammunition over the counter, too.

I would also like to see a pipsqueak 6mm round, perhaps based on a blown-out 220 Russian case. This cartridge would allow for a short-action rifle of very modest recoil, perfect for medium-range deer and antelope hunting. My own lady hunter has used her Frank Wells custom 6mm-222, which propels an 80-grain bullet at about 2,900 fps MV, for about fifteen years with perfect satisfaction. It has produced more one-shot harvests at ranges up to 200 yards than any other rifle in our experience, mainly because it is so easy to shoot accurately and because its range is limited to a maximum of 200 yards.

5

Sporting-Cartridge Ballistics

BALLISTICS is the science of missiles in motion—for our purposes, it's the story of bullets fired from rifle barrels. If the bullet is traveling in the bore, that's *internal ballistics*. If the bullet is flying through the atmosphere, then the term is *exterior ballistics*. Modern riflemen want to know, and understand, what is happening when a bullet is launched from its cartridge case all the way through the bore and from the muzzle to the target, with notes on muzzle velocity, terminal velocity, muzzle energy, terminal energy, bullet upset, trajectory, and more. Ballistics is a "hard science," belonging to that branch of study called physics, and the data are presented in cold numbers. Yet, we also apply personal experience to gain better understanding.

INTERNAL BALLISTICS

Modern smokeless powder is powerful. It's the fuel which does the work of sending the missile downrange. Internal ballistics is the study of what happens when a charge of this fuel "goes off" in the case and bore. It includes the time lapse from the fall of the firing pin until the bullet's exit from the muzzle. Nitrocellulose, a major ingredient in smokeless powder, has a potential energy of about 1.5 million foot-pounds per pound. Of course gunpowder is not pure nitrocellulose. Furthermore, solvent is used on the nitrocellulose in the powder-making process and some of this solvent is left behind in the finished product. There are also coatings on the powder, which help control burning rate. These and other factors reduce the potential of the powder to roughly 85 percent of the efficiency of pure nitrocellulose.

There are further losses in the barrel/breech of the rifle. After all, the rifle is something like a heat engine. Part of the work is used up in making heat. Plus, any form of engine, no matter how loosely the word is used, uses up some of the energy in the system. A car engine of 200 horsepower does not deliver 200 horsepower to the wheels that push or pull the vehicle. In fact, about 20 percent efficiency is considered pretty good for an auto engine. The rifle works at about 30 percent efficiency. Energy is used pushing the bullet through the rifling, in barrel friction, in heat production, and even in the actual gas velocity, the work it takes for the powder to push on the powder, you might say.

Pressure

The burning gases build pressure and that pressure forces the bullet from the bore. Sometimes the very word itself receives bad notice with riflemen. "Watch out for pressure!" Yes, watch out for *overly high* pressure, but remember that without pressure your rifle would be no more than a club. Pressures go up if the bullet is restricted, of course, and tightly crimped cases which cling to bullets may bring a rise in pressure. Also, the rifleman who handloads knows that as he adds bullet weight, he reduces the powder charge. More friction and more mass cause the powder charge to burn a bit faster, so we see, for example, a 30-06 load of IMR (Improved Military Rifle) 4350 rifle powder of 59 grains with a 150-grain bullet reduced to 56 grains of the same powder with a 180-grain bullet and down to 54 grains when a 220-grain bullet is used in the same case.

Also, we note some big changes in powder charge as the *type* of powder varies. Powders render different energy per type, but just as important is the fact that different powders may burn with different rates. For example, in the 30-06, the maximum load of 59 grains of IMR-4350 with the 150-grain bullet changes when Winchester-748 rifle powder is used. A maximum load, again in the 30-06, is listed at 53 grains of W-748 with a 150-grain bullet, 50.5 grains of W-748 with the 180-grain bullet, and about 46.5 grains of W-748 with the 220-grain bullet.

Even the so-called "slow-burning" powders get things done in quite a hurry. Everything happens at great speed, from the detonation of the primer to bullet exit. The time the bullet remains in the bore, once it is kicked in its base by the expanding gases of the powder charge, is measured in milliseconds —thousandths of a second. In one rather modest 30-06 load, for example, an elapsed time of only .00065 seconds was recorded from "blast off" until the bullet said good-bye to the crown of the muzzle, this in a 24-inch barrel.

Barrel Length

Riflemen are often interested in how internal ballistics affect muzzle velocity due to barrel length. The powder charge does need time to do its work, even if bore time is measured in milliseconds, and the longer barrel allows for that time. However, many factors are at work, including the amount of powder being consumed, what kind of powder it is, bore diameter, and so forth. And even though a rifle may pick up some muzzle velocity with a longer barrel length, you have to be practical. Riflemen don't want to tote a piece that has a barrel that resembles a vaulting pole. So we compromise. Barrels in the 22- to 24-inch range are popular in big-bore rifles, even though in many instances a longer barrel would produce a bit more velocity. In the 22 rimfire, we add barrel length for sight radius and tradition, but a barrel of about 14 to 18 inches will consume the powder charge of the 22 Long Rifle round.

Loading Density

Loading density is the ratio between the actual weight of a given powder charge and the weight of water that would fill that case. Water's maximum density takes place at a bit over 39° F, at which it

The smokeless-powder load (left) requires only 30 grains to propel a 170-grain projectile at over 2,200 fps MV out of the little 30-30 case, while a full 120 grains of black powder are required to drive a 230-grain round ball at about 2,000 fps MV.

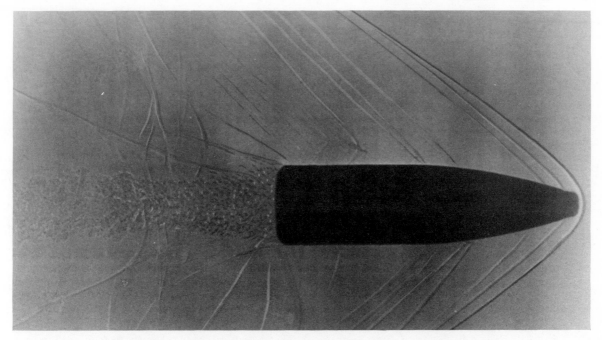

The bullet strikes a strong barrier when it hits the atmosphere. The lead tip is very slightly deformed at this time. The photograph exaggerates the actual deformation of the bullet tip.

weighs a pound for 27.68 cubic inches. If we multiply 27.68 times the weight of the actual powder charge in pounds, dividing by the volume of the powder chamber in cubic inches, the result is a number indicating load density. Or you can look at it this way—good load density with a certain powder charge tends to fill the case.

Generally speaking, you want the powder charge to occupy most of the space inside of the cartridge case. Ideally, this is supposed to prevent erratic burning of the powder when the primer ignites the charge. If your favorite rifle is not producing good groups, *one* consideration may be load density, so look in your loading manual and try a powder type and charge which does improve on that one aspect. It's worth a try.

EXTERIOR BALLISTICS

Now the bullet slams into the atmosphere. The first point to consider in exterior ballistics is that this atmosphere, the very stuff we breathe, is tangible to that speeding bullet. We know that the atmosphere has a lot more to do with slowing a bullet than gravity does. Many times more, in fact; even a

very streamlined Spitzer bullet with a sharp tip of exposed lead can be slightly blunted when it smacks the air. High-speed photos show this graphically. Not to worry, of course, because these good shapes still hold up quite nicely. However, this factor did bring about bullets such as the Remington Bronze Point and Nosler Ballistic Tip, missiles with very hard points.

These hard points do not deform and therefore the bullets retain their sleek shape, meaning they hold up better against the ravages of the air. On the other hand, there is a trade-off here, and though these excellent bullets do shoot with a flatter trajectory, they expand because the nose tip is forced back into the body of the projectile. Sometimes this action can be pretty explosive. I have used the Ballistic Tip and the Nosler Partition bullet on deer at similar distances and found more tissue disruption with the former. But, again, that hard tip certainly helps in velocity/energy retention. Another help is the use of a very small tip of exposed lead. The Hornady 162-grain, 7mm boattail bullet is an example of this style.

A bullet's change of shape when slamming into the air is a basic fact of external ballistics. And knowing such facts helps the modern rifleman understand his firearm. Bullet shape is so important to external ballistics that a term and mathematical principle were invented to describe this factor. Of course, if you set a chronograph up downrange and actually measure retained velocity, this formula is not needed, but the concept is still vital.

Ballistic Coefficient

Ballistic coefficient is noted as "C." The C of a bullet allows us to determine how well it will retain its initial muzzle velocity (MV) and that knowledge helps determine how flat it will fly from muzzle to target, as well as how much energy the bullet will have when it reaches its destination. A high C is good and a low C is bad in terms of retained velocity, energy, and trajectory. However, don't get the idea that blunt-nosed bullets are no good. Blunt bullets are very good and often preferred for hunting at woods and timber ranges. A round-nose bullet may make a straighter wound channel in the game, perhaps reaching vitals better than some sharper forms. And some very experienced hunters think that blunter bullets offer greater initial impact than sharp ones. But the latter point is hard to prove and does not show up at all "on paper," although we should remember that ballistics *plus* shooting experience is what we are considering.

There is *drag* on a bullet. The shape of the bullet has a lot to do with how that bullet reacts to drag. A standard bullet was dreamed up, sometimes called the "Krupp Standard Bullet." With this mathematical concept, the standard bullet can be compared with any other bullet in the form of a ratio. The standard bullet is "derived" at sea level values, since air density alters with elevation. A shock wave accompanies the bullet, too, and shadowgraph pictures reveal this. That shock wave is more pronounced as velocity increases. Also, drag increases quite noticeably after the speed of sound (about 1,120 fps at sea level) has been surpassed. So C covers all these factors despite its being a single number, and, therefore, all we have to do is compare that number with other C numbers in order to determine how a bullet will react to the atmosphere.

You can't just look at a racy and pretty bullet and say, "Now that one has high ballistic coefficient as compared with that other one." Maybe. Maybe not. A Hornady 60-grain, 22-caliber bullet has a C of .262. It's a fairly sharp-looking bullet. And it looks as though it would probably have a higher C

On the left is a 180-grain, 30-caliber bullet of good sectional density and ballistic coefficient. Compared with this bullet is a 54-caliber, black-powder missile of much lower sectional density and ballistic coefficient. At closer ranges the latter is extremely effective on big game, but the former will deliver its energy potential to longer ranges.

than a Hornady 140-grain, 6.5mm *round-nose* bullet, but that's not true. That 140-grain round nose has a C of .291. In theory, it should "shoot flatter" than the 60-grain, 22-caliber bullet. But what happens at the range? In fact, the 140-grain, round-nose, 6.5mm bullet does shoot a tad flatter and we see that it retains its initial velocity a bit better than the 22 bullet. Start both at 3,000 fps MV and the 60-grain 22 bullet ends up at 2,004 fps at 300 yards' distance. Start the 140-grain, round-nose, 6.5mm bullet at 3,000 fps MV and it ends up with 2,079 fps at 300 yards.

So the bullet of higher C won, despite the fact that a projectile of sharp profile was compared with a round nose. How come? The mathematical formula for C is computed as a ratio of a bullet's weight to the product of the square of its diameter along with the *form factor* itself. The form factor is a figure which is computed along with the data on weight and bullet diameter. Form factor means "shape," but C is obviously *not* shape alone. C is *sectional density* plus shape. But what is sectional density?

Sectional Density

Shooters tend to think of sectional density in terms of diameter versus height of a bullet. I had an aunt and uncle who seemed to visually depict sectional density in human form. The lady was tall and thin, something like an arrow with a hat on. The gentleman was short and heavy, something like a bowling ball with a hat on. Long and slender—high sectional density. Short and squat—low sectional density. Not quite, though certainly we can *think* of relationships between diameter and length here because they do count for something.

Sectional density is a ratio. It is the ratio between the weight of a bullet in pounds divided by the square of the diameter of that same bullet in inches. Shape means *nothing* here. Shape factors belong to C only. So a 150-grain, round nose, 30-caliber bullet and a 150-grain, pointed, 30-caliber bullet have the same exact sectional density. In formula, it looks like this:

$$SD = \frac{w}{7,000 \ d^2}$$

SD stands for sectional density. The little "w" represents the weight of the bullet in grains (7,000 grains to a pound) and d^2 is diameter of the bullet squared. The 30-caliber bullet ends up with a figure of .226. It's very easy to compute with a hand calculator. Seven thousand times $.308^2$ is the math, since a 30-caliber, 150-grain bullet is .308 inch in diameter. The result of this multiplication is 664.048. Now divide 150 by 664.048 and the result is .226, the sectional density of a 150-grain, 30-caliber bullet.

To prove that "long and lean" profiles do not mean a high sectional density all by themselves, compare a couple of bullets that have different *appearances.* A 45-caliber, 500-grain bullet looks good, but certainly it does not have the whistle-at-me shape of a 160-grain, 7mm bullet. However, the 500-grain, 45-caliber bullet has a SD of .341 and a 160 7mm bullet will fall at .283. Of course, put the form factor to work and calculate C and the 45-caliber bullet ends up with a C of only .297 with its blunt nose, and the 7mm bullet will calculate at well over .500.

Velocity

The C figure goes to work here. For our purposes the velocity is simply the speed of the bullet. We begin at the muzzle and then calculate or chrono-graph for downrange speeds. Velocities are very important to riflemen for at least two reasons. First, the most-used energy ratings, coming up next in discussion, take velocity heavily into account. Second, as the velocity goes, all other things being equal, so goes the trajectory. In other words, flat-shooting rifles do not fire low-velocity bullets.

Energy

Today, every ammo-crafter in the country notes energy in terms of foot-pounds, which is an expression of Newton's formula. A single foot-pound would be the force required to lift one pound of weight one foot high. Call it kinetic energy if you like, for Newton's formula relies on motion, the motion of that bullet measured in feet-per-second, or fps. A machine called a chronograph tells us this, for it actually measures the speed of a bullet as it is shot over the device's screens.

In Newton's formula, this velocity figure is *squared.* The formula goes like this: First, square

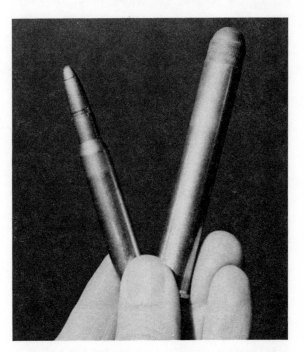

Mass or velocity? Which lends the most potency to a bullet? The kinetic energy formula, which is used by all ammo companies and bullet manufacturers today, squares the velocity, but does not square the bullet's weight. Hence, velocity is given the nod in the power story. Shown are a 50 Sharps, on the right, with a 30-06 round. The former fires a 700-grain bullet at about 1,400 fps MV. The 30-06 can shoot a 165-grain bullet at 3,000 fps MV. *On paper,* the two are ballistically very similar.

the velocity. Then divide by 7,000 to reduce from pounds to grains, since we work in the grain weight of the bullet. Next, divide by 64.32, which is twice the "acceleration of gravity," a constant. The formula at this point gives the energy per one grain of bullet weight. So you must multiply by the total weight of the bullet. Example: a 150-grain bullet at 3,000 fps. Multiply 3,000 by 3,000 and you get nine million. Then divide by 7,000 and the figure is reduced to 1,285.714 (rounded off). This is again divided by the constant of 64.32 for a figure of just about 20 (19.989). But that is for one grain, so it's multiplied by 150, the weight of our bullet, and the end result is 2,998. But 2,998 what? It is 2,998 foot-pounds of energy.

The weight of the projectile is vital in this measurement of energy, but only the velocity gets squared. Consider a big 300-grain bullet at 1,500 fps MV. Now the 1,500 is squared for a figure of 2,250,000, not nine million. Divided by 7,000, the result is 321 (rounded off) and divided again by the constant, 64.32, we have a shade less than 5. Up above we had about 20 foot-pounds of energy per bullet grain. Now we have only 5. Five times bullet weight (300 grains) gives a muzzle energy of a bit less than 1,500 foot-pounds, or about *half* of the 150-grain bullet's energy at 3,000 fps MV.

Supposing a polar bear has mistaken your foot for a seal sandwich and is putting his bib on for dinner. Which would you rather have, a modest or even light bullet at hellish muzzle velocity, or a big, heavy bullet at not-so-fast speed? The catchall answer is, of course, both—a big, fast bullet. The problem is that pretty soon you have to mount such cannons on wheels, and recoil is sufficient to make you think Saturday is Sunday after only one shot. So a choice must be made, and most professional hunters have made it—for dangerous game at close range, they go with heavy bullets at modest velocity. It is obvious, then, that pure muzzle energy, or remaining energy figures, are not completely indicative of "killing power."

My own hotshot 25-caliber antelope/deer plains rifle fires a 100-grain bullet at an average muzzle velocity of 3,630 fps. Muzzle energy is very close to 3,000 foot-pounds. Think about that hungry polar bear again. An old 45-70 is pushing a 500-grain bullet at only 1,300 fps with an energy rating of less than 1,900 foot-pounds, or about one-third less punch. Yet, given that bullet penetration and bone breaking are necessary, it's quite likely that the fat

bullet will be somewhat better than the speedball at close range. But, all in all, it is very difficult to come up with a formula which describes cartridge effectiveness with just one number.

The (comparatively) little 257 Weatherby Magnum has dropped ponderous beasts with one shot as if Zeus had struck them down with his lightning bolts. On the other hand, a lot of huge bullets have been tossed at game only to make the animal angry. A shot in the tail is a shot in the tail and no amount of foot-pounds is going to alter that. But the figures are still quite valuable for comparison. Push a 500-grain bullet at 2,100 fps (that's a 458 Winchester load) and the result is close to 5,000 foot-pounds of energy. And it shows in the field.

The Newtonian formula is the only one widely accepted by ballisticians. Many other formulas have arisen, and are still cropping up, from the pages of gun writing; however, no ammo company has adopted any of them. Momentum, for example, is a scientific measurement of force, and it has been seized upon by those who want to give bullet weight more impetus. Momentum is simply velocity times mass—speed of the bullet times the weight of the bullet in grains, for our purposes. Here, that 100-grain bullet at 3,630 would be worth 363,000— divide by 10,000 to reduce to a more workable sum, 36. That old 45-70 and its 500-grain bullet at 1,300 would be worth 65, rounded off. So you have almost twice the "power" if you use a momentum figure for the big 45-caliber bullet.

You pick your own method as you see fit, of course, but the Newtonian number for energy is going to stick for a long while. It's been used for many years and nothing has come along to take its place.

Elevations

Exterior ballistics also deals with elevations. Velocity taken at sea level may be different than for the same round fired up in the mountains where air is less dense and air temperature usually cooler. Bullets of high C are affected much less by this situation. A 270 using a 150-grain Spitzer sighted-in on the coast is going to be quite close to "on target" in the mountains, usually close enough for hunting. However, you 30-30 fans take note: A blunt bullet can strike quite differently in low-terrain shooting than in high-country shooting. That 30-30 with a blunt bullet, as one example, may

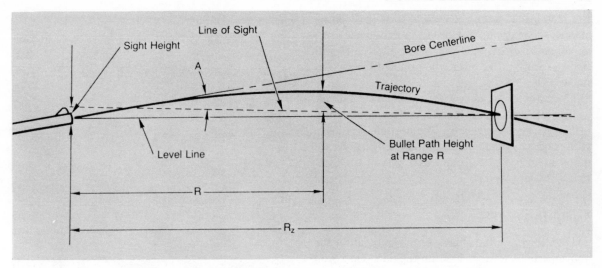

The bullet travels from muzzle to destination in an arc called a parabola, as illustrated in this Sierra Bullet Company chart.

strike the target as many as nine inches higher at 300 yards at an elevation of 10,000 feet above sea level if it was sighted-in at sea level.

Trajectory

The bullet, of course, cannot speed from muzzle to bull's-eye in a straight line. Once the push is off, the bullet begins to drop due to gravity and atmospheric onslaught. A bullet has a bit of "lift," and it is quite possible that this lift alters the above statement to a small degree, but, generally, bullets begin, for practical purposes, to drop once they exit the muzzle. They take a course described as a parabola, a curved line, and it is this line we call trajectory.

Therefore, the idea is to aim the rifle upward so that the bullet arcs on its parabola and the rifle gains the most from that trajectory pattern. Factors of velocity and C have much to do with how the bullet will fly, of course. And you must sight-in according to that arc. To sight a 270 Winchester for 100 yards, for example, ignores its ability as a flat-shooting round. It would be like taking a couple of spark plugs out of an Indy race car and expecting the car to perform normally. A 270 with a 130-grain bullet starting out at 3,100 fps MV should be sighted about 3 inches *high* at 100 yards from the bench. This will put the bullet back on target at 275 yards.

A comparison is necessary to show how impor-

tant trajectory knowledge is. Sticking with the example of the 270, the sight-in will be done in two ways. First, it will be sighted-in right on the money at 100 yards from the muzzle. At 200 yards from the muzzle, the 130-grain bullet has fallen three inches. In other words, it will land three inches below the *point of aim.* At 300 yards, a 130-grain bullet will have dropped close to a foot.

Now the same 270 rifle, with the same 130-grain bullet at 3,100 fps MV, is sighted to strike the bull three inches *high* at 100 yards instead of right on target. What happens? At 200 yards, the bullet hits four inches high. At 275 it is right on, and at 300 it is a couple of inches low. At a full 325 yards from the muzzle the bullet has only departed from the line of sight by about a half foot or a bit less. Even a small antelope is over a foot in chest depth, and a mule deer is much bigger. A hunter who has sighted his 270 three inches high at 100 yards can literally hold right in the center of the chest of his big game all the way out to 325 yards, with no guesswork or "Arkansas windage" when he is firing a 270 properly sighted.

Naturally, the figures change for various rifle classes. A 30-30 with a 170-grain, flat-nose bullet at 2,200 fps MV is not going to shoot "as flat" as a 270. A 257 Weatherby Magnum is going to shoot flatter. It's not possible to give all of the figures here; however it is entirely possible to reveal to the shooter where to find them all, or most of them.

For handloaded ammo, take a look at the loading manuals. For example, Hornady's handbook gives an excellent chart, showing where the bullet will strike at various distances when sighted for a given range.

These are terrific charts, for they show a shooter just how to sight-in for best advantage in trajectory from a particular cartridge. The next chapter deals with trajectory in more detailed terms. Here, we are more interested in trajectory as a part of the exterior-ballistics story.

Uphill-Downhill Shooting

Then there are the angles. Specifically, all of the above pertains to rifles fired on the flats. Once you aim uphill or downhill, things change a little. For our purposes, it's good to know that in *either* steep uphill *or* downhill shooting, the bullet will strike a bit *higher* on the target than anticipated. With the flat-shooting big-bore rifle normally used for long-range big-game hunting, actual differences are measured in inches, and usually not more than a couple of inches at that. Therefore, while it behooves the modern rifleman to know that there are differences in aiming point as angles increase, it is also paramount to remember that the differences are slight in practical terms. On a steep up or down angle, just remember that the bullet may hit a couple of inches higher than it normally would at that same distance on the flats.

Drift

Bullets drift off course. Why? A bullet will naturally drift a little bit in the direction of the rifling. If the bore has a right-hand twist, it imparts a rotation to the bullet which will induce it to drift a tad right, generally not enough to cause a problem.

But the drift caused by the wind is significant. Naturally, the crosswind gives the most trouble, since it hits the most bullet surface. A headwind may force the bullet to strike a tad low and a tailwind may force it to hit a tad high, but these I never concern myself with. However, a strong side wind can blow your bullet right off target and such a wind is a significant part of the exterior ballistics of your favorite rifle round.

Examples pay off here because they are easy to visualize. First, let's put a 220 Swift on the range. It's firing a sharply pointed bullet of 50 grains' weight at 4,000 fps MV. The wind flag at the range

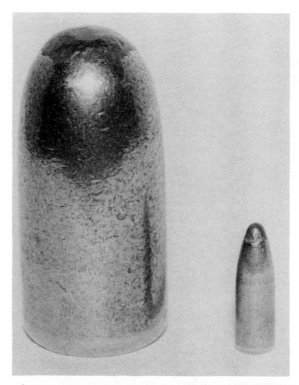

The huge 900-grain, 60-caliber bullet on the left, if started with a very low muzzle velocity, could drift more in a crosswind than the tiny 25-grain, 17-caliber bullet started at over 4,000 fps MV.

is standing straight out and wind velocity is 30 miles per hour, coming in at a right angle to your bench. In other words, a sidewind of 30 mph is hitting the bullet. At 300 yards from the muzzle, the bullet will drift over two feet off target! Many long-range shooters seem to ignore this important factor and when they "hold for the wind" it means by a few inches. Even a 20-mph wind will drift that same bullet by almost a foot and a half.

But that, you say, is due to the little 50-grain bullet that the Swift is firing. Give the bullet some weight, you suggest, and the drift caused by the wind will mostly go away. To some degree, but wind is still a big factor. A 270 firing its 130-grain bullet at 3,100 fps MV will drift off course by a full 18 inches at 300 yards in a 30-mph wind. Even the great 7mm Magnum with a 175-grain bullet at 3,000 fps MV will move over by about 13 inches at 300 yards in a 30-mph crosswind. And big, slow bullets get pushed around badly by the wind. For example, a 300-grain, flat-point bullet in the 45-70 can depart the muzzle at about 1,800 fps from the Model 1886 Winchester rifle. Drift in a 30-mph crosswind at 300 yards would be over 115 inches. One of the factors here is time. A slower time of flight allows more time for the wind to push on the bullet, so even though the big bullet is chugging downrange like the Little Engine that Could, the wind simply has too much time to work on it. Ballistic coefficient is another big factor in wind drift.

All of this sounds pretty serious, and it is for the rifleman who wants to hit the mark in a wind. The problem is compounded because we seldom know the exact velocity of the wind and we only know its general direction. I have found that awareness of wind drift is the best defense against it. The target shooter can take some practice sighters, which will tell him how much drift is involved. The field marksman is going to do best by practicing and "getting the feel" of wind drift.

Shoot a 22 Long Rifle at 200 yards in crosswinds. Such shooting is a real eye-opener. What's more, if the target is placed on a sandy area where the strike of the bullet is visible through the scope sight, and a scope is advised for 200-yard 22-rimfire shooting, the shooter can actually see the splash of the projectile when it hits. Since the 22 rimfire does not recoil enough to blot out the sight picture, a shooter can get the feel of shooting in the wind. Then he can turn to his favorite big-bore rifle for further practice.

TERMINAL BALLISTICS

What the bullet does when it gets there is a part of exterior ballistics and is often called terminal ballistics. Bullet design and construction have much to do with this story. The all-lead bullet is still quite viable, not only for target shooting, but also for hunting. A lead projectile offers good hold-to-gether. A pure lead bullet is of high molecular cohesion—fragmentation is not likely, meaning good penetration and wound channels result. The jacketed bullet is necessary to withstand the ravages of high velocity, and it can be constructed in many different ways, with bonded cores—cores which tend to stick to the jacket instead of separating—thick jackets, thin, thick at the base, thin at the nose, and so forth.

As for design, you could fill a book with various styles from flat-base to boattail, full metal jacket to hollow point, and everything in between. For the purposes of the practical rifleman, however, the best bet is finding a bullet which fires well in a given

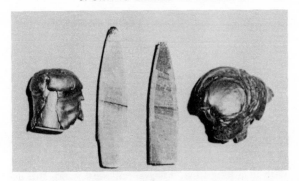

Terminal ballistics reveal that these specially constructed Allred bullets offer superior retention of original weight, since core and jacket remain intact as a single unit.

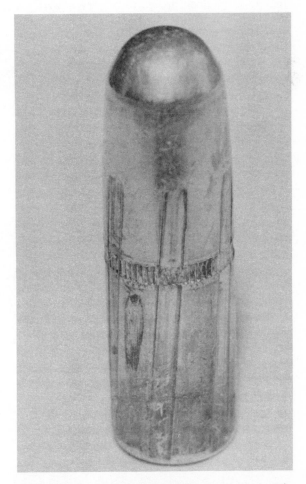

This RWS factory 375 H&H Magnum bullet of 300 grains' weight penetrated several *feet* through a big Cape buffalo without deformation of the projectile. This bullet met its test—penetration without deformation.

rifle and which is designed for a specific job. For example, the new "big game" bullets are the best we have ever had. They are designed to penetrate well, hold together, and yet expand to give large wound channels.

These bullets are now being built by every manufacturer. Hornady has its Interlock. Sierra has its Game King, Nosler the Partition; Winchester has its Power Point, and Remington makes the Core-Lokt. Some of these big-game designs have been with us a long time. They are all very good. But go with the bullet that works best in your rifle. For example, a fine big-game bullet is Speer's Mag-Tip. I found that in my 30-30 Improved a 150-grain Mag-Tip bullet fired in single-shot fashion only—it is too pointed to load in the tubular magazine—dropped deer-sized game with startling efficiency. My 7mm Magnum firing the Hornady boattail, 162-grain Interlock proved to be very powerful at long range. A Sierra 170-grain Pro-Hunter bullet from the 30-30 was excellent on deer in the brush.

The bullet for a big bore must withstand the force of being rammed through the bore at high velocity. Then it must withstand the beating the atmosphere is going to give it. And after it holds up to all of this, it has to react properly on impact. Not only that, but it is called upon to open up, but not blow apart, at close range, while still opening up instead of acting like a full-metal-jacket bullet at long range. It's a credit to the bullet makers that their projectiles offer the terminal ballistics we have today.

Boattails versus flat-base . . . that's always a good argument. While it is provable that even over hunting ranges the boattail bullet does retain a bit more of its initial velocity and energy, and does

The all-lead round ball does a surprising job on big game at close range. The ball does deform; however, it usually retains the bulk of its original weight, which aids penetration.

shoot flatter, there are many expert riflemen who simply prefer the flat-base bullet. They contend that these bullets do the job perfectly well and that over practical hunting ranges the boattail does not offer enough added value to be worth so much as a cent more. I keep away from that argument. Some of my rifles digest boattails very nicely and I use them. Others do fine with the flat-base bullet. The simple fact is both are fine and that you pick one over the other because your individual rifle shoots it better.

The shooter who wishes to explore ballistics further will find many well-blazed trails to follow. Loading manuals are replete with ballistic data and explanations, as are books on the subject. For a study of factory data, check into the Pachmayer *Extended Ballistics* manual, for example. It deals with factory loads. And remember that you, too, are an experimenter. With total safety, you can learn more about exterior ballistics from your favorite rifles. Such familiarity breeds better shooting.

6

Sights and Sight-In

THE FIRST rifles were pointed rather than aimed. Aiming was out of the question because there was nothing to aim with. The evolution of rifle sights is like a view through a fog—it's difficult to get a full, clear picture. Initially, barrels wore no sights at all. Then there was a lump which served as a front sight, somewhat similar to a modern shotgun bead. It offered a reference point and was better than nothing, but lacked precision. A gunner aligned the bead on the target, and if his face met the cheek of the stock in the same place consistently, he could probably hit a target at close range.

A groove in the breech area may have followed as the next improvement in sights. The groove served as an open rear sight, in effect, offering a reference point for consistency of aim. The true rear sight appeared next, fixed in place, no more than a piece of metal with a notch cut in it. The front sight was aligned in that notch. Meanwhile, the front sight was becoming more refined into a blade form. A talented gunmaker could mount the front and rear sight precisely so that a shooter could hit a close-range target consistently.

More sophisticated aiming systems followed. Shooters became interested in target shooting. A shade system was developed at this time. Glare on the iron sights altered the sight picture and caused misses. In order to keep the sun off the sights, a shade was constructed. It was simply a device on top of the barrel which prevented reflection of light on the sights; however, the shade system gave rise to the tube sight. A tube sight appeared very much like a telescope without lenses.

The tube sight became quite sophisticated and was manufactured until recently. It was adjustable for windage and elevation through its mounting system and was, in effect, a shaded peep sight, for the eyecup included a small aperture to look through and at the opposite end of the tube was a front sight, often of "globe" shape. The tube sight concentrated aim and omitted unwanted light. The peep sight was another early aiming device which is still constructed. It could be considered a tube sight without the tube, for there was an aperture near the shooter's eye and a front sight to align with that aperture.

No doubt, the telescopic rifle sight followed on the heels of the tube sight, for in effect the 'scope was a tube sight with lenses for magnification and a reticle which replaced the peep and front aiming devices of the tube. Scope sights were mounted on a few muzzle-loaders and were prominent during the buffalo hunting days of the middle 1800s as well. Many of the Sharps and Remington long-range buffalo rifles wore high-powered telescopic sights.

THE OPEN IRON SIGHT

Still with us and apt to be around for a good while longer is the open iron sight, essentially no more than a bead, post, or blade up front and a notch of some kind at the rear. Although this is a very old sight system, it still works well enough for much shooting. In fact, it is a preferred sight device in some instances. For example, the professional

The tube sight had no glass in it. It was, as the name implies, a tube which isolated and concentrated the shooter's view. It did contain metallic aiming devices, however. *(Arm-sport)*

Although crude when compared with a scope sight, some very fine marksmanship has been accomplished with the open iron sight.

hunter of Africa will usually prefer an open sight, especially with a shallow V-notch at the rear. Much of his game is taken at under 100 yards and the dangerous ones sometimes uncomfortably closer. This sight is fast. You settle the front sight in the center of the V at the rear and the bullet will strike the target.

Dozens of variations in the open-sight system are now found. The rear sight can be a notch with a U-shape, V-shape, shallow-V shape, or no notch at all—just a line in the center. The front sight can be a bead or a blade in many different shapes and styles, and you can also find a post up front. There are even front peep sights, the idea being to place the target in the center of that peep hole for a hit. But in all open sight systems, the idea is alignment, to line up the front sight and back sight optically in order to make a "sight picture."

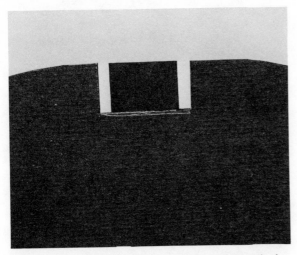

The sight picture illustrated here shows correct frame of reference. The top of the front sight is even with the top of the rear sight and there is about the same amount of light on both sides of the front sight.

In theory the human eye is not able to discern iron sights well enough to allow for much better than a four-inch group at 100 yards. However, in actual practice, the shooter learns to do far better than this by creating his own frames of reference. It is very important to open-sight shooting skill to understand the frame of reference. First, it is a mistake to have a front sight fully fill the open rear sight because the frame of reference is then lost. It is better to allow a bit of light on both sides of the bead or blade as it rests in the rear notch. This creates that frame of reference; the front sight is truly centered with the rear sight, optically speaking.

With the front sight settled into the notch and the same amount of light appearing on both sides of that front sight, the shooter can return to the same sight picture time and again for shooting consistency. Naturally, the front sight must also be matched in the notch vertically. Again, a frame of reference is necessary. I do a lot of open-sight shooting and I like to sight in, if possible, so that the front sight rests exactly level with the notch of the rear sight.

Using this frame-of-reference system, the sight picture can be altered for special effect. With the bead resting in the notch, equal light appearing on both sides of it, and that bead level with the top of the rear-sight notch, a "standard sight picture" is presented. This is the sight picture we want to use most of the time. But you have heard the oldtimers calling for a "fine bead" or a "coarse bead" picture. They might say, "Take a fine bead on that tin can."

Depending upon how the face is held on the comb of the stock, allowing the bead to rise optically above the top of the rear-sight notch or setting the bead firmly down into the notch can change point of impact on the target. I have seen shooters use the "fine bead" hold also as a device to force them to take a better sight picture, though in and of itself that fine bead is less accurate in some cases than using a full frame of reference picture. Always sight in using the frame of reference method, then you can experiment with the open sight using a "fine bead" or "coarse bead" hold.

Another aspect of sight picture with the open-sight system is the *hold* on the target. With the front-post sight it is often well to use the six-o'clock hold. This means keeping all frames of reference constant in the picture, but instead of putting the front sight on what you want to hit, you allow the target to "sit on top of" the front post, optically speaking. You can even have a thin space of light between the top of the post and the target. I call the hold-on-target picture a "hunting aim," where the sight is placed optically right on the target and the trigger is squeezed.

Which open-sight style you end up with is often a matter of chance as well as choice. Switching factory-made iron sights for sights of our own preference is not always done. So we learn to use whatever the manufacturer provided. But iron-sight fans

The "six o'clock hold" means taking a sight picture with the bead or post of the front sight directly *beneath* the intended point of impact on the target.

The hunting-sight picture, or "hold on" aim, puts the bead or post of the front sight directly *on* the intended point of impact at the target.

with a clear frame of reference, the blade or bead works equally well. My best open sights, probably, are the front-blade type, whenever a truly fine sight picture is desired.

The biggest problem with open sights is one of visual accommodation. The eye has to work hard in focusing on three levels with open iron sights. It has to keep the target, front sight, and rear sight matched up. First gain your frame of reference, then hold the rifle as still as possible while settling a sight picture on the target. Three levels of concentration are vital to good work with open sights. Young eyes do well. Older eyes don't. But with corrective lenses, even the eyes of older shooters can do the work demanded by open iron sights.

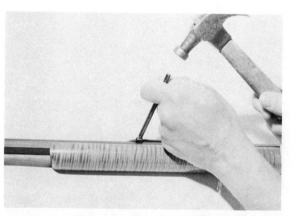

In order to adjust the "nonadjustable" rear sight, it is necessary to *drift* the sight in its dovetail notch, as shown here.

often alter the system to meet their own needs. I prefer, for example, a rather fine front sight. A large bead may fill too much of the rear-sight notch and frame of reference is lost. I prefer a 1/16-inch bead for most iron-sight shooting. But a 3/32-inch bead is also fine enough under many shooting circumstances. These fine beads allow for a good clear sight picture and yet they are big enough to put on target fast up close, too.

As for bead shape, the flat-faced bead is excellent. It offers a good picture and tends to reflect light less than a round bead. As for shape of front sight—bead, post, or blade—it makes little difference to me. As long as I can gain an optical picture

Sighting-In with Open Iron Sights

Modern muzzle-loaders have old-time sight systems because they are in effect old-time rifles. Many of these quite correctly carry the "nonadjustable" open sight. We sometimes call these *fixed* sights, which is not quite correct. Take a look at some police revolvers and you will see true fixed sights. There is no movement of either sight. In order to alter these sights, you must file or bend them. The nonadjustable sights spoken of here are not like that. They do move in dovetail notches.

Just remember this of all open sights: The rear sight is moved in the direction you want the next bullet to land—up, down, left, or right.

With these so-called fixed sights, you drift the

rear sight to the left for a hit to the left, obviously, and the reverse of that for a hit to the right. But they do not go up and down. So if you wish to move the point of impact on the target either up or down, the front sight must be altered. The front sight is the opposite of the rear sight in that if you want to hit lower on the target, you buy a taller or higher front sight. If you want to hit higher on the target, then get your file out and lower or shorten the front sight. The same goes for left-right or horizontal movement. Want the next bullet to land more to the right? Then move the front sight to the left.

True fine-tuning is possible here, but only by trial and error measurements. I have sighted in many muzzle-loaders and have been able to get them all to print on target right where I wanted them to, but only after patient and careful work, gentle filing of the front sight, gentle drifting of the rear. However, once sighted in, these sights tend to remain so if they are fixed in place. This is done, using a punch, by forcing metal (from the dovetail slot in the barrel) down flat around the bases of both front and rear sight. The metal is pounded down with the punch until it firmly holds these sights in place.

The adjustable rear sight makes sight-in simpler. Usually, these sights preclude the movement of the front sight at all. There is an elevator bar or other element which literally moves the rear sight up or down. There may also be a left-right adjustment without having to actually drift the rear sight in the dovetail notch. So you simply adjust the rear sight until the group prints on target right where you want it.

THE PEEP SIGHT

The aperture sight or peep sight dates far back in the history of aiming devices. While this sort of sight is not vastly popular today, it is still one of the best iron sights ever developed. Remember that in using the open iron sight the eye had to focus back and forth from target to front sight to rear sight. In effect, one of these three operations is totally removed with the peep sight.

The rear sight is there, but you do not consciously use it. You simply look through it. Period. Shooters make too much fuss about the peep sight. They try too hard. Just look *through* the hole and put the front sight on the target. The brightest concentration of light is dead center in that peep. Your eye will find that automatically. No need to "line it up." The image of the front sight will end up dead center in the aperture. Then all that is left to do is hold the front sight on target and master the con-

Here is an aperture sight, also known as a "peep" sight. This Lyman model allows for very close shooting from this custom Model 94 Winchester.

trol of rifle-hold and trigger squeeze. I cannot emphasize this enough, for every season I run into a peep-sight shooter who is having trouble lining up that front sight in the hole. Just don't try. Your eye will do it for you with no strain at all.

Another factor which applies to the peep sight is an elongated sight radius. Sight radius is the actual distance between the front sight of the rifle and the rear sight. Obviously, as you move the rear sight rearward in the peep system to get it closer to the eye, you elongate the sight radius. With open iron sights, an increase in sight radius can help *sharpen* the sight picture and this is why some shooters marvel at how sharp the open-sight picture is with those old long-barreled muzzle-loaders. It's not really the sights, but rather the increased sight radius at work.

The peep sight is fast. The eye has less work to do than it does with the open iron sight. You simply look through, not at, the aperture, put the front sight on target and squeeze the round off. In fact, a peep sight which rests on a well-fitted rifle is no doubt faster than open irons in putting the first shot right on target. Naturally, aperture size has much to do with this phenomenon. A tiny target-type disc aperture is not going to allow speed in the hunting field. Such a small aperture is totally unnecessary for most shooting. I prefer a ring size of approximately one-third inch with an aperture size (hole in that ring) of about a tenth of an inch.

In poor light, a peep sight is a boon. The front sight seems to stand all alone, nothing around it. A shooter can see the bead clearly and he merely puts the bead on target. If shooters simply look through the peep without consciously trying to center the bead, it would be agreed, I think, that the peep is easier to master than the open.

Of the many types of peep sight, the tang-mounted is not seen often these days, but it used to be quite popular. It was, actually, an auxiliary sight. The tang is a peep sight mounted on the upper tang of the rifle as shown in the illustration on page 60. It is very close to the eye and very fast to use, though it generally doesn't offer the ease of sight-in associated with other sights. Another type of peep sight was found on the Model 71 Winchester—a bolt-mounted peep, quite effective, but not popular enough to enjoy wide use. It mounted, as the term implies, on the locking bolt of this lever-action rifle and it was close to the eye and as neat and clean in appearance as one could ask for.

Called a receiver sight, the peep can be mounted

The tang sight was common on rifles of yesteryear. This is an original tang peep sight mounted on a Savage Model 1899 rifle. It locks in either the up or down position.

on the receiver of the rifle, and usually is. There have been dozens of different styles in the receiver-sight realm, some with simple adjustments and others with much more precise movements, the latter being the micrometer peep sight. The micrometer is, no doubt, the best of the peeps in terms of sight-in. It allows accurate movement of point of impact through click adjustment. Usually, the value of each click is a quarter minute. However, there have been many micrometer peep sights with other click values. Remember that a minute of angle, for shooters, is an inch at 100 yards, two inches at 200 yards, three inches at 300 yards, and so forth. Scientifically, this is not quite correct, but for our purposes, it is a workable definition.

The quarter-minute click is designed to move point of impact one fourth of one inch at 100 yards. That's quite precise. Naturally, we are dealing in averages and theory, as well as fact, because a sporting rifle is not going to place its bullets into a quarter-inch group at 100 yards. However, in effect, this fine micrometer sight does allow for a quarter-inch adjustment in the *point of impact* (center of the actual group) at 100 yards from the muzzle.

Sighting-In with the Peep Sight

The values of the clicks are important to understand. If they are quarter-minute, remember that this means a quarter inch at 100 yards. At only 25 yards, it takes *four* clicks to equal a quarter inch of movement. So in that initial sight-in at 25 yards, each inch of motion requires sixteen clicks of the sight. At 200 yards from the muzzle, the value changes again. Now a single click is worth one-half inch, or twice its 100-yard value. In other words, if the rifle is shooting an inch lower than you desire at 200 yards, two clicks up would bring it on target.

Remember you are dealing with a group, not one bullet hole. In order to determine how many clicks to take in changing point of impact, fire *groups* of five to ten shots. Look for the *cluster* center of that group. Ignore any bullet holes well out of that cluster. Find the center of impact for the majority of holes which are clustered closest together. Measure center to center. This means from the center of one bullet hole to the center of another. If, of the five shots fired, four are clustered in an inch grouping, locate the center of that group and measure from that center to the center of the bull's-eye.

Begin sighting at 25 yards or closer. This advice goes for all sighting-in. It saves ammo because it's much simpler to get on the paper at 25 yards than to figure out where the bullets are going when you can only see them strike the dirt bank behind the target. Furthermore, at 25 yards click values are diminished, so you can make a whole lot of adjustment—many clicks—right now and put that sight very close to zero. Fire five to ten shots. Determine the center of the point of impact of this group. Measure the distance from the center of the group to the point on the target which you want to hit. Make the appropriate adjustments. Now shoot again. Hopefully, the cluster or group will be dead center at 25 yards following the adjustment. It should be. Move the target out to 100 or 200 yards and refine the sighting.

THE TELESCOPIC RIFLE SIGHT

There is absolutely nothing new about telescopes. Jim Bridger used one in the early 1800s as he advanced through the far reaches of the West, and it took no time at all for shooters to realize that if you stuck a scope, which is the shortened term we use today, on top of a rifle, you'd get magnification of

The Bushnell Banner Trophy scope, 3×–9× variable power, offers a wide-angle view, bullet-drop compensator, along with a clear optical picture.

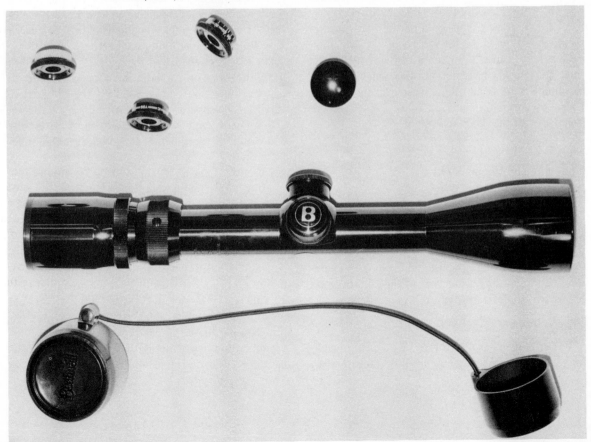

the target, a precise aiming point, and a flat image with that reticle "pasted" right on the target, optically speaking. The advantages of the scope sight became evident a long time ago, and yet it was not until fairly recent times that the scope reached the rank of number one in sighting instruments.

Even in the 1950s and early 1960s, it was common to see scopeless big-game rifles in the West. But soon enough, the scope earned its wings. Early scopes may have fogged a bit, and the wires might have been off in one corner of the scope's view. They were more sensitive to failure and less sensitive to sight change, and the mounts that held them on the rifle were often bulky and ugly. All that has changed. Fog is a word I have not heard connected with scope-sights for a very long time. Constantly centered crosswires are commonplace. A positive adjustment system is ordinary on today's better scopes. And the only scope I have ever put out of commission in the field was banged against a rock. Even a rugged iron sight may well have been knocked out of whack with such a blow. Accuracy of adjustment, optics, ruggedness—all of today's top-of-the-line scopes have these features.

Properly mounted scope sights are fast to use and easy to sight in. Today's mounts hold the scope on target very well and they are pretty to look at. All in all, there is no doubt in my mind that for most rifle shooting the scope is the king of all sight systems. I do not use a scope on a few of my own rifles for three reasons: I do not use a scope on my muzzle-loaders because they do not fit the image of the rifle. I have a few lever-action rifles which I use for handmate hunting and these wear iron sights. And I also use irons on some 22 rifles just to keep in practice with the older-style sight.

Choosing the Scope Sight

Optics

My first criterion is optics. I want a bright scope with good resolution, one which will clearly show the target, and also give good *definition*. Such optics allow for a more precise aiming point. Therefore, as in choosing a fine pair of binoculars, good optics are the foremost feature to consider.

Power

Power is listed as $3\times$ or $4\times$ or $6\times$, etc., meaning the target is visually magnified by that number.

If I were to shoot in brushy or woods settings with a given rifle, and never use it for long-range work, I would mount a $2.5\times$ or $3\times$ and leave it at that. Conversely, if I were to hunt with a rifle just on the plains, then it could possibly wear a $6\times$ scope or even an $8\times$ and no further range of magnification would be required. However, I have found that in brush hunting there is always a clearing and an opportunity to shoot across that clearing, while on the plains, I have entered a little dip in the land only to be surprised at close range by a buck. In other words, brush country offers an occasional long shot and open country an occasional close shot.

While I find no fault whatever with a $3\times$ or $4\times$ scope as a good all-around choice, I have gone more and more to the *variable*. I have found all of my variables totally reliable and I prize the ability to switch from low to high power. Too many shooters tell me they would not buy a variable because they almost always seem to set it at one power without ever moving it again. That makes as much sense as never putting your car in overdrive even though the car has the feature.

I switch power on my variables all the time. My favorite long-range plains rifle for serious shooting is a 257 Weatherby Magnum. It wears a $2.5\times$–$8\times$ scope sight. I have taken game with that sight at just about all of its settings. Even on the plains, there are pockets of brush and when I enter one of these, I switch to $2.5\times$ for the wide field of view. I have found game at long range with my binoculars, stalked it, and then had to settle for a long shot using the scope on $8\times$ because of its great ability to discern the exact aiming point on the target. I've carried the scope at $4\times$ when tramping the open areas where game might show up in a hurry and $8\times$ would be too much but $2.5\times$ not enough magnification.

Recently, I set up a Ruger 77-22 for small-game hunting and general shooting. Certainly, a $2.5\times$, $3\times$, or $4\times$ scope would have worked well. But as I thought it over, I realized that I'd like to use the little rimfire for running rabbits, would put it to work on varmints at modest range, and might also go squirrel hunting with it, besides employing it on mountain grouse (perfectly legal where I live). The 22 rifle got a Bushnell $2\times$–$8\times$. At $2\times$, I could pick up on a running rabbit. At $4\times$ it was just right for grouse. On the upper powers it was good for varmints and any shooting where a highly magnified target was desirable—putting a bullet right on target in squirrel hunting, for example. The variable has come of age. It's a wise choice if the rifleman will take advantage of it.

Construction

Most modern scopes are strongly built, internally as well as externally. Some scopes use lens clips internally, yet I own such models and the accuracy and dependability have remained high over the years. Today, most scopes are well constructed. Of course, you must pick the right scope for a certain task, especially if that task is a rugged one. For example, do not stick a little scope made for a 22 rimfire on a spring-piston air rifle. It's quite likely that the air rifle will destroy the scope. For such an air rifle, special models are available. They are made to withstand the uncoiling of that powerful spring and its rather unique "double" recoil. Also, look to rugged scopes for big-game rifles of high recoil.

Eye Relief

Watch out for eye relief when choosing a scope sight. Eye relief is the normal distance between the eye and the ocular lens of the scope that still allows you to see the entire field of view. Some scopes have a very limited eye relief. Others have much more latitude. Be sure that on a high-recoil rifle, the scope can be mounted so that the ocular bell never reaches your forehead during recoil. Also be sure that you see the whole picture in the scope without blackout. Most big-game scopes offer eye relief in the 2.5- to 5-inch range. A "long eye-relief scope" can be purchased for those who need to mount the scope forward of the receiver of the rifle.

Field of View

Associated with the magnification of the scope, the field of view is a measurement which reveals how many feet in width may be seen through the scope at 100 yards. A 4× scope may have a field of view of 30 feet, for example, meaning that your eye will view a width of 30 feet at 100 yards. I have a 2.5× to 8× variable on one rifle which gives a 45-foot field at 2.5× and a 14-foot view on 8×. Obviously, the lower setting with its wide field is preferable for closeup, fast-shooting situations.

Reticle

Also known as the reticule, this is the aiming device in the scope, usually a crosswire. Put the

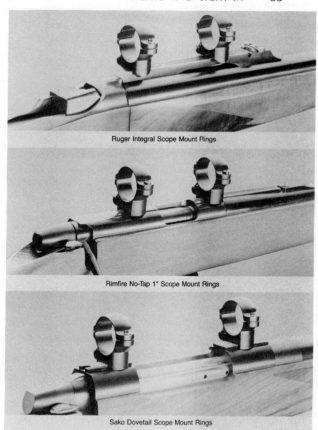

Ruger Integral Scope Mount Rings

Rimfire No-Tap 1" Scope Mount Rings

Sako Dovetail Scope Mount Rings

Leupold rings: handsome as well as functional. *(Leupold & Stevens)*

cross on target and you are ready to fire. The crosswire has been popular for a very long time. Today, however, a variation of this reticle is common. It offers a system of heavy crosswires, easily picked up by the eye, in combination with finer crosswires in the center for precise aiming. One cannot go wrong with this reticle. A dot is excellent for range estimation and close-range shooting in the brush; however, the heavy/fine crosswire combination does not blot out as much target as the dot and is far easier to sight on a small bull's-eye.

Mounts

Once the nemesis of the scope fan, the mount has been vastly refined today. A few foreign mounts are still uglier than a bucket of frogs and higher than they need to be. But generally, modern scope mounts are handsome, strong, and functional. Some are custom-made as integral parts of the receiver of the rifle. Dean Zollinger, for example, mills his own scope bases to match the style of his custom rifles. Ruger has long offered an integral base system as well. Redfield and Leupold manufacture excellent one-piece bridge-type mounts. Select a mount to match your rifle's style and function.

OTHER AIMING DEVICES

The Aimpoint sight is a small unit, internally lighted, without lenses for magnification. It is easily seen under low-light shooting conditions. Lighted reticles have also found their way into telescopic sights. Having tested the Thompson/Center scope with lighted reticle and the Bushnell Lite-Site system, I discovered that both did exactly what they were advertised to do—they allowed for quick and easy placement of the reticle, in low light. Incidentally, the Aimpoint device mentioned above can be magnified via optional devices. Millet Sights also makes a custom sight instrument which does not magnify the target. It's called the Cyclops 22 Reflex Sight and it has a base which easily attaches to the dovetails on a 22-rimfire rifle. It has a bright fluorescent reticle and uses no battery, but works with mirrors.

No matter how good the sights are, a shooter must still observe all of the tenets of good marksmanship, from firearm control to trigger letoff.

Conversely, no matter how good a shooter is, he's no better than his sights. Putting the best sight on a rifle is a matter of application—the actual use of the rifle—and appropriateness—what truly fits the lines and style of the rifle. Fortunately, the modern rifleman has a wide choice of the best sight devices ever designed.

SIGHT-IN CHART

Rifles are sighted in commensurate with range potential. The trajectory of the cartridge is first discerned. The usual MRT table (midrange trajectory) is valuable because it shows the height of the bullet at a point halfway between the muzzle and the target. However, the following chart gives the reader a more direct route to sight-in.

Sight in from a benchrest to remove as many human variables as possible. Portable benchrests, such as the Cabela unit, work well. These benches are collapsible for portability. The local shooting club will have solid, heavy benches to fire from, benches which are designed to offer maximum stability. The human elements of heartbeat, tremor ("shake"), and breathing effect are reduced somewhat by the bench. The following list does not contain every possible cartridge of course. If your favorite round is absent, choose a ballistically similar one and use that data as a guide.

The benchrest is the proper place for sighting-in and accuracy checks. This portable Cabela rest can be taken into the field with minimal effort.

SIGHT-IN CHART

22 LONG RIFLE
40-grain bullet at 1,300 fps MV

0	+ 1"	0	− 2.5"	− 7.5"
20 yards	50 yards	85 yards	100 yards	125 yards

22 HYPER-VELOCITY ROUNDS (Stinger, Spitfire, Yellow Jacket, etc.)
33-grain bullet at 1,500 fps MV

0	+ 2.5"	0	− 6"	− 9.5"
25 yards	50 yards	100 yards	125 yards	150 yards

22 WMR (Winchester Magnum Rimfire)
40-grain bullet at 1,900 fps MV

0	+ 1"	0	− 6"	− 20"
25 yards	50 yards	100 yards	150 yards	200 yards

17 REMINGTON
25-grain bullet at 4,100 fps MV

0	+ 1"	+ 2"	+ 3"	0
25 yards	50 yards	100 yards	200 yards	300 yards

22 HORNET/218 BEE
50-grain bullet at 2,800 fps MV

0	+ 3"	0	− 9"
25 yards	100 yards	225 yards	300 yards

222 REMINGTON/222 REMINGTON MAGNUM/223 REMINGTON
50-grain bullet at 3,300 fps MV

0	+ 3"	+ 4"	0	− 2"	− 15"
25 yards	100 yards	200 yards	285 yards	300 yards	400 yards

220 SWIFT/22-250 REMINGTON/224 WEATHERBY
50-grain bullet at 3,900 fps MV

0	+ 2.5"	+ 3.5"	0	− 8.5"
25 yards	100 yards	200 yards	310 yards	400 yards

243 WINCHESTER/6MM REMINGTON
100-grain bullet at 3,100 fps MV

0	+ 3"	+ 4"	0	− 3"	− 13"
25 yards	100 yards	200 yards	275 yards	300 yards	400 yards

240 WEATHERBY MAGNUM
100-grain bullet at 3,400 fps MV

0	+ 3"	+ 3.5"	0	− 9"
25 yards	100 yards	200 yards	300 yards	400 yards

250 SAVAGE/257 ROBERTS
100-grain bullet at 3,100 fps MV

0	+ 3"	+ 4"	0	− 3"	− 10"
25 yards	100 yards	200 yards	275 yards	300 yards	400 yards

25-06 REMINGTON
120-grain bullet at 3,200 fps MV[1]

0	+ 3″	+ 4″	0	− 10″
25 yards	100 yards	200 yards	300 yards	400 yards

257 WEATHERBY MAGNUM
100-grain bullet at 3,630 fps (chronographed) MV

0	+ 3″	+ 4″	+ 1.5″	− 7″	− 20″
25 yards	100 yards	200 yards	300 yards	400 yards	500 yards

264 WINCHESTER MAGNUM
140-grain bullet at 3,200 fps MV

0	+ 3″	+ 4″	0	− 9″
25 yards	100 yards	200 yards	300 yards	400 yards

270 WINCHESTER
130-grain bullet at 3,100 fps MV

0	+ 3″	+ 4″	0	− 3″	− 13″
25 yards	100 yards	200 yards	275 yards	300 yards	400 yards

7MM-08 REMINGTON
150-grain bullet at 2,600 fps MV

0	+ 2.5″	0	− 6″	− 10″
25 yards	100 yards	200 yards	250 yards	300 yards

7×57 MAUSER/284 WINCHESTER
150-grain bullet at 2,900 fps MV

0	+ 3″	+ 4″	0	− 4″
25 yards	100 yards	200 yards	270 yards	300 yards

7MM REMINGTON MAGNUM/7MM WEATHERBY MAGNUM
139-grain bullet at 3,400 fps MV

0	+ 3″	+ 4″	0	− 9″
25 yards	100 yards	200 yards	300 yards	400 yards

30-30 WINCHESTER
170-grain bullet at 2,200 fps MV

0	+ 1.5″	+ 2″	0	− 5.5″
15 yards	50 yards	100 yards	150 yards	200 yards

300 SAVAGE/308 WINCHESTER
150-grain bullet at 2,800 fps MV

0	+ 2.5″	0	− 7″
25 yards	100 yards	225 yards	300 yards

30-06 SPRINGFIELD
150-grain bullet at 3,100 fps MV[2]

0	+ 3″	+ 4″	0	− 4″
25 yards	100 yards	200 yards	270 yards	300 yards

[1] Handload/64 grains of H-870 rifle powder, Winchester case.

[2] Handload using 63 grains of Winchester-760 rifle powder, Winchester case.

*300 H&H MAGNUM/300 WINCHESTER MAGNUM/308 NORMA
MAGNUM/300 WEATHERBY MAGNUM*
165-grain bullet at 3,200 fps MV[3]

0	+ 3″	+ 4″	0	− 10″
25 yards	100 yards	200 yards	290 yards	400 yards

338 WINCHESTER
225-grain bullet at 2,900 fps MV

0	+ 3″	+ 4″	0	− 3″
25 yards	100 yards	200 yards	265 yards	300 yards

35 REMINGTON
200-grain bullet at 2,000 fps MV

0	+ 2″	+ 3″	0	− 7″
25 yards	50 yards	100 yards	150 yards	200 yards

358 WINCHESTER/356 WINCHESTER[4]
200-grain bullet at 2,500 fps MV

0	+ 3″	0	− 12″
25 yards	100 yards	200 yards	300 yards

35 WHELEN (wildcat)
200-grain bullet at 2,700 fps MV

0	+ 2.5″	0	− 10″
25 yards	100 yards	200 yards	300 yards

358 NORMA MAGNUM
200-grain bullet at 2,900 fps MV

0	+ 2.5″	0	− 8″
25 yards	100 yards	225 yards	300 yards

45-70 GOVERNMENT
350-grain bullet at 1,900 fps MV (new Marlin 1895 rifle)

0	+ 2.5″	+ 3″	0	− 8″
25 yards	50 yards	100 yards	150 yards	200 yards

458 WINCHESTER
500-grain FMJ bullet at 2,100 fps MV

0	+ 1.5″	+ 2″	0	− 5″
25 yards	50 yards	100 yards	150 yards	200 yards

SUMMARY

Other cartridges of similar ballistics may be plugged into these tables with good results. Note that an initial sight-in of 25 yards often puts the bullet into its best trajectory pattern. Naturally, fine-tuning at longer range is vital; however, it is suggested that the shooter can save much time and ammo if he will begin the sight-in process at close range, usually the 25-yard mark.

[3] Specifically, the 308 Norma Magnum reaches closer to 3,100 fps MV with this bullet, and the 300 Weatherby can achieve 3,300; however, sight-in with all four is quite similar and these data are accurate.

[4] 356 Winchester with RN bullet should be sighted for 175 yards, 3″ high at 100.

Accuracy and the Sporting Rifle

WHAT IS ACCURACY? Not long ago, the shooter next to me at the target range let out a war whoop. "She shoots!" he exclaimed, and, wanting to share the good news with somebody, he advanced a couple of steps over to my bench to locate a set of interested ears. His hand poked out toward me. I could see a bunch of bullet holes scattered about a large black bull's-eye. From a distance of only 100 yards, the man's rifle had managed something like a five- to six-inch group. He was firing a muzzle-loader. He explained that this was the first time five shots landed together on the paper. He had found his load! Accuracy was chained.

I hardly knew what to say. My own 54-caliber Mulford custom long rifle printed two-inch groups when I did my part. We once mounted a scope sight on her as a test run and the grouping shrank to an inch, center-to-center. Accuracy, then, is a relative thing, but we can pin it down to some degree. Accuracy is more meaningful if attached to specific *classes* of rifles. My match-grade RWS 17-caliber air rifle creates a .20-inch group at 10 meters, which is one little hole in the bull's-eye.

Within the air rifle's range and limitations, such accuracy is superb. At 50 yards, the little pellets get tossed around in a wind, and 100-yard shooting is out of the question, since the light pellets are prey to the atmosphere. My best muzzle-loader will produce two-inch groups at 100 yards, with iron sights. I have a couple of big-game rifles which will group their bullets into the one-half-inch realm at that distance. My most accurate big-game rifle, a 7mm Magnum with a Douglas air-gauged barrel, has achieved several .75-inch three-shot groups at 200 yards.

I can live with a black-powder rifle which will average three-inch to four-inch clusters at 100 yards because such muzzle-loaders are for hunting and seldom are shots taken at game beyond 100 to 125 yards with a frontloader. I prefer my modern big-game rifles to group in the one-inch domain at 100 yards, or better. I feel that the 22-rimfire rifle should produce the same group size at 50 yards. There are, of course, many factors pertaining to accuracy. The wise rifleman learns how to squeeze the best accuracy from his personal rifles.

MEASURING ACCURACY

"Boy, is that rifle accurate!" We have all heard that statement made about a particular firearm. But what does it mean? That the bullets will group into a washtub at 50 paces? "My rifle shoots into a minute of angle." That statement is better. This means that the rifle prints inch groups at 100 yards, two-inch groups at 200, three-inch at 300 and so forth. This is a better way of talking about accuracy. However, a rifle which groups into an inch at 100 yards does not always group into two at 200 or three at 300. Maybe the bullet's stability is all gone at 200, so at 300 yards the projectile is tipping and may not hit the target point-on.

I prefer a simple statement of accuracy—"This rifle groups into an average of two and one-half inches at 200 yards." A group could, by definition,

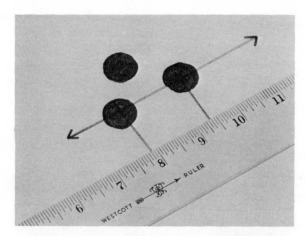

7

A group is measured "center to center," as illustrated here.

consist of two shots or two hundred shots, but a three-shot group will give a shooter a pretty good idea of where his *hunting* rifle falls in regard to accuracy, and a five-shot group is even better. Statistically, the more shots, the better reliability, all other things being equal. In practical terms, five shots tells a pretty good story.

THE BULLET AND ACCURACY

Many factors affect accuracy. The bullet is certainly one of them. We can oversimplify the whole accuracy story by simply saying that good bullets fired from good barrels are accurate. But what are good bullets? Years ago, bullets often were manufactured at a campfire or hearth. Lead melts at about 621° F, so it's possible to create your own missiles with a pot, mold, and heat source. The molds were sometimes fairly good in days of yore. I cast a few projectiles from an old-time mold, believing that they would not shoot accurately in my muzzle-loader. They shot just fine.

How could out-of-round balls shoot well in that muzzle-loader? By formation of the bullet in the bore itself. Obturation it's called, the actual foreshortening of the projectile as the expanding gases push on it. The projectile fills out and engages the lands of the rifling for a pretty good fit. Therefore, the less-than-perfect products of my old-time mold shot quite well.

Now comes the modern bullet. While the term obturation isn't used, there is some *upset* of the missile in the bore as it is blasted out by the powder charge. Even the jacketed bullet undergoes some of this upset. Coupled with the modern bullet, which is a miracle of uniformity, bullet upset helps to create a very precise projectile in the bore. I have used a micrometer, only to find that I cannot discern any difference in the diameter of modern bullets. I measured ten before writing these lines and all ten were .3085 inch in diameter. Then I weighed the same ten. There was not one-tenth of one grain difference between them.

So the factor of good bullets in accuracy is a foregone conclusion in modern bullet making. But what about the bullet that is battered by hot expanding gases and then is slammed into a hostile atmosphere? There are instances of bullets failing because they are improperly constructed to withstand the rigors of high velocity. I once fired some thin-skinned 50-grain projectiles from a 220 Swift at close to 4,000 fps MV. The bullets never made it to the target. There was a blue trail of smoke in the air, and nothing on paper at 100 yards to show a hit. The bullets disintegrated in the air.

And what about the "bottle of molten lead" theory? A rather surprising number of very astute shooters have believed that one problem with bullet accuracy has to do with the notion that a bullet at very high speed must be a veritable bottle of molten lead. After all, the bullet races through the bore at 3,000, 3,500, even 4,000 feet per second. Heat must be terrible. And lead melts at only 621° F. Does it not follow that the bullet would be a jacket loaded with liquid lead? No. The bullet is in the bore too little time for it to get that hot. It's like passing your hand through the flame of a campfire and not getting burned. If you hold your hand in the flame for a moment, it will be badly scorched. Check the base of a Nosler Partition bullet. It's of the open-base style, lead showing. Pick one out of the sand-bank at the range and it's intact. The lead has certainly not leaked out, no matter what the muzzle velocity.

Dr. Franklin Mann, famous for his many shooting experiments, declared that the projectile was the single most important factor in accuracy. It's quite difficult to separate the bullet from the bore, of course, because the best bullet in the world is not going to be accurate from a badly worn bore. Today, we shooters can rest in total assurance that the bullets we buy are uncanny in their excellence, uniform to a fantastic degree of reliability, and, of themselves, highly accurate. Yet, not all bullets fire accurately from all rifles. Why not? Because many other factors are at work.

DAMAGED BULLETS AND ACCURACY

Bullets do not normally become damaged, but there is a wide belief that a smashed bullet would steer away from its appointed course to the target. Fear not. In fact, the shooter is invited to try this. At the range, sort out five good cartridges loaded with soft-point projectiles. Take three of them and rap their noses on the bench until the lead point is smashed flat. Now shoot all five. The group will be quite normal. Nose damage is of no important consequence.

How about the base of the bullet? In the first place, the only natural damage I have ever seen done to the base of a bullet is through handloading. Sometimes handloaders fail to chamfer the mouth of the case, and the bullet has to scrape its way past the mouth in order to be seated. Does this sort of base damage spoil accuracy? If I were involved in world shooting competition, I'd avoid such damage. However, for the usual sort of marksmanship most of us engage in, minor base damage won't hurt anything.

I've also filed away a corner of the bullet base. Results have varied for me. With some black-powder missiles, the damaged base destroyed accuracy. And yet, I cut the corner away on a 7mm, 162-grain bullet and it remained with the group at 100 yards and was only slightly out of the group at 200. The results were not totally conclusive. Perhaps bullets of high C are less susceptible to base damage than bullets of low C, and that could be why my short, low-C black-powder bullets were out of the group with base damage while the 7mm bullets were not. However, there seems to be a pretty good indication that base damage is more serious than nose damage, and that the rear end of the bullet does most of the "steering."

TWIST AND ACCURACY

The whole idea of rifling is to spin the bullet on its axis, giving it stability. As the bullet changes in sectional density, twist must be altered, too. The essential factor is the RPS (revolutions per second) that twist imparts to a bullet. Bullets vary widely in the RPS required to stabilize them. For example, a round ball requires very little RPS. Twists in a 50-caliber rifle of 1:66, a turn in 66 inches, all the way

The rifling of the bore allows for bullet stabilization through gyroscopic effect. The rate of twist is established on the basis of bullet configuration and mass. The correct twist for one bullet may be all wrong for another, although there is a range of acceptable bullet weights.

beyond 1:75, proved adequate for shooting up to 200 yards.

A bullet of higher sectional density (a round ball has very low sectional density) requires greater rate of twist. However, even here there is another factor at work—exit velocity. RPS is derived from the rate of twist, but it is twist in concert with muzzle velocity. For example, a 117-grain bullet fired at 2,200 fps MV from a 25-35 Winchester requires a fast rate of twist. The Model 94 25-35 has a 1:8 rate, a turn in eight inches of barrel. The 257 Roberts, shooting the same 117-grain bullet at perhaps 2,900 fps MV, stabilizes with a 1:10 rate of twist.

In order to gain sufficient RPS to stabilize the long bullet in the 25-35 at only 2,200 fps, more twist is needed. But with the greater velocity of the 257 Roberts, the bullet stabilized with less rifling twist. Remember that twist is *not* a function of barrel length. It's confusing because twist is described as a turn in so many inches of barrel. A 1:10 rate of twist means that the bullet will turn one complete revolution in the bore in 10 inches of barrel. However, it is the *rate* of twist which counts, and that is established right away. If you keep the muzzle velocity just the same, RPS is going to be the same in a 1:10 rate of twist 24-inch barrel or a 1:10 rate of twist 12-inch barrel using identical bullets. Revolvers have faster rates of twist not because of their shorter barrels, *per se,* but because those shorter barrels produce less muzzle velocity. In order to get the RPS up, rate of twist is quickened.

If the twist is sufficient to stabilize the bullet, then it is the right twist for accuracy. If the twist is not suitable for stabilizing the bullet, it's wrong. For example, I own a very accurate 6.5mm-06 rifle. It has a 1:10 rate of twist. Accuracy is supreme with 120-, 129-, and 140-grain bullets. But a 160-grain bullet is not accurate in this rifle. I believe that the latter fails at the target because the 1:10 twist is not stabilizing the bullet in flight. It is yawing and even keyholing, rather than humming smoothly along on course. Therefore, try various bullet weights in your rifle to determine which are more accurate.

What about overstabilization? Is it possible? I know that in testing a round-ball rifle, I learned that with fast rates of twist, accuracy fell off. This occurred with high-velocity powder charges, but not with low-velocity charges. I feel that the RPS was too high in that fast rate of twist and the ball simply "stripped" the rifling, riding on them, not being guided by them. On a few occasions I have sensed similar problems with modern rifles; however, I have little hard data showing accuracy loss from overstabilized bullets in modern big-bore firearms.

Everything else in the bore is taken care of. We don't worry about depth of groove, for example. A depth of groove may be about .004 inch, for example, with a 30-caliber rifle, and that's fine. Gunmakers have already done the work for us here. We need not worry about the numbers of grooves/lands in the bore, either. There may be four or six or more. Rates of twist per given cartridge have also been chosen wisely by our barrel makers. There will be some variation, because the factories don't always agree. For example, buy a Remington 308 Winchester rifle and the twist will be 1:10. Buy a 308 from Winchester and it will be 1:12. Most 30-06s are 1:10, a few are 1:12.

FREEBORE AND ACCURACY

It's the consensus, and has been for a very long time, that the best accuracy is obtained when a bullet is seated out far enough to just touch or engage the lands in the chamber of the rifle. Handloaders, of course, have control over this factor and they should seat bullets in the cartridge case far enough out to just meet the beginning of the rifling in the throat of the chamber. Experiments seem to validate the claim that this will improve a rifle's accuracy.

I have only one problem with the theory. Given that best accuracy is obtained when a bullet just meets with the lands of the rifling, then freebore should definitely bring a deterioration in accuracy. Freebore is the cutting away of rifling for a distance in the throat of the chamber. The very curse of accuracy, many say, is allowing the bullet to jump from the neck of the cartridge case into the rifling. Freebore causes just that problem, if indeed it is a problem.

We also know that a rise in pressure occurs when the bullet is restricted in any way in the rifle. A very tight crimp can cause an upswing in pressure. So can loading a bullet so that it touches the lands. Again, I have to add "So they say." Some tests just don't show significant surges in pressure when the bullet touches the lands before takeoff. At any rate, freebore was designed to lessen pressure with hot-rock rounds that burn lots of powder and give lots of ballistic performance.

I have a freebored 6.5-06, custom made by Dale Storey, with a Bauska barrel. Bauska gave us his usual well-designed barrel and we proceeded to stick a throat in it that would swallow a hotdog before the lands were touched—plenty of freebore in other words. The rifle promptly repaid us with half-inch five-shot groups at 100 yards. Consequently, more freebore rifles were built, also very accurate. When we have a physical law, we'd like that law to work all the time. If, indeed, there is a law stating that freebore is damaging to accuracy, and that loading bullets out to engage the rifling promotes accuracy, then the law should hold up. It has not.

Therefore, the best advice I have at the moment is testing in individual rifles. Naturally, a bullet is loaded so that the round is the correct length to function in the rifle. I have been loading for magazine length, mainly because my tests with bullet seating depth and accuracy have not been entirely productive. Therefore, overall cartridge length is correct for functioning in the magazine of a specific rifle. And bullets are not loaded to touch the lands, lest they stick in the throat of the rifle when working rounds through the action. I load them so they do not engage the rifling, but miss by a minute degree. So far, accuracy has not suffered.

ACCURACY AND LOAD DENSITY

Load density is the condition of using a powder type and a certain charge of that powder, as recommended by the loading manual, which takes up most of the air space within the cartridge case. Actually, it is slightly more complicated than that, but this explanation is close enough for our purposes. I set out to prove (or disprove) that load density is indeed vital to accuracy, but the results were less than convincing. For example, an extremely accurate load was built for a 30-06 using a charge of IMR-4895 powder which rendered only 2,700 fps MV for a 150-grain bullet. Load density here was denied. Accuracy was not.

Load density is another factor which some shooters believe contributes to accuracy in a cartridge. This round enjoys 100 percent load density. Its full case capacity is taken up with powder. *(Remington Arms)*

Using only 45 grains of IMR-4895 in a 30-06 does not produce high load density. Therefore, accuracy should have been diminished as compared with a previous load, 63 grains of W-760 powder and the same 150-grain bullet. In fact, both loads were very accurate in the test rifle, the first at only 2,700 fps MV, the second at 3,100 fps MV. Alas, proof was flitting about the range like a mischievous puppy getting away from its master. In another test—and I use the word "test" in the everyday sense, knowing that these are not scientific experiments, but rather *demonstrations*—a 270 Winchester using 59 grains of W-785 with a 140-

grain bullet proved more accurate than 55 grains of W-785. Load density seemed to have an effect this time.

I know that in some rifles and cartridges, high load density has proved a boon. I also know that in others, it has not. Proof is lacking. The idea of more uniform powder ignition through higher load density may be a good one, but more testing is needed. Rifles may vary with load density. Test yours with approved loads.

THE ACCURATE CARTRIDGE

Are there simply accurate cartridges? Is it true that a 30-06 is inherently more accurate than a 30-30 by virtue of case design, case capacity versus bore size, shape of the case—shoulder angle and so forth—or is one round potentially as accurate as another? I would say that the vast majority of shooters in this country believe that there are indeed certain rounds which were simply born accurate.

I go along with Dr. Mann, who suggested that accuracy is more in keeping with good bullets from good barrels. Case shape, for example, is important to powder-burning characteristics, yet I have seen a wonderful-looking 6mm International round and a rather slouchy-looking 32-40 on the range at the same time, both chambered in good rifles, both quite accurate, and the 6mm did *not* outshoot the 32-40.

In choosing a round strictly for accuracy, I'd prefer a modest-sized case of whatever shape, and that only because of recoil factors and ease in arriving at a good balance between the powder charge and the bullet weight. In other words, load density notwithstanding, I'd rather work on accuracy loads in a 308 over a 300 Magnum. If case shape were indeed such a big issue, rounds such as the 30-30 would be in big trouble. Over the years, a number of shooters thought the 30-30 a rather inaccurate cartridge. While it was always adequate in the hunting field, on the bench the 30-06, for example, outshot the 30-30. However, experimenters such as Al Barr disproved the idea once and for all. Barr built a fine single-shot in 30-30 caliber and proceeded to show his friends many half-inch 100-yard groups. Certainly, if the 30-30 were, by birth, lacking in accuracy, no rifle could have salvaged it.

Therefore I am not a believer in cartridge shape or size as leading to accuracy. However, there may be some rounds which burn the powder in a manner inconducive to best accuracy. Personally, I never fired a 22 WRF rifle (and I've shot several) which gave the accuracy of a plain 22 Long Rifle chambering. However, is that cartridge design, or the actual care in the manufacturing process of the ammunition?

STANDARD DEVIATION AND ACCURACY

A vital accuracy factor is standard deviation from the mean velocity. It's a numerical figure which relates the amount of variance in ammunition. Recently, chronographs have been designed for standard-deviation readout—no more long mathematical calculations are necessary with these machines. A button is pushed. The datum is given. In concert with standard deviation figures, these chronographs, such as Oehler's models, read highest velocity in the string, lowest, average, and extreme spread.

Standard-deviation numbers relate the reliability of ammunition. Mathematically, standard deviation is the square root of the variance. It tells how far a given sample varies from the average. Therefore, a low figure is desirable. A high figure is undesirable. For example, if five rounds of ammo are fired and the standard deviation is 10 feet per second, that figure denotes very reliable ammunition. Accuracy of this ammunition will be good commensurate with bullet and bore precision. Conversely, a high figure, such as 90-feet-per-second standard deviation, denotes ammunition of less reliability.

Standard deviation is an excellent checkup on *potential* ammo accuracy. I have found that from good barrels firing good bullets, the standard deviation factor of the ammo is an excellent predictor of accuracy. I use this check on my handloaded ammunition, and also with factory fodder. Not all factory ammo is created equal. For example, my tests have shown a very low (excellent) standard deviation for 30-30 ammo. Standard deviations in the 10-foot-per-second range are common.

BARREL BEDDING

Barrels vibrate during firing. Bedding can alter the pattern of vibration. For that reason, barrel bedding in the stock is important to accuracy. Bolt-action rifles may have free-floated barrels, meaning that the action is tightly bedded, so the barrel makes no contact with the channel in the stock for the majority of its length. Or the barrel may be fully bedded, firmly resting in the stock channel from action to forearm tip. Pressure points may be installed at given locations along the channel, using a leather shim, small piece of playing card, or other material.

Tuning, a topic soon discussed, often includes alteration of the barrel bedding because this factor plays a major role in accuracy. Which type of bedding is best? It depends on the rifle, and no one has proved that one bedding style is actually better than another overall. My Storey Conversion, a custom Model 94 Winchester 30-30, registers minute of angle groups, with an aperture sight, not a scope. I contend that part of the reason for such high-level accuracy from this lever-action design is barrel bedding. A stiff octagon barrel is fitted to the action with extremely close tolerances. For all intents and purpose, the barrel is free-floated. There are no barrel bands. The fore end is attached via a tenon. The barrel is allowed to vibrate without constraint.

The bolt-action rifle is said to gain its accuracy from the stiffness allowed by the strength of the action and by the rifle's one-piece stock. This is a Remington Model 700. *(Remington Arms)*

TUNING

A rifle can be tuned for better accuracy by altering the bedding of the action and especially of the barrel. A free-floated barrel can be given a pressure point, for example. A small bit of tanned leather has worked well for me. I place a piece of thin leather near the fore end, right in the barrel channel. Sometimes this pressure point works well and a free-floated barrel delivers better accuracy. The reverse has also been true. A rifle can be taken to a competent gunsmith (stockmaker) and he can free-float the barrel. He can also glass-bed it—seat the action in fiberglass—to make that section of the rifle more rigid.

The shooter can also use a shim, again a thin bit of tanned leather or other material, on a fully bedded rifle. I have altered the grouping of many pre-1964 Model 70s by cinching the bedding screw down tightly, then backing off a quarter turn, while also providing a shim under the fore end. Another tuning trick is relief of pressure at various points. My own Model 94 carbine was made to shoot much better by careful removal of pressure at the barrel bands. A professional smith is recommended for this procedure.

BARREL WEIGHT

Another aspect of accuracy is the heft of the barrel. Target barrels are often of the "bull" type. That is, they start out big at the action and stay that way without taper. Two things happen. The big barrel is less sensitive to bedding, and the big barrel reacts better to heating up. As a barrel gets hot, its dimensions change and it can actually push on its own bedding and alter pressure points. But the big barrel prevents this for a number of shots because there is so much more metal to heat up. So big barrels are more accurate, right? Not really. I have some rifles with very light tapered barrels which shoot with tremendous accuracy; however, they do heat up quickly and may string shots after heatup. However, I won't carry a bull barrel into the hunting field, so I stay with the accurate, light barrel weight. Just remember that after many shots, point of impact and group size at the target can be expected to change with the light barrel.

Barrel shape itself may have quite little to do with accuracy. Proof is lacking. One of my shooting friends uses octagon barrels whenever he can, believing that they are stiffer per inch than round ones. Another believes that the octagon barrel heats up all wrong and may even vibrate crazily. I am afraid that neither can prove his point.

ACCURACY AND APPLIED PRESSURES

Pressures against the exterior of the rifle may alter grouping and point of impact. Rest a rifle firmly over a tree limb, settling the fore end wood on wood and that rifle may not shoot the same as it did when it was sighted-in at the bench. More than this, rest the *barrel* of the rifle across that limb and you will most likely see a change in point of impact, sometimes a big change. Sight-in with fore end, not the barrel, rested on sandbags, and when you are in the field, remember that resting your fore end on a hat instead of directly on a hard surface may mean the difference between hitting and missing.

ACCURACY FALLOFF

Few things are sadder to the rifleman than sighting-in, producing super groups, and then watching the accuracy of his firearm gradually fall off. Many

Barrel stiffness is another attribute which is supposed to contribute to accuracy. A target or benchrest rifle will often have a bull (heavy) barrel. This is a Remington Model 40XB target rifle. (*Remington Arms*)

things can cause this. Remember that part of the bedding consists of the screws and bolts which hold the barrel and stock together. If pressure on these connections is altered, accuracy may suffer. Check the screws and bolts first. Insure that they maintain their fit. Barrels and stocks may tend to "set," too. Pressure points can change. If accuracy falls off badly, the problem could be a change in pressure points of the bedding. Stocks may also warp.

I had a fine Frank Wells rifle made up for me a long time ago. It wore a Douglas air-gauged barrel and it was bedded perfectly by this master craftsman. However, accuracy was always good and never spectacular, usually in the 1.25-inch range for five shots at 100 yards. Several years later it had improved to the point where .75-inch groups were common and half-inch groups ordinary. I found that the fore end had warped very slightly away from the barrel. That rifle simply shot much better with relief at that point. It is still shooting with super accuracy.

Indirectly, triggers contribute greatly to the accuracy of a rifle by allowing the shot to be fired with minimal disturbance of aim. These double-set triggers offer a very light trigger pull. The rear trigger sets the front. The front, or hair trigger, is touched off for firing.

ACCURACY AND THE PET LOAD

Reloaders have found that rifles vary and that each rifle may be a law unto itself. Because of this, the pet load has always been admired. The pet load is that specific handload which uses a certain bullet, certain powder, and powder charge in a given brand case which that rifle digests like a wolf eats meat. The concept of the pet load is an old one, but still viable. If you don't reload, then try different factory ammo, but never rest contented until you have given your favorite rifle a varied diet to see which ammo works best.

TRIGGERS AND ACCURACY

While a trigger has no direct bearing on accuracy, good groups with a lousy trigger are rare. A good trigger is crisp. That means it breaks cleanly without creep. Creep in a trigger is like lumps in your mashed potatoes. You can live with it, but you're much happier without it. Letoff, the actual pounds of pressure needed to pull the trigger (which releases the sear and allows the firing pin to fall), is measured in ounces and pounds. Most factory triggers fall into the five-pound realm, but I've seen some with seven- and eight-pound pulls.

When I run into one of these, the rifle goes directly to the smith, nonstop. My own triggers are quite light. I prefer them that way. However, the average good trigger need not be ultralight in letoff if it is crisp. I can tolerate a five-pound pull if the trigger is crisp and without creep. A four-pound pull is nice and three pounds is about minimal for most shooters. I also like the multiple-lever trigger system (often called a "set" trigger). One of my modern rifles and most of my muzzle-loaders have the set trigger. By mechanical advantage, one trigger is activated to set the other trigger. When built correctly, set triggers are quite safe, yet letoff can be reduced to a few ounces for a very clean pull. There are also single-set triggers, a single trigger which is shoved forward to set it for a lighter pull.

SIGHTS AND ACCURACY

The sight is not directly linked with accuracy. The best sight on an inaccurate rifle won't help. However, before you hit the target you have to see it, and this is why the peep sight generally gives a better showing than the open iron. The scope sight is king, magnifying the target and giving a fine, clear aiming point with its reticle. So sights do indirectly affect accuracy. In other words, before you can realize the full potential of a rifle's accuracy level, you must give it a set of sights which will offer a clear picture of the target.

The crown of the muzzle has a final influence on the bullet as it departs the barrel, and damage to the crown can cause a decided loss in accuracy.

This Remington Model 40-XR rimfire position rifle shows the kind of stability which is built into the target rifle—heavy stock, heavy barrel, stiff action, and particular attention to overall rifle balance. Note scope blocks for sturdy mounting of the telescopic target sight. *(Remington Arms)*

TARGETS AND ACCURACY

Good targets are a must in testing the accuracy potential of your rifle. I've seen groups on huge black bull's-eyes which diminished in size when the aiming point on the target was refined. If the bull gets so small it cannot be discerned, that is no good, of course. But it should be small enough to give a *specific* aiming point. I use inch- and under-inch-size dots at 100 yards with my variable-scope rifles, for example. Recently, I tried a rifle at 100 yards on a six-inch bull. Two-inch groups resulted. Then I pasted a bright orange one-inch dot in the center of the black bull. Groups shrank immediately. I had refined the aiming point.

Good bullets from good barrels do produce good accuracy, but not without correct twist for missile stabilization, decent sights and trigger, correct bedding or relief of pressures on the barrel, good ammunition of high reliability, trial and error testing of different ammo, and even a workup of a special pet load for that specific rifle. The knowledgeable rifleman looks at all aspects of accuracy potential, correcting faults where he can, searching for the right load, and keeping his rifle in tune through proper maintenance.

Reloading Rifle Ammunition

8

CAMPFIRE FLAME licked the darkness like the darting tongue of a mythical beast as the firelight played across the face of the lone man who had come to the Rocky Mountains to trap beaver. Coals were raked from the burning hunk of rockhard pitchpine with its turpentine volatility, and a little bellows extracted from the possibles bag (the real possibles bag was a provision sack, not a loading pouch) breathed puffs of cold mountain air which made the coals glow angrily. A ladle full of galena rested on the coals and soon the melted metal was poured into the mold, where it cooled rapidly.

The mountain man pried the iron handles apart and the globe of lead fell onto a bed of soiled buckskin. There it shone like money in the bank, only it was better than money. Money couldn't buy much in the mountains, but the lead ball could make meat or even save the man's life.

American riflemen have always been do-it-yourself oriented, first from necessity and later by choice. Early riflemen cast their own projectiles, loading each one down the muzzle. It was handloading, all right, and the tradition is carried on today.

WHY RELOAD?

An earlier chapter on factory ammo applauded its excellence. Factory ammunition is entirely reliable, accurate, powerful, and available. Then why reload? There are several reasons—economy, cartridge versatility, custom loading (pet loads), creating ammo for obsolete rounds, and for the sake of

handloading itself. The art has become a hobby in its own right. A savings of 50 to 75 percent, depending upon the cartridge and the components, may be realized. However, shooters are attracted to reloading by much more than thriftiness.

A reloader can make one cartridge do the work of many. Just about any round will serve as an example, but how about the powerful 7mm Remington Magnum, a large, belted big-game round? Can it be everything from rabbit getter to moose harvester? Yes, for the reloader. A lead bullet, such as the Lyman No. 287448, which weighs about 119 grains cast in Alloy No. 2 metal, backed by 15 grains of SR-7625, provides only 1,750-feet-per-second muzzle velocity with good accuracy. Mild report and light recoil make this load ideal for small game.

On the plains, the 7mm Magnum becomes a flat-shooting, long-range antelope round using a load extracted from the *Hornady Handbook,* Vol. II, p. 182: a 139-grain bullet exiting at about 3,400 feet per second, with H-4831, Remington case, Federal 215 primer. In the mountains, the 7mm Magnum serves as a ridge-to-ridge mule deer round, firing bullets in the 160–162-grain niche at over 3,100 fps MV using H-870 powder. The same H-870 powder drives the long 175-grain bullet at over 3,000 fps MV for elk hunting, and a big 195-grain Barnes bullet reaches 2,750 for moose and bears. All of these ballistic features can be realized from the 7mm Magnum, if you are a handloader.

Even the 30-30 "brush round" becomes versatile when handloaded. A low-velocity lead bullet can be loaded for small game. A 110-grain jacketed bullet

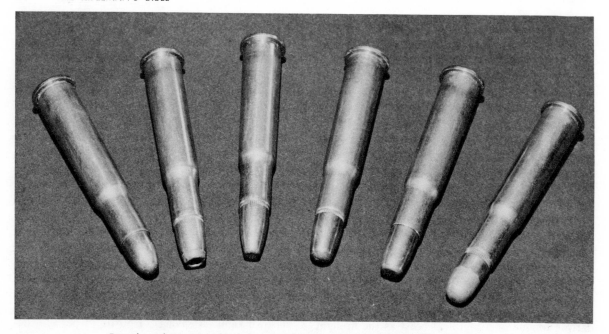

Even the ordinary 30-30 becomes quite versatile through handloading. From the left: a 110-grain round-nose soft-point loaded down for small-game hunting, a 125-grain hollow-point for modest-range varmint work, a 130-grain bullet for plains hunting, a 150-grain bullet for deer hunting, a 170-grain flat-point for woods and brush hunting, and finally a 190-grain bullet for big game at close range.

can be underloaded for the same purpose. My 30-30 carbine drives the 125-grain Sierra hollow-point bullet at over 2,600 fps MV for varmints. The longer barrel of my 30-30 custom pushes that bullet still faster. The accurate 130-grain Speer flat-point bullet, at over 2,600, has harvested several antelope from my 30-30 rifle. The 150-grain bullet has taken deer in the mountains and the 170-grain bullet has harvested the same game in the thickets. I also handload the 190-grain Silvertip for up-close big-game hunting, the latter extracted from 303 Savage (Winchester brand) factory ammo, as the bullet is no longer offered as a reloading component. The mundane 30-30 can perform all of these tasks for you, if you are a handloader.

Custom loading means preparing a special handload for a personal rifle; this charge is often called a pet load. Handloaders experiment with various loads listed in the manuals until that one ideal combination of powder, bullet, case, and primer is found for best accuracy, or for a special shooting chore. Handloaders may also build ammunition for obsolete rounds. For example, a friend of mine owns a Marlin 40-82. Were he not a handloader, his rifle would be a wallhanger, for no 40-82 ammo has

been available for years. He makes his own. The ammunition factories are simply not able to provide shooters with every possible load for a given cartridge. But the reloader can build personal ammo for his favorite rifle.

Reloading is an enjoyable hobby. Often, I've slipped out to the loading bench for relaxation. Handloading can be a slow, deliberate, contemplative endeavor. It can also be very interesting, and advanced reloaders have created wildcat rounds so good that factories have tamed them. The "wildcatter" has altered or invented many different cartridges and quite a few of them have "gone factory." A few of these are the 22-250 Remington, the 25-06 Remington, the 7-30 Waters, and the 7mm-08 Remington. There are many more.

RELOADING TOOLS

Without hocking the family jewels, a very respectable reloading outfit can be assembled. There are starter kits which contain all the basic tools required for reloading. Central to handloading is the cartridge case itself, often composed of 7030 cartridge brass, a very malleable metal. The case can be reformed to near original specs after firing, so it may be reused several times, depending upon the handload. "Hot loads" will, of course, stretch the brass more than mild loads, thereby reducing case life. Eventually, even with light loads, the brass will fatigue. However, some of my more mild loads have rendered ten to as many as fifteen reloads per case.

The Press

Firing the cartridge swells the brass to match the interior dimensions of the rifle chamber. Therefore, a tool is needed to reform fired cases to approximate new case dimensions so that the reloaded cartridge will once again fit the chamber without undue camming action of the bolt. The resizing die does this, but the power which forces the case into the resizing die comes from the *press*. A press can be small or massive. Handheld reloading tools date back to the last century and are still with us. I have one of the small "nutcracker" type tools. It is a Winchester model carrying an 1884 patent. It decaps, resizes, and reprimes the spent case, also seating bullets. The tool has a built-in bullet mold as well. The old-time shooter had no trouble measuring powder, for the case was bulk-filled with Fg or FFg granulation black powder, leaving room to seat the bullet.

The modern press for heavy-duty work is benchmounted. These presses are well made and will last a lifetime. They have sufficient camming power to resize brass cases efficiently. Various press types are available, some with automated features for speedy reloading. The prospective handloader must study the lineup of presses for himself, deciding on the right press for his needs, desires, and pocketbook.

The Shell Holder

This small unit fits into the ramhead of the press. It holds the cartridge in place during various operations, such as resizing, bullet seating, and, in some designs, repriming of the brass case. It must be strong enough to hang onto the head of the case for extraction from the resize die and it must also be precisely cut to accept the head of the case. Shell holders are numbered, the number corresponding to the specific cartridge to be reloaded. For example, RCBS's No. 5 shellholder accepts brass of magnum head size, which includes many different

Another good reason for handloading—creating ammo for those gone but not forgotten cartridges of the past. Shown here are cartridge cases from B.E.L.L., a company dealing in hard-to-find brass. *(B.E.L.L.)*

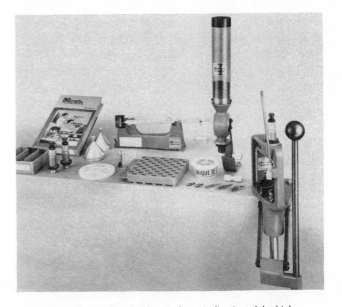

These Hornady/Pacific reloading tools are indicative of the high quality reloaders have come to expect. *(Hornady Manufacturing Company)*

rounds, 7mm Remington Magnum, 338 Winchester Magnum, 300 Winchester Magnum, 300 Weatherby Magnum, 458 Winchester Magnum, and many more. There are also presses which have auto-adjustable "universal" built-in shell holders. The Big Max press from RCBS has this feature. However, even the Big Max requires standard shell holders for some rounds, such as the 222 Remington, for example. The automatic shell holder will not grip this small head and a regular shell holder must be used.

Priming Devices

Most presses allow for repriming with the case in the shell holder. A priming arm may swing into place for the installation of a new primer, for example. In some presses, repriming is automated to a degree, examples of these being the Hornady Pro-7 unit and the RCBS 4×4 press. Handheld repriming tools are also very popular. They allow good "feel" for correct primer insertion into the primer pocket and they can be used away from the press while the shooter is relaxing in his easy chair.

Dies

The resize die may be full length or neck only. I much prefer the former in which the body of the case is returned to near-factory dimensions, whereas the neck-only die leaves the body expanded. Some shooters feel that this custom fit enhances accuracy. In benchrest competition, such a minute edge may be valuable. In practical terms, it is not. I always resize the full length of my cases. The seating die calibrates overall cartridge length by gauging bullet depth in the cartridge-case neck. Some seating dies also crimp the neck of the case, forcing the edge of the neck into a bullet cannelure. Most rifles do not require crimped ammo. There are also three-die sets with one die belling the mouth of the case to better accept the base of the bullet. This feature is desirable on some straight-wall cases, such as the 45-70 Government. Some dies are constructed of special metal so that lubrication is not necessary. Most are not.

The Scale

Simply an accurate device for weighing powder and bullets.

Powder Measure

This handy device meters powder. It is adjustable for various powder charges. It can be omitted from the loading bench, but without this tool, the reloader must weigh each charge on a scale.

Funnel

Small but important, the funnel allows transfer of powder from the pan of the scale into the cartridge case.

Case Block

Plastic or wood, this is the unit which holds the cartridges during the reloading operation.

Trimmer or Trim Die

A rotary trimmer tool or a trim die is essential for keeping cases at normal length. Brass stretches and the case can become too long after a few firings. An overly long case could pinch the bullet in the throat (leade) of the rifle, raising pressures. The trimmer cuts the neck back to proper length.

Deburring Tool

This tiny tool deburrs and chamfers the case mouth, leaving a beveled edge that promotes easy entry of the bullet.

Primer-Pocket Cleaner

A little bristle brush which removes fouling from the primer pocket.

Bullet Puller

The bullet puller allows the dismantling of a loaded cartridge. The inertia-type puller resembles a small hammer. The round is inserted and the tool is rapped on a hard surface, expelling the bullet. I use a puller to extract bullets from one cartridge to be loaded into another (the example of 190-grain 303 Savage Silvertips was given above). The bullet puller can also be used to retrieve components, especially the bullet, from a loaded round which does not fit the chamber of the rifle correctly.

Case inspection can uncover a problem. Note the small, but very significant crack in the shoulder area of this case. The case is now valueless and must be discarded.

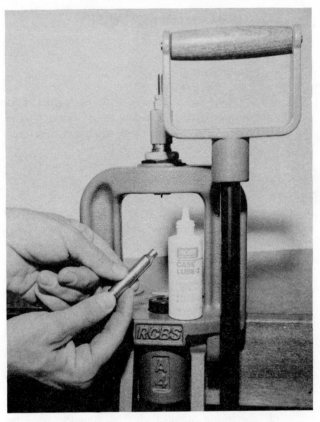

The case must be lubed in order to prevent its being stuck in the resize die (except with special dies that require no lube).

The case tumbler does more than polish cases. It also aids in revealing incipient case damage. Of course, the polished case also lends a professional look to the finished handload.

Reloading Manual

These guidebooks are essential. Never handload without such a reference.

Tumbler

The tumbler or case polisher is a device which shines the brass to like-new appearance.

Case Lube

While not a tool, case lube is essential in most rifle-cartridge reloading. Unless the die is of special metal which prevents the sticking of the round, such as carbide dies, the case will stick in the resize die without lube.

STEPS TO HIGH-QUALITY HANDLOADS

Inspect the Case

Each fired cartridge case must be inspected for split necks, cracks, and any other brass fatigue. Any case which exhibits the least sign of wear must be discarded.

Clean the Case

With a medium such as ground nutshells, the case is vibrated or tumbled until it shines. Cases may also be cleaned with polishers, such as Brasso. Clean cases make for a professional-looking reload. After case polishing, check again for brass fatigue. Incipient cracks are easier to locate in a cleaned case.

Lubing Cases

I use my hands. Some reloaders use pads. A thin coating of lubrication is applied to the cartridge case. With a cotton swab, apply a very light coating of lube inside the neck as well. Should a case become stuck in the sizing die, there is a device appropriately called a "stuck-case remover" which will extract it. Properly lubed cases seldom become stuck.

Decap and Resize the Brass

The empty, polished case is placed in the shell holder and rammed up into the resize die. The decapping pin within the body of the die will expel the spent primer from the primer pocket. The case is now deprimed and full-length resized. In order to insure full-length resizing, insert the die so that its base makes contact with the head of the shell holder in the ram.

Clean the Primer Pocket

The primer pocket may now be cleaned with a few twists of the primer-pocket cleaning tool.

Reprime the Case

The polished, resized, and deprimed case must now be reprimed. I use the handheld tool because I prefer to reprime as a separate operation, and be-

The lubed case is run up into the resizing die. In one stroke of the press handle, the case will be resized and decapped. The empty primer pocket can now be cleaned before a new primer is inserted.

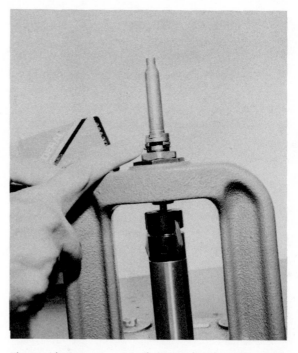

The cartridge case, now resized, is primed. In this press, priming takes place singly, and not during the sizing/decapping stroke.

cause I can leave the loading room to accomplish the task. Primers are seated fully within the primer pocket in the head of the case, but are never strongly forced into the pocket. There is a primer-depth-gauge tool which can be used to determine proper depth. I seat primers so that the case head does not wobble when rested on a flat surface. If it does wobble, this indicates that the primer is protruding too far from the pocket.

Primers are available in *pistol* or *rifle* sizes. They are not interchangeable. Use only rifle primers in rifle cartridges. These come in two sizes, small rifle and large rifle. Small rifle primers are approximately .175 inch in diameter. Large rifle primers are approximately .210 inch in diameter. There are also standard or magnum primers. Use the type of primer called for in the reloading manual, because the load has been tested with that primer.

Charge the Case

This is perhaps the most important part of the operation for obvious safety factors. Powder must be weighed or metered out with precision. The reloading manual is the bible. Remember that the components listed in the manual must be adhered to, especially the brand of cartridge case. Do not switch from one type of case to another without consulting a reloading manual, for case capacity can vary with brands. For example, 270 Winchester cases made by Remington and 270 Winchester cases made by Winchester do not have the same volume capacity. If your loading manual calls for 58 grains of H-4831 in a Winchester case, you cannot gain the same results by trying to use that charge in a Remington case or in military brass (which has been necked down to 270).

In this example, both Remington and military cases have less volume capacity than the Winchester case. In short, the brass is thicker. Significant pressure increase may occur if the powder charge intended for the Winchester case were used in the Remington or the military case in the 270. I was visiting a friend in western Wyoming prior to a hunt. He was having a bad time with a 25-06 rifle. The bolt was sticking after each fired round and some primers were pierced, a sign of very high pressure. The brass was necked-down military 30-06. But the load my friend was using had been intended for Winchester cartridge cases. The powder charge was cut by 3 grains and the rifle then shot well.

An across-the-board reference to case-volume variation cannot be given. A difference of about 2 grains in capacity between Winchester and Remington brass is correct for some cartridges, but not for others, depending upon the round itself. For example, I have not noted a 2-grain difference in 30-30 Winchester and Remington brass. I have found a 2-grain difference between 270 Winchester and Remington brass. The easy way to avert any possible trouble is to stick with the component data given in the reloading manual, using the case, powder, primer, and bullet called for.

Another aspect of charging the case appropriately is powder designation. Refer to the *entire* notation, including brand as well as powder number. For example, H-4831 from Hodgdon's Powder Company is *not* the same powder as IMR-4831 from duPont. Although the numbers are the same, these powders burn at different rates and do not deliver the same pressure per charge. Avert any possible problem. Refer to the entire powder designation as listed in the manual.

Scale-weighed or powder-measure-dumped—which is best? The former is the more precise; however, for most reloading the powder measure is quite adequate and will deliver accurate loads. The use of the powder measure does not preclude the use of the scale, however. The scale is used in calibrating the measure. The stem on the measure is adjusted until the charge is correct according to the powder scale. I have found greater uniformity from load to load with the measure using ball or spherical powders. The tiny beads course through the measure more easily than the kernels of extruded powders. For some cartridges, such as my 257 Weatherby Magnum, I still rely on scale-weighed charges when using extruded powders, such as H-4831. But for the majority of my handloading, the measure is put into service.

Seat the Bullet

Bullets are seated by aligning them with the case neck and operating the handle of the press to force the bullet down into the case. The die must be set correctly for precise overall cartridge length. Begin by inserting the die until the base touches the shell holder. Back the die out so that there is a visual gap between the base of the die and the face of the shell holder. Cinch the ring now and the die will always return to this position in the press. Withdraw the bullet-seating stem several turns. Insert a cartridge

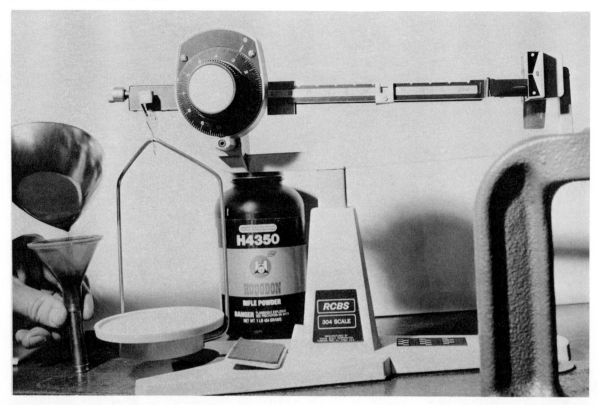

The cartridge case is now charged with powder. Powder may be weighed with a bullet/powder scale, or distributed through a powder measure. Here, a scale was used, and the powder introduced to the case with a funnel.

The bullet is seated by resting its base on the case mouth, and then running the cartridge up into the seater die. The seater die is preset to determine overall cartridge length.

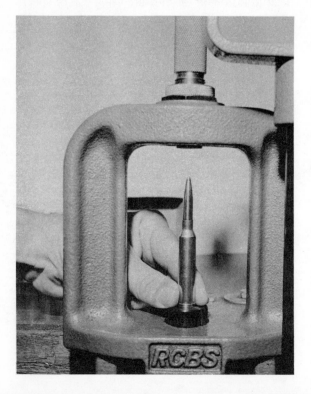

of proper length (trimmed case) into the shell holder and run the round up into the seating die, then screw the stem downward until the stem just touches the nose of the bullet and set the ring. Every future cartridge reloaded with the same bullet shape will seat to the same depth henceforth.

Some cartridges call for a crimped bullet. My 30-30 rounds are crimped because they are carried in a tubular magazine and recoil may force the bullet down into the body of the case if not crimped at the neck. Crimping means that the very edge of the case mouth folds slightly into the cannelure (ring) provided on the bullet. To set up for crimped bullet seating, place an empty case in the shell holder. Screw the seater die into the press, but leave a quarter-inch gap between the base of the die and the shell holder.

Screw the seater die downward in the press until contact is felt. Operate the press handle and lower the case away from the seater die. Now give the seater die a minute turn downward. Run the cartridge case back up into the die and then check the mouth of the case to see if it is slightly rolled back. If not, repeat the above, screwing the die slightly downward again and running the case back into the

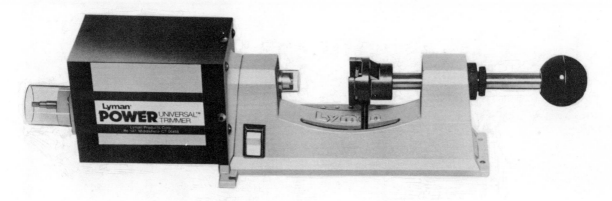

Use a case trimmer to insure proper case length. This Lyman power case trimmer does a fast and neat job. *(Lyman Company)*

die until there is a slight rollback at the mouth of the case. That fold must correspond with the cannelure of the bullet, so the seating stem has to be set to align the cannelure and the neck. This is done by trial and error, moving the stem up or down. Once the seater die is properly set, it need not be set again unless a different bullet is used.

Other Important Loading Procedures

Case trimming is vital. A rotary case trimmer will reduce overly long brass to acceptable length. Another type of trimmer is the trim die, which is inserted into the press. The trim die is manufactured of extremely hard metal. It is set flush with the shell holder. The cartridge case is run all the way into the trim die and any portion of neck protruding *above* the die is filed away. Since the die metal is so hard, the die is not damaged by filing. After the excess brass is removed, chamfer the mouth of the case.

Case-neck chamfering allows easier bullet seating and prevents thickness at the mouth of the neck. I always chamfer brand-new brass to thin the metal at the mouth. The deburring tool is used.

Make a habit of inserting empty cartridge cases upside down in the loading block. As each case is charged with powder, its upright posture immediately indicates a loaded cartridge case. In this manner, double charging is avoided.

Try Your Loads

Wipe each round with a cloth. Oily rounds may

not offer proper case cling in the chamber of the rifle. Then chamber and eject each cartridge through the action of the rifle. Cartridges which do not chamber correctly are broken down, their bullets pulled, and the cases discarded. The last thing a hunter wants in the field is a stuck case. I was javelina hunting with a lever-action 243 one season when a lone boar left a catclaw thicket and began to climb the hill in front of me. I attempted to lever a

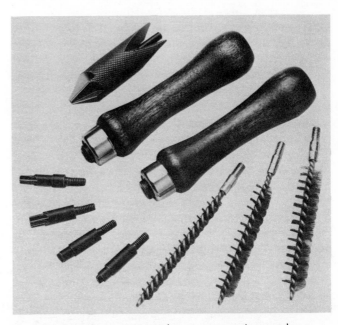

The deburring tool (topmost) is used to remove any minor metal aberrations at the neck of the case. Inside-neck cleaning and primer-pocket cleaning are accomplished with ease using these Lyman tools. *(Lyman Company)*

This Lyman case block will insure that powder does not spill out of charged cases. It is also a safety device when properly used because it can prevent double-charging. *(Lyman Company)*

A sign of excessive pressure—gas leakage—is seen here around the primer of this fired round. Note also that the primer itself is quite flattened, another sign of strong pressure.

round into the chamber, but the cartridge stuck. No boar. That never would have happened had I prechambered the round at home. And it never has happened to me again.

Signs of Pressure

The only certain pressure reading is with the proper machinery, which yields either psi (pounds per square inch) or LUP/CUP figures (Lead or Copper Units of Pressure). However, the reloader can use many checks which reveal *signs* of pressure. The first and best check is case-head expansion. The head of a once-fired round is measured with a micrometer. On a magnum case, measure across the belt of the once-fired case. After sequential firings, remeasure. Expansion at the head is a sign of unduly high pressure (or fatigued brass). I use .001 (one one-thousandth of an inch) as a guideline. If a case head or belt expands by .001 inch, it is discarded. If expansion is noted across the board with a given load, the load is reduced.

The primer reveals signs of pressure, too, though the hardness (or softness) of the primer may be the real problem. A crater may be evident where the metal of the primer was forced up around the firing pin. You can feel as well as see this crater. Naturally, a pierced primer is screaming out, "high pressure—beware!" The inclusion of so obvious a sign may seem ludicrous; however, I have known of shooters who ignored pierced primers. Pierced primers may also indicate a headspace (see Glossary) condition. If reducing the charge does not

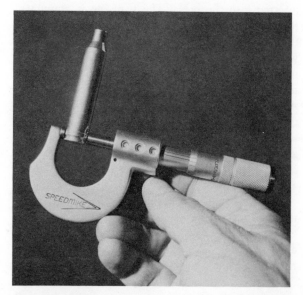

The careful reloader may wish to measure the head of the case or the belt as described in the text. Here, a 7mm Magnum case is measured across the belt, as is proper with magnum type cases.

correct the situation, see your gunsmith. Read the headstamp as another pressure sign. A hot load may engrave this area. The imperfections on the face of the bolt are actually impressed into the headstamp area of the round. Check for similar marks left by the ejector. Slight engraving of the headstamp is normal. Heavy engraving is not.

Difficult extraction is another sign of high pressure. The fired cartridge case should expel easily from the chamber. If it sticks, the chamber could be pitted or even very dirty, but it's more likely a pressure indicator. Another good check for high pressure is during the repriming step in reloading. If a primer slips into the pocket of the cartridge-case head without requiring much pressure, chances are the pocket is swelled. Throw the case away, but also check your load. It may be too hot.

Using Your Loading Manual

Loading manuals vary one from the other for several reasons. Test guns are not all the same. Chambers differ. Sometimes different barrel lengths are used. Many variables are at work during the testing procedure. Therefore, no two manuals will reveal the exact same figures. This is why I consult several manuals when looking for a pet load for a given rifle. When I was seeking a powerful 30-30 deer load using a 150-grain bullet, I checked several reloading books.

The third edition of the *Hornady Manual* listed a charge of N201 powder, 35.2 grains, for a muzzle velocity of 2,400 feet per second from a 24-inch barrel, using a 150-grain bullet. Speer's tenth edition manual showed a muzzle velocity of 2,319 feet per second, from a 20-inch barrel, using 29 grains of RE-7 powder and a 150-grain bullet. Sierra's second edition manual called for 27.2 grains of RE-7 for 2,300 fps MV from a 26-inch barrel. Hodgdon's twenty-fourth edition manual listed a muzzle velocity of 2,409 fps with 34 grains of H-4895. And Lyman's forty-sixth edition handbook called for 39 grains of H-335 powder for 2,473 fps MV with the 150-grain bullet, with a listed pressure of 35,800 CUP.

The Lyman load was impressive, so I began testing it in my own 30-30 with its 24-inch barrel, beginning with 35 grains of H-335 and working up. Although there was no case-head expansion nor any adverse signs of pressures with the full 39-grain charge in my rifle, accuracy was better with 37 grains, and velocity was almost 2,600 feet per sec-

Chronographs are now within the financial reach of most shooters.

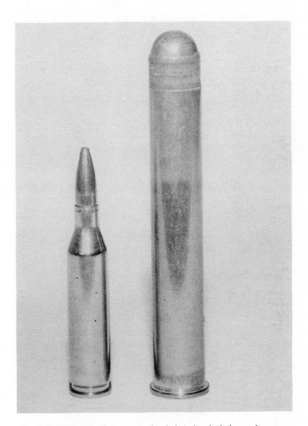

The little 243 Winchester on the left is loaded down for some pleasant practice, and the big 50 Sharps on the right could not be fired at all but for reloading. The 50 Sharps is not commercially available.

ond. I settled on the 37-grain H-335 charge with the 150-grain bullet for my own 30-30 rifle.

Rifles vary. Generally, these variations are minor. Sometimes they are not. Testing two 270 Winchester rifles with identical handloads, both rifles having 22-inch barrels, a difference of 200 feet per second was registered. Actual bore dimensions and chamber dimensions may have been the cause, though the rifle which attained the higher velocity showed no adverse signs of pressure in doing so.

Experimentation with different loads is all right as long as the loads are always derived from a reloading manual. Never concoct your own loads. The average shooter does not have the pressure-testing devices necessary to discover possible pressure problems. Although case-head expansion and other criteria do reveal high pressures, in creating new loads, a pressure gun is necessary. Maximum means maximum, too. A friend of my son's was boasting about the magnum performance he was getting from a 30-06. I asked about the load and he said it was over max. Such practice is foolhardy. Consider a maximum load as just that. Do not exceed it.

Bullet casting is another part of handloading. Supreme accuracy can be obtained from a cast projectile, and some shooters mold their own missiles as a hobby. Cast bullets also serve in some hunting, especially small game, but also big game under certain circumstances. For example, using a 180-grain cast bullet in a 30-30, deer were cleanly harvested in a brush-country, close-range shooting area. There are manuals on the art of bullet casting. Shooters interested in making their own cast bullets should consult these textbooks.

Rolling your own gives more shots per dollar. But I think it is the other aspects of handloading which carry the greater weight. Although factory ammo is certainly accurate, pet loads are usually more accurate. Factory rifle cartridges are powerful, but handloads can usually exceed factory ballistics. Factory ammunition is versatile, but handloaded ammo is more versatile. And you either handload for an obsolete cartridge or you may not be able to shoot it at all. For these and other reasons, handloading is a big part of the modern shooting scene.

9

Rifle Handling

A PERFECT RIFLE with perfect trigger, high-grade accuracy, and the best sights in the world will not a rifleman make. The rifle must be mastered. That mastery is rifle handling, which is a combination of many things at once, all blended into one controlled and flowing motion, *execution* with *follow-through*.

MOUNTING THE RIFLE

Mounting the rifle means more than jerking it to the shoulder. Depending upon stock style, weight of rifle, sights, balance, and other factors, each rifle is handled differently. The goal is one smooth motion, with the rifle traveling from a position of rest to the shoulder and with the sights aligned almost automatically. Rifle control and body control are handmates to rifle management, the rifle moving to the shooter more than the shooter moving himself forward to meet the buttstock of the upcoming rifle. Good marksmen are good rifle handlers. Good rifle handlers mount their rifles with control and grace.

ACTION MANAGEMENT

Action management is linked with rifle handling. Each action style calls for a different set of mastery rules. The semiautomatic rifle is an exception because activation of the action is taken care of by the system itself, although all other tenets of rifle handling still apply. Slide-action rifle handling also re-quires little hands-on effort from the shooter. The rifle must be mounted smoothly, with all of the management rules in play, and the action is worked with the rifle at the shoulder at all times. The rifle is not lowered each time it is fired in order to eject one round and chamber a new one. The left hand, for a right-handed shooter, simply flicks the rifle forearm back and then forward again smartly.

The lever-action requires more action management than the semiauto or pump rifle. Good shooters handle the lever gun this way—they fire the rifle without moving it from the shoulder, maintaining the sight picture as closely as recoil will allow, and using a quick down-up motion of the fingers in the finger lever to eject the spent round and bring up a fresh one. Some shooters prefer to lower the lever-action between shots, claiming that this motion gives them a better perspective of the target, se-quencing the rifle more readily. The shooter reaf-firms his target without moving his eyes from it; the action is worked with the rifle lowered, and then the rifle is remounted. Having tried both methods, I lean toward the first with the lever gun. Mount. Fire. Flick the lever down-up. Once mounted to the shoulder, the buttplate remains firmly implanted there. The rifle is not lowered between shots.

The bolt-action rifle is often mismanaged. Shooters tend to fire a round, lower the rifle, and, in some instances, actually *look* at their hands as the action is activated. Practice will chase these bad practices away. The bolt-action requires a four-step process. The bolt is lifted upward, pulled back, pushed forward and then locked down. Many shooters pinch

Mounting the rifle to the shoulder is a matter of practice and experience. Here, the hasty sling method is used to help control the rifle.

the bolt knob between thumb and forefinger. They also lower the piece between shots. Both methods are time-wasters. The bolt knob should be settled in the *palm* of the hand, slightly pinched there for control. The whole hand moves smoothly and swiftly and the action is mechanized with a rolling motion of the palm. There is no reason to lower the rifle in order to expel a fired cartridge case and bring another round up from the magazine.

Modern shooters choose single-shot rifles for the challenge. The goal is to fire one, and only one, well-placed shot. However, in actual practice, at the range or in the field, the single-shot turns out to be a multiple-round rifle after all. We would all like to master marksmanship so that the first bullet from the barrel finds the mark as if guided like a heat-seeking missile. However, being human, we don't always place the first bullet in the bull's-eye and follow-up shots become necessary. Repeated fire with the single-shot has always been the rule, not the exception. Expert riflemen can reload the single-shot in the blink of an eye. Practice makes it so.

The shooter can practice reloading his single-shot at home with dummy ammo. He takes a stance, eyes forward. When the firing pin falls on the snap cap, the rifle *is lowered;* however, the eyes are not. There is no reason to look at the hands at work. The fingers activate the action, move to the shell loop (or pocket) for a fresh cartridge, feed the round home, and close the action as naturally as you reach into a back pocket to extract your wallet without looking. Eyes remain riveted to the target. You should no more move your eyes downward in single-shot rifle action management than you do to shift gears in your automobile. Practice with your particular rifle action until you can work it with unconscious fluidity. Familiarity breeds confidence.

THE SCOPE SIGHT AND RIFLE MANAGEMENT

The scope must be mounted so that the shooter sees a full picture the moment his face comes to rest on the comb of the stock. The head should not have to slide forward or back once the face touches the comb. Scope eye relief is the key to placement. The scope is mounted fore or aft on the rifle, whichever is comfortable. The relationship between comb height and scope height is paramount to fast sighting. Sometimes a change in scope rings can accommodate for a mismatch of eye level with scope-sight level. Sometimes not. Stock alteration may be necessary.

Scope focus is another aspect of rifle handling. When a scope is not focused to the individual eye of the shooter, the eye must accommodate for a clear picture. It should not have to. Thousands of shooters never bother to focus their rifle scopes. In fact, a check of scope-sight focus at the National Matches in Camp Perry, Ohio, revealed that about 25 percent of those expert riflemen had never focused their scopes.

Pointing the scope at a blank wall or the sky, revolve the ocular bell until the reticle appears very sharp. Once the reticle image is sharp, control the rifle at the benchrest, and focus your eyes *(not through the scope sight)* at a distant object. Try to discern the details in that object with your eyes. Now quickly look at the same object through the scope sight. The reticle will probably be blurred. Adjust the eyepiece in or out. Only trial and error will tell you which way to turn it. Over and over

The lever has been worked, the spent case expelled. The rifle is firmly butted into the shoulder, left hand relaxed, and the lever worked while the rifle remains on the shoulder. Bill Fadala will get off a fast, but well-aimed, second shot.

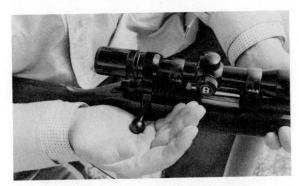

The bolt is *rolled* in the palm of the hand, not pinched between the fingers.

again, look at the distant object with the naked eye and then look quickly back into the scope sight, adjusting the eyepiece. Eventually, there will be no visible blurring of the reticle as you switch your view from naked eye to scope because your eye will no longer be accommodating for a difference be-

tween the unaided view and the magnified view through the scope. Your scope is focused *for you.*

RIFLE CONTROL

Execution and follow-through, the same attributes vital to many sports, from tennis to baseball, are paramount to good rifle handling. A steady hold, sight-picture maintenance, and proper trigger release are required. These are executed and mastered through body control.

A white-knuckle grip on the forearm of the rifle generally leads to lack of control. High-recoil rifles, such as the 338 Winchester, 375 H&H, or 458 Winchester, require firm support on the fore end for obvious reasons. However, most calibers can be fully managed without a deathgrip on the forearm. Pressure should be no greater than required to support and guide the rifle. I prefer a slim forearm because there is less surface to grasp, and consequently less chance of a choking grip. The heavy fore end is good at the benchrest, but is not necessary for field shooting.

The wrist of the rifle, straight-grip or pistol-grip design, can be more tightly held. Much control of the rifle is maintained at the grip. The right hand (for a right-handed shooter) tugs back on the grip, pulling the buttstock of the rifle firmly into the shoulder. Forearm grip does not do this. Again, a white-knuckle deathgrip is not necessary, except for certain high-recoil rifles. Sufficient pressure is applied to control the rifle, and no more. The buttstock is snugged into the "pad" of the shoulder, especially with the common shotgun-style buttplate (flat). The rifle-style buttplate (curved), may rest more easily into the joint of the arm than into the pad of the shoulder.

The face *must* rest firmly on the comb or cheekpiece of the stock. If the head is raised above the stock during shooting, poor marksmanship will result. A shooter who finds himself moving his head up or down, back or forth on the comb prior to firing the rifle has a problem: rifle fit, rifle management, or sight location. The first is attended to by a gunsmith who may alter stock dimensions for better fit. The second is bettered by understanding proper rifle management and practicing the rules. The third requires sight alteration, such as moving the scope forward or aft, or acquiring new rings for it to change its height.

Proper trigger control and good marksmanship go hand in hand. The "jerked trigger" causes many misses. First step to good trigger control is a good trigger. I can't think of a factory rifle I have owned which has not gone to the gunsmith for trigger-pull refinement. Heavy trigger pull and creep are to trigger control what rust is to steel. Ruinous.

There are many ways to control trigger squeeze. One is to apply pressure with the whole hand, squeezing the wrist/grip of the rifle and the trigger simultaneously. I find no advantage in this method. Others do. A second method calls for wrapping the hand fully around the wrist of the rifle, with the *second* joint of the trigger finger, not the pad of the first joint, applying letoff pressure. I fire my lever-action, straight-grip rifles using this method. A third way comes from the world of handgun shooting. The trigger finger acts independently of the rest of the hand.

This takes practice. The hand squeezes the grip of the rifle for control, while the trigger finger remains as relaxed as possible. The forefinger, using the pad of the fingertip, moves onto the trigger and gently squeezes until the rifle goes off. Trigger squeeze or controlled jerk? If the rifle is steady, the squeeze method is best. The trigger finger applies pressure so gently and steadily that the shooter actually does not know exactly when the rifle will fire. Using this method, I have actually been surprised by the fall of the firing pin. When the sight picture

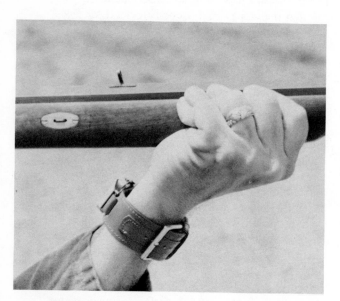

Choking down on the fore end with a "white knuckle" grip generally means a loss of control.

This is the shotgun style buttplate, most used on rifles today. Note the Pachmayer recoil pad. Recoil pads are found on most big-game rifles today. (Pachmayer)

is not perfectly steady, as from the offhand position, the shooter may have to nudge the trigger when alignment of sights on target is best. Use gentle pressure whenever possible, but master the controlled jerk as well.

The Feet

A shotgunner may approach his target face-on. But the rifleman points his feet away from his target. The right-handed shooter aims his feet at about 45 degrees to the *right* of the target, with feet spread apart at about shoulder width for stabilization. As with all points of stance in rifle control, there are exceptions to the norm. My wife, an excellent rifle shooter, points her feet toward her target. When she is finished firing, there are a lot of holes in the bull's-eye. She is an exception.

The Hands

Part of rifle control is hand grip. The hands should apply sufficient pressure to guide and manage the rifle, and no more. Too much pressure prevents a smooth swing of the firearm on a moving target. Furthermore, excessive pressure may introduce a tremor. Double your fist and squeeze as hard as you can. You will notice additional body shake when you do this. *Balance* the rifle with the left hand (for right-handed shooters). *Control* the rifle and trigger-squeeze with the right hand.

Knees

Do not lock the knees. Shotgunners who lock their knees diminish swing potential and often miss the moving target. Riflemen who lock their knees find more body tremor and less fluidity of motion for the moving shot. Relax the knees. Stiff-kneed shooting prevents follow-through, which is vital to good marksmanship. At the report of the rifle, the body responds by maintaining a relaxed control. That is follow-through. Locked knees prevent such controlled relaxation.

Two points of good shooting are shown here. The trigger finger acts almost independently of the rest of the hand. It flows into the trigger guard and applies individual pressure on the trigger. Also, the face is firmly planted against the cheekpiece of the stock, not raised above the stock.

Elbows

Target shooters in the offhand stance are taught to hold the right elbow high for greater control. In the field, a more relaxed elbow height is called for, with the elbow maintained at the horizontal or slightly below. The shooter may wish to practice with various right-elbow positions until he finds one which suits him. The left elbow is placed directly beneath the forearm of the rifle (right-handed shooter) for best rifle support. Do not lock the elbow. That brings tension and tension hinders steadiness.

Eyes

Shoot with both eyes open if you can. Don't give up if at first this seems unnatural. Squinting one eye shut removes part of the field of view and has no benefit in taking aim. Even with the scope sight, shoot with both eyes open as a part of correct body control. Three-dimensional viewing is also impaired by closing one eye.

The shooter who has a problem with two-eye shooting should check for master eye domination. He may be one of the few who are right-handed but left-eyed, or *vice versa*. To check for master eye, hold a forefinger out in front of you at arm's length. Aim the forefinger as if it were a front sight, placing it on an object in the room a few feet away. Wink the left eye shut. If the right eye is dominant, the forefinger will remain "on target." If the forefinger optically jumps off target, the left eye is dominant. As a double-check, take aim again, but wink the right eye shut. If the right eye is master, then the forefinger will jump off target.

Breathing

Hold your breath and your pulse rate will climb. A higher pulse rate can induce body tremor, bad for rifle control. The rifleman should draw a full breath, exhaling part of it, then holding the remainder in the lungs until the rifle is fired. Do not hold the breath too long. As rifle mastery increases, the rifleman gets his shot off faster. The beginner sometimes has a problem with breath control because it takes him longer to gain aim, and meanwhile he runs out of breath.

PUTTING IT ALL TOGETHER

1. While maintaining a relaxed grip on the rifle in the "at rest" position, unmounted to the shoulder, look at the target. Size it up. Try to judge distance if it's a field shot.

2. Adjust the placement of the feet, about 45 degrees to the right of target for a right-handed shooter. Spread the feet about shoulder-wide.

3. Mount the rifle smoothly, fluidly, left hand guiding the fore end, right hand controlling the pressure of the buttstock against the shoulder.

4. Sight with both eyes open.

5. Unlock elbows and knees.

6. Draw a breath. Let part of it out. Hold the rest.

7. Control the trigger. Squeeze it if you can; nudge it off when the sights are on target if the offhand stance prevents gentle trigger squeeze.

SHOOTING POSITIONS

Offhand

Least steady, the offhand position is nonetheless vital to the rifleman for it is often the only available stance. Aim the body first, as previously described, controlling all aspects of body control. Do not *cant* the rifle. Cant is the rotating of the firearm off of the perpendicular and it may cause a miss. Right arm out at the horizontal, left arm underneath the fore end for control, follow the points listed above, and the bullet should find its mark.

Sitting

Poise the body about 45 degrees off target. Maintain the aspects of body control with both elbows planted firmly into the legs for support. Maintain breathing and trigger-squeeze rules and the reward will be good groups from the sitting position. Open-country big-game hunters should use the sitting position in favor of the offhand whenever possible.

Kneeling

Not as steady as the sitting position, the kneeling stance is sometimes assumed when high grass or other obstacles prevent seeing the target from the sitting posture. The left elbow is planted on the left knee. The right elbow assumes the same position it normally takes in the offhand stance. The left hand controls aim and the right controls buttstock pressure and trigger squeeze.

Prone

Steadiest of nonrested positions, the legs are spread for stability, toes pointing outward for balance. The left elbow controls the forearm as usual, and it should rest directly underneath the rifle. The body is bent upward at the waist, upper torso directed toward the target. Both elbows are on the ground for steadiness.

Field Rest

When possible, use a rest in the field. I often carry a walking staff and will rest the rifle on the upper padded portion of the stick for steadiness. If using a rock or tree limb as a field rest, the forearm of the rifle should be padded, as with a hat or coat, because the pressure of the rifle on a hard surface may cause the bullet to fly off target. All tenets of rifle control are observed. A shooter may be lulled into a false sense of stability when using a field rest. Then he forgets to squeeze the trigger and the shot is missed.

Running Game

Just remember this—never stop the swing. If follow-through ever had application, it's for running game. The sight picture is swung out ahead of the moving target for lead and the rifle goes off *in motion*. Do not swing, stop, and fire. A miss will result because lock time and human reaction time will delay the exit of the bullet from the muzzle long enough so that the shot will fall behind the target. Even a slow-trotting animal requires lead, the amount depending upon distance from the rifleman. An antelope moving at only 20 miles per hour requires a one-foot lead at 300 yards using a 243 Winchester with a 100-grain bullet at 3,100 fps MV. But antelope can move much faster than 20 miles per hour. A lead of several feet may be required, the rifle "going off" with the barrel still in motion.

Here is the offhand stance using the hasty sling method, demonstrated by Dick Reitz, an expert rifleman. Feet are spread apart about shoulder-wide. Left hand is relaxed. Right hand pulls buttstock into the shoulder. Elbow of right arm is straight out from the body. Elbow of left arm is directly beneath the rifle forearm.

This is the sitting position, feet dug in at the heel of the boot, elbows firmly planted in line with the shin bones. Right hand controls the rifle. Left hand is relaxed.

The kneeling position. Reitz maintains control of the rifle by making firm contact between left elbow and left knee. Left elbow is also directly beneath forearm for stability.

The prone position, an extremely steady stance. Reitz demonstrates toes-out stability, with left elbow directly beneath forearm and right elbow planted firmly on the ground.

Benchrest Shooting

Observe proper benchrest technique. Keep feet flat on the ground. Rest *both* elbows. Pad the right elbow (for right-handed shooter) to avoid skid on the bench during recoil. Use a firm rest beneath the forearm of the rifle, not underneath the barrel. Control breathing and trigger letoff, as well as observing other tenets of marksmanship. Use a spotting scope to prevent having to walk back and forth from bench to target to check groups. If no scope is available, be sure to rest between hikes in order to regain body control.

THE RIFLE STOCK

As athletes treat their bodies and their equipment, so do riflemen. The body is adjusted to the situation. Equipment is altered to fit the user. The rifle stock must fit the shooter. The stock should be comfortable. Length of pull should match the build of the shooter so that he does not have to *reach* for the trigger, nor find his nose too far forward on the stock. I used to prefer a 14.5- to 15-inch length of pull, but have learned that a shorter pull is faster in operation.

The stock should match the recoil of the rifle. My favorite stock style is very slight fore end and rather narrow butt end. But the recoil is managed better with a bit more forearm and a thicker buttplate to distribute the energy. A straight stock (not too much drop at the comb) will also deliver the energy of recoil with less disturbance to the shooter than a stock with a lot of drop, which may act to lever the comb into the shooter's face. If your stock is not comfortable, consult a gunsmith or stockmaker. Adjustments may be possible.

But don't forget that the body bends, too. Some riflemen get carried away with the notion that a stock must have perfect lines in order for them to shoot the rifle well. Ideally, the rifle will fit the shooter; however, perfect fit is not likely. Practice generally overcomes those nuances of imperfect fit. I like a stock of simple, classic design; however, with practice I've been able to shoot various stock styles successfully. I believe that any rifleman can.

PRACTICE

There are no born great shots. There are people who have good eyesight and hand-eye coordination, but all in all, riflemen are made, not born, and they are made through practice. There are many kinds of practice. I have been doing a lot of basement shooting with an RWS 17-caliber air rifle lately. The high accuracy of the rifle has allowed some very serious shooting for groups, and the novelty-type targets have supplied the interest. I consider the modern air rifle ideal for shooting improvement.

Dry-firing is another viable means of improving marksmanship. The trigger is pulled on an empty rifle. A snap cap can be installed in the chamber to prevent firing pin damage. Dry-firing is accomplished by aiming at a target with the goal being a matchup of click and sights. It's like a called shot. When the trigger is pulled, the sights should be optically planted on the target. If the sight picture is off-target when the snap of the trigger release is heard, it's a miss. Because there is no recoil to contend with, much is learned through dry-firing, including refined trigger mastery and body control.

Small-game hunting also constitutes practice for the rifleman, as does varminting. Target shooting, from informal to competitive, is another means of practice, as is plinking, the targeting of tin cans, wood blocks, and other objects in front of a safe backstop. Shooting games are enjoyable as well. There are many ways to practice. But practice seriously. Buzzing off a burst of 22-rimfire ammo in the direction of the backstop does not teach the shooter anything.

ANALYZING RIFLE-HANDLING TECHNIQUES

Self-analysis is possible, though not always practical. I have caught myself and others in obvious infractions of good rifle handling, such as flinching and trigger jerk; however, the finer points of shooting are not always self-evident. The professional rifle-shooting coach is trained to observe shooting style and to help improve marksmanship, but when no coach is available, I have used a camera.

A 35mm camera, employing fast film, such as Tri-X (400 ASA), will "freeze" a shooter's motion, often stopping the action at a crucial point so that the developed photo clearly demonstrates a shooting problem. A motor drive camera works best, but is not essential to this effort. The photograph can show locked knees or elbows, clench-fisted fore-end grabbing, flinching, incorrect face placement on the comb of the stock, faulty buttstock placement, and poor rifle mounting, as well as much more.

Successful rifle handling is a blend of many details. It is a coming together of man and tool. Mastery comes from refining the tool, the rifle, to meet the requirements of the shooter. But more than fitting the rifle to the shooter is fitting the shooter to the rifle, and that is accomplished through understanding and practicing good rifle-handling techniques, and through practice. Although there are no great "born shots," just about anyone can learn to become a competent rifleman.

A steady field rest is assumed by "hugging a tree." Note that the author's left hand supports the forearm of the rifle. The rifle is not actually making contact with the tree. A very useful stance when sedentary game is spotted in the field, or, as shown here, when hunting tree squirrels.

Dale Storey shoots on his padded benchrest top. The padding helps to avoid elbow skid during recoil and it offers a nonslip surface as well. Note that the forearm of the rifle rests upon a shooting pad, and not against a hard surface.

10

Your Custom Rifle

EVERY RIFLEMAN deserves at least one custom in his life. The custom rifle is special, unique, personal. At one time in this country, most rifles were "custom crafted," made one at a time. Henry Ford and his assembly line policy put automation into American manufacture and the trend moved from cars to rifles. It was a good trend. Today, we have excellent over-the-counter rifles, and, because of automation, the average shooter can afford them. But they all look alike. The custom rifle is an individual piece.

What qualifies a custom rifle for the title? It must be one of a kind, though individual gunmaker traits are often evident in a given line of rifles. Some collectors of fine rifles can look at a custom piece and tell you the builder by noting checkering styles, lines, metalwork, and other highlights which denote that builder's work. But each rifle constructed by that gunmaker will still be an individual unit, made by hand.

A true custom rifle is expertly made. Sadly, there are gunmakers who call themselves craftsmen, but who do not produce quality work. At a recent gun show, I inspected a table of supposedly custom long arms. The lines were all wrong, a mix of European and American classic styles. The workmanship was untalented. Checkering? There wasn't any, and when I asked about it, the fellow admitted he *didn't know how to checker.* Unfortunately, the rifles lured buyers. Such "customs" only hurt the professionals who work so hard to create beautiful rifles.

A custom rifle is designed with *purpose* in mind. The purpose may be multiple, a combination of big game and showpiece, for example. But the custom should exhibit a function. It may be chambered specially. I have a Dean Zollinger custom 257 Weatherby Magnum rifle, its function being long-range plains hunting. Its caliber and 26-inch Shilen barrel mark it as an open-country firearm. While it is art, it is not in the same class as an expensive vase or painting. It is a rifle and rifles are for shooting.

Although I say rifles are made for shooting, it is true that some fine custom pieces are never fired. Dennis Mulford, a talented riflemaker who specializes in muzzle-loaders, has handcrafted several pieces which will never be loaded by their owners. They are for enjoyment of another nature, pleasure of eye to see and hand to touch. But they do have a special purpose. They are correct in every detail, emulating beautiful long arms of the past. They serve as modern replicas of guns of long ago.

VALUES OF THE CUSTOM

Part of the value of a custom rifle is, of course, its firing. The above-mentioned 257 is a fine harvester of game, flat-shooting, accurate, high on long-range delivered energy, a premier plains rifle. Another value is uniqueness, having a one-of-a-kind rifle, *your* rifle. There is also value in the artistic beauty of the custom. This beauty is often shared among friends who understand fine rifles. Dollar values range from modest to very high, depending upon quality and rareness of wood, special metalwork, engraving, and other details. Recently, a custom rifle made in 1920 sold for $4,000 at a gun show, far more than it was worth several decades ago.

CUSTOM VS. CUSTOMIZED

The gap between custom and customized is as wide as an ocean. The customized job can be anything from an off-the-shelf model with a shortened barrel to a factory rifle with a refinished stock. Never pay a custom price for a customized rifle. The custom is a from-scratch effort created individually for an individual. Customized rifles are often parented by woodshop hobbyists.

The ordinary customized rifle may be a factory or military rifle for which a new stock has been made. The stock is generally a semi-inletted model of medium-grade wood. The original barrel contour may be altered, the action glass-bedded, old sights removed, a new scope installed, rebluing applied, a new trigger added, and the rifle weight-trimmed by removal of excess metal and/or wood . . . but the rifle is still customized, not custom.

I recently saw a table of so-called "custom" rifles which were actually customized (restocked) factory models. The stocks were simply huge. King Kong's hand couldn't encompass the wrist of these rifles. But there was a reason for the girth of the stocks—carving. Oh, yes, *lots* of carving. There were all manner of animals cavorting and frolicking over the wood, lions jumping, gazelles leaping, deer clearing farmyard fences. You name it and these carved animals were doing it. Walk away from such stuff.

This custom rifle was made by Frank Wells of Tucson, Arizona. *(Nick Fadala)*

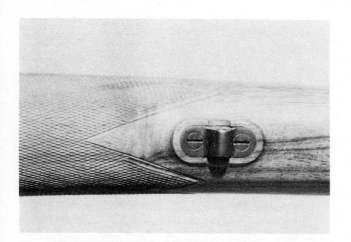

Custom versus customized—this fine stock, custom-crafted by Dean Zollinger of Rexburg, Idaho, shows the mounting of the sling swivels on a pad of raised wood, definitely a custom touch.

THE SEMI-INLETTED STOCK

Granted that the meticulous gunmaker will usually eschew the semi-inletted stock, there are applications for this stock style. For example, a craftsman may send a blank to a commercial stockmaker for semi-inletting. This is a time-saving effort, and the final fitting is accomplished by handwork. I see nothing wrong with semi-inletting under these circumstances, even for a custom rifle. The commercial semi-inletted stocks, the ones with "90 percent of the inletting done" often have 90 percent of the *work* remaining, but they can be dandy stocks for the talented home-workshop fan.

GLASS BEDDING

I surveyed a number of custom stockmakers. The majority considered a glass-bedded stock beneath the dignity of true custom rifle makers. One gunmaker disagreed. He felt that glass bedding was strong and accurate and he used it. I side with him because I defy anyone to detect glasswork in his rifles. The fiberglassed action and barrel channel are done so expertly that only by removing barrel from stock will the glass be seen.

There are many applications for good glasswork. A custom rifle maker glassed my 458 Winchester because the barrel and action were splitting the stock. He reinforced the cracked areas and the rifle has remained solid ever since. Magnabed, a newer fiberglass compound, was given a trial run on a restocking job and the rifle's bullets grouped better than they had ever grouped in the past. Finally, glass bedding may stabilize a rifle which changes point of impact frequently due to unstable wood. So there's a place for fiberglass, even in the world of customs.

This stock was fiberglassed behind the upper tang to prevent stock splitting. It's a 458 Winchester "elephant rifle."

ORDERING YOUR CUSTOM RIFLE

But is the custom worth it? (Price tags of $3,000 to $6,000 are commonplace these days for better custom rifles.) I think so. The value is there. The two major ways of obtaining a custom rifle are buying a spec gun or commissioning a rifle maker to prepare a special rifle just for you. The former may seem to fall out of the guidelines for a custom rifle. However, finely handmade custom rifles are made on speculation. They are unique. They have a special purpose. They are customs in every sense. And there is no *waiting* for it.

The special-order custom rifle may take a year to reach your hands, often longer. You contract for it. First, find the gunmaker of your choice based upon work of his you have seen. Gunmakers advertise in arms journals, such as *Rifle Magazine,* and these magazines often carry profiles of various craftsmen as well. The prospective buyer can contact the rifle maker and, usually, arrange to see his work.

You and your gunmaker decide mutually on the rifle of your dreams. And it is a mutual decision. I once decided to have a custom muzzle-loader built by Dennis Mulford. I wanted a heavy plains rifle, large caliber, long barrel, full-length stock. Dennis refused. He preferred the style and grace of the Lancaster school Pennsylvania rifle. We compromised when he located an original long rifle which had been modified by its owner. I ended up with a beautiful, balanced, large-caliber, but correctly designed long rifle of high accuracy. Had I gotten my way entirely, the graceful piece would never have materialized.

It's your money, yes. But it's his reputation. Work with the rifle maker and be ready to compromise to a degree. You deserve what you want as a buyer; however, the rifle maker is an expert and his advice should weigh heavily. As part of the pre-riflebuilding agreement, price must be established. The price will be based upon the cost of raw materials plus labor, and there can be significant labor in a custom rifle. Stock blanks have also increased in price significantly in the past few years, and good wood of high figure is expensive.

Finally, the contract must include a time period. Before paying the usual 50 percent deposit, an approximate date of delivery should be promised. Custom rifle making takes time, but even the Almighty gave himself a cutoff date. He rested on the seventh day, not every day. Professional gunmakers work for themselves. It takes motivation to sit at a workbench instead of picking up a fishing rod. I waited a year for my last custom rifle. I might be willing to wait eighteen months. But I do not believe in two- and three-year waiting periods.

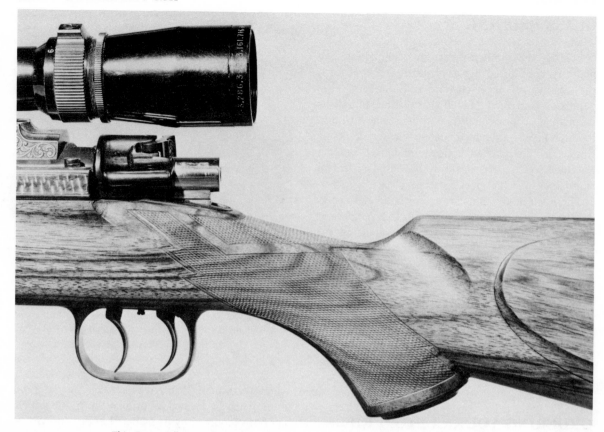

This Dean Zollinger custom rifle exhibits the guncrafter's skill in producing beautiful checkering in fine-line style. The distinctive checkering pattern consists of fine diamonds with sharp edges.

ENGRAVING

Relatively few gunmakers are engravers. Engraving is an art unto itself and the best engravers are professionals. Unless qualified to criticize engraving, the prospective custom rifle buyer is wise to have someone who knows engraving look at a craftsman's work before the rifle is embellished. Engraving is more than lines cut in metal. It is an art form. Be sure an artist is doing your work. An exception is a simple pattern which may be handled by a gunmaker. But extensive engraving requires extensive talent. If first-rate engraving is not affordable, consider no engraving at all.

THE CUSTOM VS. THE SEMICUSTOM RIFLE

An alternative to the full custom rifle is the semicustom piece. This is not the *customized* rifle.

Today's semicustoms are often very beautiful pieces and just right for the person who does not wish to part with a fat roll of folding green, but who still wants a special rifle. These rifles exhibit handwork. They are not assembly line products. And yet, they do have a lookalike nature because they follow a pattern. For example, the beautiful Hatfield muzzle-loader rifle is a semicustom. Though the company does have a custom shop and can produce very individual pieces, a Hatfield is recognizable. The lines are unmistakable.

The semicustom rifle shows excellent workmanship. It's a good buy. The Remington custom shop, for example, can make a very fine rifle based on the Model 700 action. Particulars of stock dimension can be custom-ordered. Various woods can be selected, and checkering patterns can be varied. These excellent rifles, however, are recognizably Remingtons and I call them semicustoms.

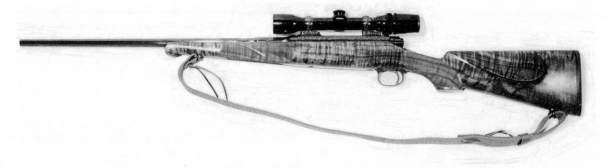

This custom rifle, made by Dale Storey of Casper, Wyoming, is a very lightweight model in 6.5-06 Improved caliber. It makes one-half inch five-shot groups at 100 yards from the bench.

A rifle may be custom-ordered from a large gun company. This Remington Model 700 is a Grade II model. *(Remington Arms)*

BUILDING THE CUSTOM RIFLE

The overall rifle design has to be planned, especially the stock. The gunmaker may draw a pattern describing the lines of the stock. He may also pencil in appropriate stock lines and checkering patterns right on the wood blank. Using these outlines, the stock is *shaped.* A great deal of wood must be removed from the original chunk, called the blank. The wood is selected on the bases of stability and suitability to withstand inletting and shaping, but also on the basis of beauty. Curly maple (tiger stripe maple) is often chosen for the custom muzzle-loader. English/French walnut (actually the same wood) may be picked for a fine modern rifle. American walnut is still available in modest quantities and good quality.

After the stock is shaped, it must be inletted. The mortise for the action is prepared. The barrel channel is cut. Further shaping is done. But there is still a great deal of wood to be removed, slimming of the fore end and wrist, cheekpiece design, thinning of the comb, and all the while aspects of stock dimension are being considered, such as drop at comb and cast-off or cast-on of the buttstock.

After inletting and final shaping, the stock must be checkered. A design is decided on and perhaps penciled on the wood, describing the panels, usually at the wrist and fore end of the stock. Stock finish is an art within the art of gunmaking and most artisans have their own secret methods. The best stock finishes are *in the wood,* not on it. That is, the finish has penetrated for protection as well as beauty.

Metalwork is often extensive on a fine custom rifle. Some gunmakers have professional metalcrafters do the work. Others have learned the craft themselves. Recently, I had a chance to inspect the metalwork of gunmaker Dean Zollinger, who is now altering Mauser actions for smooth and flowing lines as pretty as pre-1964 Model 70s. He also makes his own safeties and scope bases.

Bluing may also be accomplished by a specialist; however, gunmakers are now doing this work in-house. Although the blue-black high-luster finish is still popular, many custom rifles are now receiving handsome, nonglare (sand-blasted) satin-metal finishes. Telescopic rifle sights with matching matte finishes are prevalent now with these pleasing blue jobs.

Nothing has been said about chambering the barrel; however, many rifle makers do their own chambering and barrel-contour jobs. In this manner, they can purchase barrels of a given caliber, such as 6mm, deciding on the cartridge later. Many custom rifles are offered in wildcat calibers, partly for the individuality of the nonfactory round, sometimes

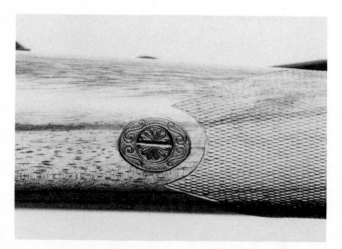

Daniel Paul, the engraver, accomplished this nice work on the escutcheon of this custom rifle.

for ballistic reasons. My wife's custom 6mm-222 wildcat, for example, has been a superb harvester of deer and antelope, its caliber unavailable commercially. (The 6mm-222 is the 222 Remington necked up to accept 6mm bullets.)

Custom crafting allows the matching of action, barrel, stock, and caliber that would be impossible to find in commercial firearms. The 6mm-222 spoken of above has a tiny Sako L-461 action. Because of the petite action, a rifle of small dimension could be built. It weighs but seven pounds with scope sight and sling, and small hands can work the equally small bolt effortlessly.

The gunmaker completes his work by testing the rifle. If the rifle does not perform to expected levels, he tunes it. He is interested in overall function as well as beauty. And he usually obtains a high degree of reliability and accuracy because of his careful work. My often-mentioned, and often-carried, Storey Conversion is an example of handcrafted reliability. Built on the Model 94 action, one might expect bullet grouping in the three-inch to four-inch domain at 100 yards from the bench, but the fine custom barrel, well fitted to the breech, has been responsible for inch center-to-center groups at 100 yards.

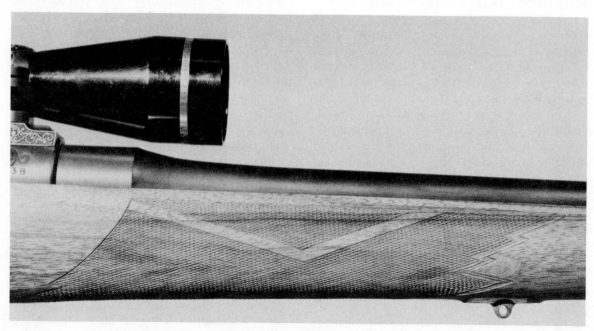

If the gunmaker cannot checker, he should not call himself a custom guncrafter. Note the straight lines of this Dean Zollinger checkering of a forearm.

The custom rifle is the apex, the ultimate. It is aesthetically functional—working beauty. However, the prospective buyer of a custom rifle must be forearmed with knowledge. The customized, not custom, piece, hewn from mediocre materials by hands less talented than the task demands, must be avoided. Purchased with care and know-how, however, the fine custom rifle is never a mistake. It's a lifetime investment that will pay continued benefits.

A custom rifle may also come in a "custom" caliber, such as the wildcat 6mm-222, left, compared with the 30-06. This excellent little cartridge, chambered in a Frank Wells lady's bolt-action rifle, has compiled an amazing record of one-shot harvests on deer-sized game at up to 200 yards.

Author's Storey Conversion is a prime example of what can be done with a custom rifle. This rifle began life as a very plain Model 94 Winchester lever-action 30-30.

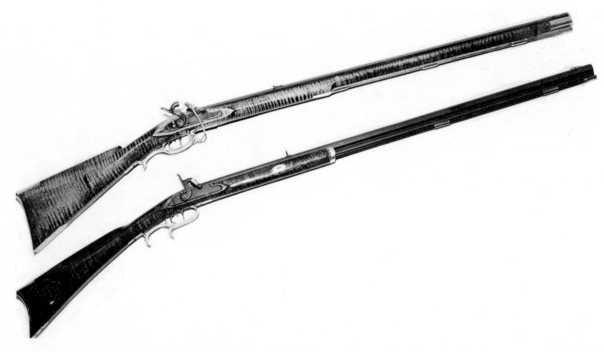

Two black-powder rifles, one a custom, the other a semicustom. Top is a Dennis Mulford 54-caliber full custom rifle, bottom a 40-caliber semicustom from Ozark Mountain Arms Company.

11

The Air Rifle Now

THE PRINCELY SUM of seven or eight dollars eluded me, though I did whatever work I could find for whoever would hire me. Nobody had heard of minimum wage in those days, and being a small boy with no particular skills precluded my asking a lot for my labors. I dug some holes. I carried a lot of trash. And I pushed a lawn mower. But still, the pig that guarded my money looked pretty anemic. What was worse, the route from school to home brought me right by the hardware shop that imprisoned the Daisy Red Ryder BB gun I wanted. Every day I stopped to look it over. Had the building not been torn down many years ago, my fingerprints, and noseprints, too, would still be pressed against the glass showcase.

And then she came through for me. I'll never know why. An aunt, who declared that she didn't really like guns, took pity on me, and one day when she arrived home from work she was carrying a long box. "If so much as one sparrow gets hurt over this," she said, or words to that effect, "it goes back to the store." There was even a leather thong attached through the saddle ring and I imagined that BB gun to be the most powerful and most accurate single carbine to ever leave the Daisy plant.

Today, air power continues to launch the careers of many young marksmen. But those no-powder rifles have certainly changed a lot, and for the better. The "adult" air gun has been with us for a long time, but never was there anything to compare with the modern powderless rifle. These rifles have been around since at least the 1500s, if not earlier. In modern times, air rifles have been used to train

soldiers, and there is argument that air rifles may have gone to war as well, though hard proof is lacking. Lewis and Clark, in the westward expedition of 1804–6, had a large-caliber air rifle with them. The Indians feared it more than the smokepoles and it was often used "for effect."

A glance into a 1932 Stoeger's catalog reveals just how serious the air rifle was taken at that time. A Webley air rifle is listed at $33. In the same catalog, a Model 94 Winchester 30-30 sold for $36. Air rifles were of high quality, and they commanded a high price. But there were also many of serviceable quality, and they cost but few dollars. But what, over the years, has been the true value of the air-powered rifle? In short, what is an air gun good for?

Economy of shooting pops up as a first consideration in air-rifle shooting. No powder, no primer, the little lead pellet or steel BB costs less to shoot than powder-burners. This factor allows for more pops per penny. Naturally, the air rifle remains a teacher of youth. Recoil is nil; though the new spring-piston powerhouses do jump, they don't bump the shoulder with real force. And they are not noisy. Combine economy with lack of recoil and report, and you have a perfect rifle for shooting at close quarters.

That brings up another plus in favor of air power. Basement shooting, or backyard, or campsite, or any locale in which a good *safe* backstop and pellet trap can be set up. Pellet traps are prevalent today, offered by many air-gun manufacturers, such as RWS, Sheridan, Crosman, and others. The beginner can build or have built for him a safe place

Many shooters "cut their teeth" on a BB gun such as this one. *(Daisy Manufacturing Co.)*

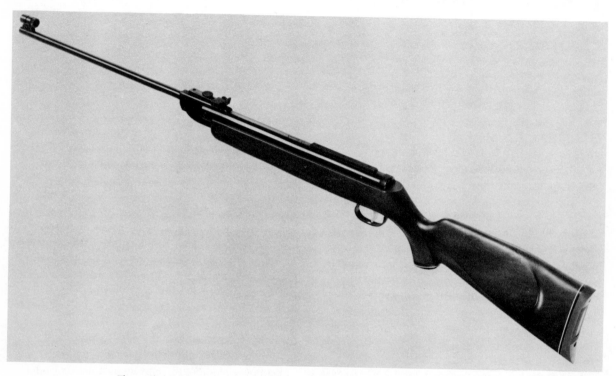

The modern adult air rifle, such as this powerful RWS model, may achieve about 1,000 fps MV with a 17-caliber pellet. *(RWS)*

to practice. And he can practice rain or shine if the range is indoors. But that's not all. The most astute rifleman of many years' experience can also take advantage of the economy, quietness, and recoilless shooting of the air-powered rifle, practicing in his basement, too, and keeping his shooting skills honed to icicle-point sharpness.

There is also competition with air rifles, even Olympic-level competition. Precision air rifles today are capable of chewing one ragged little hole in the bull's-eye at 10 meters, about 33 feet, a common range for air-rifle competition. These fine rifles are so accurate, so precision-made, that some of us—including this shooter—have purchased target air rifles for personal practice. My own RWS Model 75 goes to work in the basement several times a week. And by the way, one factor of air-rifle shooting not yet touched on is an obvious one—fun. Shooting the air-powered rifle is a great deal of fun.

So today's air rifles are accurate, the most accurate in history. But they are something else, too. Powerful. The shooter can purchase an over-the-counter air rifle which will drive its little pellet at over 1,000 feet per second. I realize this seems piti-

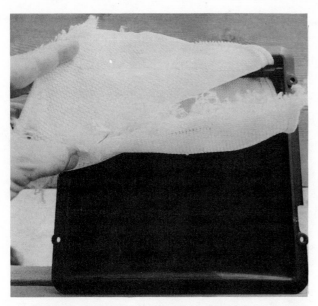

This pellet trap will allow the shooter to practice in his basement. It has a nylon curtain to stop pellets.

ful when compared with modern ballistics for big bores. And the 22 rimfire is much more powerful than the air pellet. But the fact remains that no garden pest will stand up to a well-placed pellet from one of the faster air rifles. And the same can be said for rabbits and squirrels, the number one and number two small-game animals in the country.

My RWS Model 36 air rifle will dispatch a cottontail with one shot at 20 yards. I know this because I've collected some wonderful edibles for the frying pan with a 17-caliber air rifle. One snowy day a winter ago I found myself at the dooryard of a rancher friend who has big problems with small bunnies. They simply eat almost everything the man and his wife try to grow, including shrubs and grass and other landscape greenery. This overabundance of rabbits is no good for my friend, and also no good for the rabbits. So some of the rabbits are harvested for food. But what do you shoot when so close to a building?

You don't shoot at all, of course, without permission and without a rigidly controlled safety setup. I would not think of touching off a single shot in that ranchyard except in a direction away from the house itself. But when you are going to hunt on farm or ranch where longer-ranged firearms could be a hazard, leave the powder-burners at home and grab your air rifle. That cold but sunny day I col-

lected my legal limit of ten wonderfully edible rabbits, all with a single pellet each. So the air rifle, when used at close range and with careful aim, is indeed a viable small-game hunting tool.

THE BB GUN NOW

The year, 1888. A company called Plymouth Iron Windmill was doing very well for itself making windmills. But the company came up with a good idea. Why not offer its customers a premium, something like the little toys found in breakfast cereals? The premium turned out to be a little BB gun. In 1889, the company's windmill business had blown away. But the air rifles were still there. And by 1895, the Plymouth Iron Windmill Company had a new name—Daisy.

The Daisy Manufacturing Company went on to offer many different models of its air rifle. The look-alike lever-action style of these rifles didn't hurt sales, and a pump-gun model found a following, too. But I think the association with Red Ryder marked one of the smartest moves in rifle-selling history. Red Ryder (and his sidekick, Little Beaver) were known to all kids, being comic book favorites and also characters in movies and in books. In fact, the Daisy Red Ryder is available even today in a 650-shot carbine model. Daisy also offers many other models, including a Spittin' Image carbine which closely resembles the Model 94 lever-action rifle.

Crosman also offers excellent BB guns, a pump gun with 200-shot capacity, for example, and a Classic holding 180 BBs with a velocity up to 795 fps with ten pumps. Crosman also offers many different kinds of BB-gun targets, a swinging unit, for example, or siluetas, which are miniature iron cutouts of the four animal silhouettes used in big-bore competition. A good Target Trap from Crosman will stop BBs in the basement, too. The BB gun is still a strong force in rifle-shooting today.

THE AIR RIFLE NOW (PELLET)

The BB gun performs its function excellently. It is very cheap to shoot, has repeatability, with many shots possible between loadings; it is not a long-range rifle, which allows for shooting at close quarters with proper backstops, and if the light is right a shooter can see the course of the BB, actually noting a miss and correcting for the next shot. During World War II, Daisy introduced a BB gun to help soldiers gain skill rapidly, and part of the training hinged on actually watching the flight of the BB. Aerial targets of various size could be used, too, and it's said that some riflemen could even hit a BB in the air.

But the pellet-shooting air rifle has been the more accurate and powerful of the no-powder guns. Generally speaking, there are two styles of pellet rifle today, a sporting/hunting/plinking/target rifle and a true competition rifle. Three major types exist, CO_2-powered, pneumatic (pump), and spring-piston. The shooter is going to select a sporting-style air rifle most of the time. The match rifle is really a precision instrument for serious target shooting. Of the various types of air rifle, each has its strengths and weaknesses.

AIR-RIFLE TYPES

CO_2-Powered

The CO_2-powered air rifle uses a cylinder or compartment filled with liquid carbon dioxide. Commercially, the gas is captured and held in a chamber, or it may come in a small, disposable CO_2 cartridge. Either way, the principle is the same. The release of the gas forces the pellet through the bore. The CO_2 design is hardly new. A patent was granted in 1889 for one CO_2 design and Crosman offered a workable CO_2 rifle in the United States

many years ago. CO_2 guns are still quite popular today. Here are some of their features:

1. The CO_2 system is quite precise in its emission of gas quantity. Some of the earlier CO_2 guns were not quite so perfect in shot-to-shot consistency, but today the high-class CO_2 system is very consistent. A perfect example of this is the Crosman Model 84, a CO_2 rifle of match-accuracy quality. Called a Challenger, the 84 has a readout panel which shows the exact muzzle velocity for each shot. It is powered by a pressure-regulated device and muzzle velocity may be altered to meet the demands of the shooter, up to 720 fps. It allows about 100 shots per cartridge.

2. The CO_2 system is convenient. There is no pumping or cocking of a heavy spring in order to gain thrust. The CO_2 push is provided by that prefilled chamber.

3. Because there is no uncoiling spring, the CO_2 air rifle does not have a jarring effect upon firing. In order to be clear on this point, it is necessary to state immediately that the jarring spoken of here does not spoil accuracy in the spring-piston air rifle. The pellet is gone before the recoil effect can damage pellet flight. However, the CO_2 system is easier on scope sights than the spring-piston design, unless an opposing double-piston system is used in the latter. More on that later.

4. The CO_2 is easier to fire rapidly than most spring-piston or pneumatic models. In fact, CO_2 air-gun repeaters are quite possible because of the nature of the CO_2 design. No time is lost in pumping or even in cocking a lever.

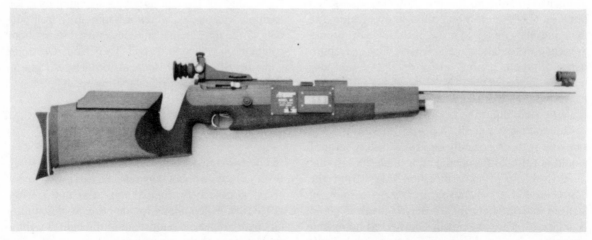

This Crosman Model 84 Competition Air Rifle is CO_2-powered. *(Crosman)*

5. The CO_2 is quiet compared with the other major air-rifle types. All air rifles are quiet, of course, compared with the powder-burners. But the CO_2 is really capable of very quiet shooting.

6. On the negative side, the CO_2 air rifle has not, to date, proved quite as powerful as the spring-piston design. One must be careful with such assessments because the ever-changing world of the air gun may produce a CO_2 super-speedster at any moment. Also, this is not to say that CO_2 rifles are slowboats. There is ample muzzle velocity for most air-rifle chores.

7. The CO_2 is more expensive to shoot than the spring-piston or pump. The spring-piston and pneumatic use muscle power to produce the pellet-pushing thrust. But the CO_2 rifle requires the purchase of the gas itself or a little cartridge which contains the gas.

The Pneumatic System

There are two types of pneumatic air gun. The first, the pump gun, has been with us for a very long time, with names such as Benjamin, Sheridan, Crosman, and Daisy household words among the shooting fraternity. The other type is the single-stroke. By working a device, air is forced into a chamber, but the device is activated only once per shot.

The pneumatic works by using a piston to force air into a holding chamber. The captured air, now under pressure, is then released by a valve when the trigger is pulled and the jet escapes down the barrel behind the pellet giving the little lead projectile its thrust. The pneumatic is a very old design, too, and the big bores of yore were so powered, including the Lewis and Clark model. The 13mm Austrian military air rifle would require many, many pumps to bring it up to full power. Some of the big bores needed as many as a couple of hundred strokes to fill the air chamber. Here are some traits of the pneumatic air rifle:

1. It requires only arm power to get it ready for firing.

2. Many pneumatics are quite inexpensive, yet they are fully functional and are used by countless shooters for target work, plinking, and hunting.

3. There is instant power variability available in the pneumatic. It is true that there may be a minimum of pumps necessary for accuracy, and perhaps an optimum number of pumps for best accuracy, but all in all, the shooter can adjust his muzzle velocity through a pretty satisfying range by simply altering the number of strokes he uses in pumping the rifle.

The pneumatic, or pump air rifle, requires several strokes of the lever in order to build power.

4. There is also, unfortunately, a bit of built-in variation in muzzle velocity in this system. To get good power several pumps are necessary. But as the pumping continues, the air gets hotter and hotter. Hot air then cools in the holding chamber, thereby altering the actual pressure in the chamber. Shoot a pneumatic immediately after pumping it a given number of times and you get Velocity X, but if you wait for the chamber and its air to cool off, you may end up with Velocity Y. Such varying pressure means varying muzzle velocity and this factor can damage accuracy.

5. The pneumatic can be difficult to pump up, too. The first few strokes are easy, but later on a force of 40 or more pounds can be needed. Therefore, the weak of arm may not always enjoy readying the pneumatic air rifle.

6. The pneumatic may be a bit slow between shots. Of course, the single-stroke is the faster design, and it may also be a bit more accurate than its pump-up cousin because the air in the chamber is not badly heated, but the pump is far more popular today, and at the moment generally more powerful.

7. A pneumatic can also be loud, louder than a CO_2, though still very quiet compared with powder-burning rifles.

The spring-piston air rifle requires only one cocking for full power; however, there is no power variability as with the pneumatic. John Fadala readies his RWS 17-caliber rifle for a rabbit hunt.

The Spring-Piston Air Rifle

Actually, the spring-piston design is rather easy to understand. Basically, there is a cocking lever and the lever cocks a powerful spring. When the spring is released, its forward thrust compresses air and the compressed air forces the pellet out of the barrel. That is an oversimplification, but close enough for our purposes. The lever may in fact be a lever, such as the old underlever or currently used sidelever, but usually it is a barrel-cocking or break-open design which cocks the spring. It's best to go right into the traits of the spring-piston air rifle because they help explain this fantastic system:

1. No pumping is required. A bit less convenient than the CO_2, perhaps, but then there are no CO_2 cartridges to fool with. The spring-piston requires only one single cocking and it's ready for full power.

2. The spring-piston is a high-velocity/high-power air rifle. At the moment, the spring-piston is the most powerful of the three general types of air rifles, and velocities in the 1,000-foot-per-second range are possible.

3. The spring-piston is economical. It requires no CO_2 supply. Also, it is highly efficient. Without any valves to wear or break, the spring-piston is generally long-lived and will normally require less maintenance than the other types.

4. The spring-piston is quieter than the pump-style air rifle.

5. Loading is fast. Certainly, it takes less time to break the barrel and insert a pellet than it does to pump the pneumatic rifle.

6. Velocity is very uniform. There is no gas chamber that can leak. And as we know, hot air cools rapidly. The hot air of the pneumatic cools in the chamber, but the air temperature for the spring-piston is quite constant from shot to shot. Hence, velocity is very constant and accuracy is sterling.

7. Less force is required to ready the spring-piston than the pneumatic. Of course, the CO_2 requires the least physical effort.

8. The spring-piston has no detrimental recoil. That is, the uncoiling of the spring, though we feel it during the firing process, does not harm accuracy. This is proved at the target range as well as on the engineer's table.

9. But the somewhat strange "double-recoil" of the spring-piston air rifle does wreak havoc upon scopes. Cheaply built scopes, or even good telescopic sights designed for 22 rimfires, can end up with scrambled egg interiors after use on a spring-piston air rifle. There is, however, a double-piston, spring-piston design which is virtually recoilless. It works according to Newton's Third Principle of Motion: Every action has an opposite and equal reaction. There are, as the name implies, two pistons. One delivers the power; the other simply counteracts the first. This interesting design is found on fine match air rifles such as my aforementioned Model 75 RWS.

10. Finally there is no variability of power in the ordinary spring-piston air rifle. One cock sets the spring. The spring unleashes and the air is compressed. And that is that. One cannot vary the velocity through altering the number of pumps or adjusting a gauge to increase or decrease the jet of CO_2 gas expelled downbore.

Calibers

As with any other projectile, larger and smaller pellets have their advantages and disadvantages. Today, one will find calibers of 17 (.177 inch, or

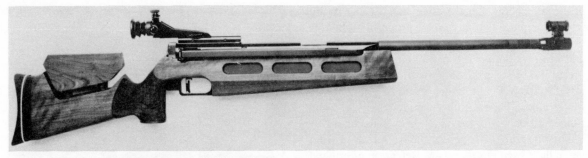

The high-grade RWS Match Rifle is sufficiently accurate to chew one ragged hole in the center of the bull's-eye at the 10 meter range. *(RWS)*

The 17-caliber air-rifle pellet is offered in many styles. These are from RWS. From the left: the Superpoint, the Hobby, the Diabolo, and the Meisterkugeln, a match pellet for serious target work.

almost 18 caliber), 20 caliber (or 5mm), and 22 caliber among the pellet rifles normally encountered. I believe in the 17 caliber overall. In my experience, the .177-inch pellet shoots flatter than its bigger cousins and I found penetration on small game and varmints better with the 17 than with the others. Also 17-caliber pellets are cheaper. As for wind deflection, none of the pellets I tried stayed on course in strong winds.

Just because I opt for the 17 caliber does not mean that the others are no good. The 22-caliber pellet is accurate, as is the 20-caliber pellet. Potential accuracy of either is on par with the 17. As air rifles progress, as they are doing so rapidly, the 20- and 22-caliber pellets may end up kings after all. Given that their velocities will increase, a 20- or 22-caliber pellet will whip the 17. I look for an increase

in big-pellet study. I'd like to see, for example, a 20-caliber pellet of new design, especially suited to small-game hunting, and my leaning toward the 17, even for hunting, may then be tilted toward the larger pellet. Right now, however, for putting holes in paper or game on the table, I'll take the .177-inch pellet.

BALLISTICS

Obviously, anything as small and lacking in mass as a pellet, even a 20- or 22-caliber pellet, is not going to render exciting ballistics. In my own tests, I found a pellet velocity of 1,110 fps maximum at the muzzle, this for a pellet of 17 caliber weighing 8.2 grains. That only amounts to 22.4 foot-pounds of muzzle energy. On the other hand, I can testify from experience that any rabbit properly hit by this pellet and its ballistic mini-force will expire rapidly and cleanly. So, on the one hand, the figures are pretty low. Even a 22 Short with a 29-grain bullet at 1,150 fps MV will render a muzzle energy of 85 foot-pounds. On the other hand, results *at close range* and on *small targets* are very satisfactory.

For one thing, the pellets I have retrieved from game have been mostly intact. Retention of original weight has been good. Given a pure lead pellet, this is as it should be. Lead has high molecular cohesion —it sticks together, in other words. Weight retention aids penetration, even with a little pellet. Usually, the 17-caliber pellets I have been using will ventilate the chest region of a cottontail rabbit at up to 20 or 25 yards. At only 8 or 9 grains in weight (and recall that there are 437.5 grains in an ounce), the pellet is no giant force, but it does have David's (of David and Goliath) strength when properly placed.

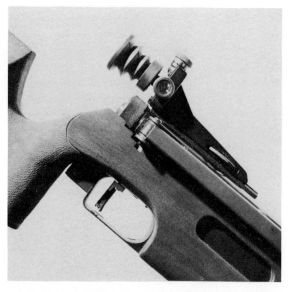

The two-stage trigger of this match rifle allows for excellent trigger control, but the shooter used to a single-stage trigger will have to practice with it in order to gain proficiency. Two-stage triggers are not common on American rifles.

ACCURACY

The high accuracy potential of the modern air rifle allows for exacting pellet placement. Perhaps the shooter not acquainted with today's air rifles doesn't realize that with a scope-sighted model it is no trick at all to hit the two-inch-wide head of a rabbit at 25 paces. That feat is nothing special. One evening a shooting friend came by my home. I was busy, in the basement at my little range, putting a lot of 17-caliber pellets into the pellet trap. Dick wanted to give the rifle a try. He sat down, took aim with the RWS Model 75, and hit the target. The target was an old business card. But it was set *on edge.* He shot several times, splitting the cards with each shot.

TRIGGERS

Those two-stage triggers on a lot of today's imported air rifles bother some shooters. But, it is no trick to master the two-stage or military-type trigger. It is only a matter of taking up the slack first and then continuing to apply pressure with the pad of the finger until the rifle goes off. The pointers given in our chapter on rifle handling are followed as usual. Practice with the two-stage trigger will bring perfection in its use.

This is a forward-facing view of the rear sight on an RWS Model 75 Match Rifle. It is a fully adjustable aperture sight.

RANGE

The air rifle is not a long-range instrument. The farthest I have used mine on small game is 40 yards, approximately. My sight-in is for only 25 yards. A 10-meter range is popular in match shooting and a basement range is whatever distance space allows, usually fewer than 30 feet from muzzle to pellet trap. A breeze that will lift a scrap of paper and waft it off will drift a pellet away from the target. So we air-rifle lovers learn to get very close to our quarry, and we do our target shooting from short range, too.

PELLETS

Pellet uniformity is astonishing. Weighing a group of RWS Meisterkugeln target pellets on a scale sensitive to one-twentieth of one grain, I noted 8.2, 8.2, 8.2, 8.2 over and over again. That scale could detect no difference in these pellets. I tried a

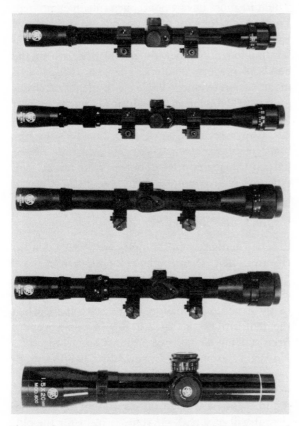

The air-rifle scope is constructed to withstand the vibration of the uncoiling spring in the spring-piston rifle design. These scopes from RWS come in various magnifications with either adjustable or nonadjustable objective lenses. *(RWS)*

few pellets designed for plinking next, thinking that the match-grade Meisterkugelns were, after all, specialized projectiles, but even the least expensive pellet I could find proved highly uniform.

Furthermore, there are various pellet styles offered the shooter. The RWS company alone has a long lineup of various pellet types. For example, the Meisterkugelns mentioned above are not the recommended plinking pellet. They cost too much. However, RWS has its Hobby for that work. While the Meisterkugeln pellet is smooth-skirted, the skirt on the Hobby is striated with lines. Both are wadcutter style, however. The RWS Diabolo is another flat-nosed pellet, striated skirt, hourglass shape. Its profile is slightly different from the Meisterkugeln. It's an all-purpose design, target and small-game work. But the RWS Superpoint, for hunting, is quite different again from the first three pellets mentioned. It has a very pointed, sharp nose and a smooth skirt. The RWS Super-H-Point is another hunting pellet, smooth-skirted, with a flat but hollow frontal section. And the RWS Superdome is skirted, striated, but with a round, heavy nose section, another hunting pellet designed for good penetration.

Remember that if you sighted in with one pellet, another may not be on target. These pellets not only weigh out differently; they also have different flight characteristics. Be certain to resight your rifle when going from one pellet to another.

SCOPES

Because some air rifles will jar a scope severely, special air-gun scopes are available. These are recoil-proof scope sights. Moreover, some of these scopes are offered with an adjustable objective lens. This means that the scope can be focused for various ranges. When shooting indoors, this adjustment comes in very handy, for the scope will focus down to a few feet. Most ordinary scopes won't focus that closely and the target may be a blur in them, or, at least, the crosswires will not be sharp.

The world of modern air-rifle shooting is fascinating, replete with superior rifles and ammo to go with them. Air rifles of any sort were never toys. That goes double today. Treat all air rifles with the same respect due any gun. But at the same time, enjoy the mild-mannered, air-powered shooting implement, for it is, after all, a very special and specialized tool, one which will do its work quietly, without recoil, but with stupendous accuracy.

12

The Muzzle-loading Rifle

ROMANCE, NOSTALGIA, AND HISTORY are intertwined in black-powder shooting. But so is challenge. Shooting the muzzle-loader requires more experience and know-how than firing the modern rifle. The two rifle systems are reversed. It is the modern long arm which is simple to use and the muzzle-loader which requires the real savvy. Once sighted-in, a modern rifle simply swallows a prepackaged load and, after firing, the spent case is expelled and a new load shucked home. But the frontloader demands much more. Each load is made by hand, individually, right down to the ignition of the powder charge via a percussion cap or priming powder in the pan of the flintlock. Once mastery is achieved, however, black-powder shooting is a great sport.

CHOOSING YOUR MUZZLE-LOADER

Choosing your muzzle-loading rifle means deciding your needs and desires for a black-powder firearm. Do you want a replica of a historical model, or will a modernized version do? Which ignition style do you prefer, caplock (percussion) or flintlock? Do you wish to shoot the patched round ball, or is the conical projectile your choice? What about caliber? Muzzle-loading rifles normally run from 32 to huge sizes spoken of in bore or gauge. Study the art of muzzle-loading and the rewards are great—shoot the frontstuffer haphazardly, and you will get little more than smoke for your efforts.

Replica or Nonreplica?

Dyed-in-the-buckskin black-powder shooters would no more have a nonreplica rifle in camp than Louis Armstrong would have played a kazoo at Carnegie. Yet, there are many good reasons why a few million nonreplica muzzle-loaders are in the hands of modern shooters. They are rugged, well made, accurate, and reliable, with plenty of power to boot. The replica is historically more correct than its modernized counterpart, but the former is not always better. Choose according to your *personal* requirements and pay no attention to the hardcore black-powder shooters who might look down on your nonreplica rifle.

Caplock or Flintlock?

If the flintlock were as faulty as modern gun literature often claims, the pioneer would have quickly become bear bait. One problem with modern flintlocks is that some of the locks are not correctly structured. They make no more spark when the flint strikes the frizzen than I can engender from rubbing a couple of ordinary stones together. No spark, no ignition. On the other hand, a properly loaded flinter—and the key word is "properly" —will fire on command. Sure, it's prone to a few failures. But it will go off on cue far more often than it will misfire. So if your desire is for the old-time flintlock design, buy a good one. Buy one that showers sparks down into the pan as if it were the Fourth of July.

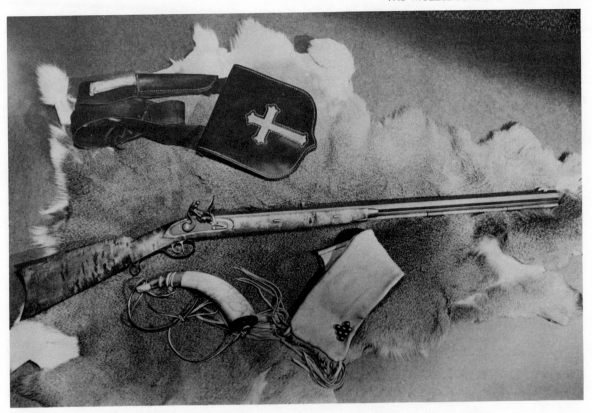

A replica Hawken muzzle-loader from the Ozark Mountain Arms Company. It is patterned after an original Hawken from the middle 1800s. *(Ozark Mountain Arms)*

A Seneca muzzle-loading rifle from the Thompson/Center Company. *(Thompson/Center)*

There can be no doubt, however, that the percussion or caplock system is more surefire than the older flinter. The flinter was eventually replaced by the percussion-cap system, and rightfully so. We find many original flintlock rifles which were converted years ago to the caplock design through the addition of the "drum and nipple" system. The flinter's lock was exchanged for a percussion lock with percussion-style hammer, and where the touchhole used to be a drum has been inserted and screwed into place.

For the average black-powder shooter the percussion rifle is the way to go. While I would not trade my favorite 36-caliber Hatfield Squirrel Rifle, which is a flintlock, for anything, the fact remains that most modernday Daniel Boones will do better with the caplock system of ignition. The percussion cap emits quite a jet of flame, and if the lock and

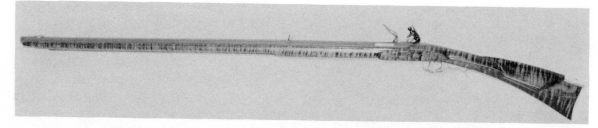

The fine workmanship of the Hatfield long rifle gives it great aesthetic as well as functional appeal. The Hatfield design comes from an original rifle made famous by the Hatfield/McCoy feud.

This Navy Arms Mark I Hawken model dropped an impala ram. The Hawken Mark I gave 100 percent ignition reliability on the hunt.

route to the "chamber" of the rifle are well designed, the flame is going to find the main charge in the breech quickly, making for surefire ignition. Go with the percussion, but don't malign the old flinter. A good flintlock rifle in the hands of a rifleman who knows his gun will put holes in the bull's-eye with unerring consistency.

Caliber

Consider the work you want your frontloader to do. But remember that caliber in the oldtimers is far different from caliber in modern rifles. A 32 caliber is just a squirrel rifle in black-powder talk, but to the modern rifleman a 32 caliber is rather large. The old round ball is part of the reason for this. A 32-caliber squirrel rifle will fire a ball in the 31-caliber class. Why? Because the ball is wrapped in a patch, so it is under bore size. Weigh a 31-caliber ball (.310-inch size) and it will be about 45 grains, or not much more than the weight of a 22 Long Rifle bullet.

For plinking and small-game hunting, I like the 32-caliber rifle. In breaking down black-powder cal-

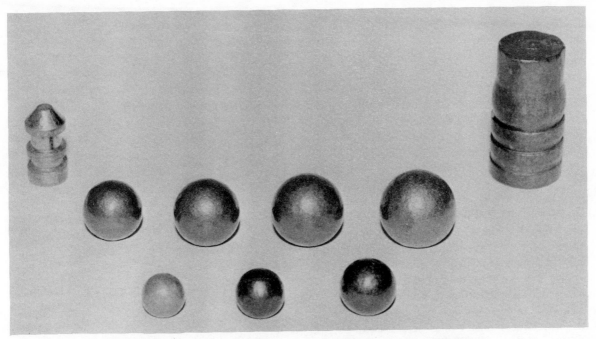

Many calibers and projectile styles are available for the muzzle-loading rifle. Popular for small game and plinking are the 32-, 36-, and 40-caliber round balls, below. The top row of balls, from the left, are 45, 50, 54, and 58 calibers. At the upper left is a 32-caliber Thompson/Center Maxi-Ball. Upper right is a 58-caliber Shiloh maxi.

iber, let's agree that the small-bore clan runs from 32 caliber to 40 caliber, with the latter bridging the gap between small and big bores. We will call the big bores 45, 50, 54, 58, and up. The beauty of the little calibers lies in excellent plinking/small-game power with little expense in either lead or powder. A 32-caliber long rifle can be fired for less than the cost of a 22-rimfire rifle. A load of only 10 grains of FFFg black powder behind a single 45-grain, .310-inch round ball will deliver near 22 Long Rifle ballistics. That means seven hundred shots for a one-pound can of powder. And if you cast your own lead ball you can make more than 150 of them from a pound of metal. You can even make your own percussion caps using the Tap-O-Cap tool from Forster, which turns aluminum beverage cans and toy caps into percussion caps.

I have found the 32-caliber long rifle excellent for everything from tin cans to wild turkeys. But I only have one 32 while I own three of the more popular 36s. The fine 36 fires a .350-inch round ball of 65 grains' weight, and it does a great job with as little as 15 to 20 grains of powder. But most 36s will also handle as much as 40 grains of powder for 2,000-feet-per-second velocity.

After the 32 and 36, there is the 38 caliber. This size is not well represented today. It offers one advantage over the first two small bores, a .375-inch round ball of 80 grains' weight, sufficient for game larger than the wild turkey with good shot placement. And the 38 uses the same .375-inch round ball required for the popular 36-caliber revolver, so ammo is readily available. A 40-caliber rifle gaps the bridge between the small bores and big bores. In many states, it is legal for deer and similar game, though it is a minimum caliber for such game. Ball for 40-caliber rifles runs in the 93-grain weight range for the .395-inch size.

For small bores, the 36 reigns supreme for the time being, with the 32 another excellent choice. The target shooter may wish to look into the 38s and 40s for their low recoil, but slightly more stable performance in the wind. But big-game hunting requires larger projectiles. A 45 is, in the opinion of many, about minimal for deer hunting. A ball in the 45-caliber domain, .44-inch diameter, is going to run about 128 grains. Not much for deer. But a good shot can do wonders with a 45, so it remains legal for deer in many states.

I prefer a 50 caliber for deer and antelope. A 50

using the .490-inch round ball is throwing a missile of 177 grains. That is more like it. You don't achieve really high velocity with black-powder rifles, so you have to make up for that with mass—projectile weight, in other words. My all-around favorite is the 54. I've taken deer and antelope, even elk and larger game with a 54, mainly using a .535-inch round ball in the 230-grain weight class. The larger-than-54s present a few problems.

Nothing wrong with a 58, for example. The ball is of good weight, a .570-inch sphere of lead going 280 grains. But it is rather difficult to propel a 58 or larger ball much beyond an 1,800-feet-per-second muzzle velocity with normal powder charges. The large volume of the bore size itself precludes gaining the type of concentrated pressure behind the ball which makes for high velocity. So after 54 caliber, we find that great gobs of powder are required to gain a respectable trajectory.

Do not confuse this with the true huge-bores of the past. These monster rifles were often of 80, 90, and even greater caliber. The 4 bore, 105 caliber, for example, propelled a missile over an inch in diameter. It only took four of these 4-bore missiles to equal a full *pound* of weight. The rifles were heavy, often 16, 18, 20 pounds, and more, and very large doses of black powder were burned. Expert riflemen could drop big game at 300 yards, even farther, with these superbores. But we do not use them today, and our 58s and 60s are the heavyweights of the league now.

Naturally, the shooter should never turn down a rifle he enjoys because it does not happen to be the caliber he wants most. Black-powder large-bore rifles can be altered in powder charge right on the spot, changing their character instantly from firebreather to pussycat.

Round Ball vs. Conical

Somewhere along the line, the black-powder shooter realized that he could gain more mass per caliber if he would make bullets that looked more like cylinders than like bowling balls. The elongated, conical projectile was the answer in gaining mass per caliber, and we all know that the round ball was replaced by the conical lead projectile and then the jacketed conical bullet. On paper, the round ball is one of the worst missiles possible. It is the smallest and lightest projectile which will touch land to land in the bore of the rifle, with the possible exception of some contrived disk. But I always

This round ball, recovered after passing through the breadth of a bull bison's chest, retained most of its original weight.

The conical is another very useful black-powder missile. These, from the Buffalo Bullet Company, are very effective, offering good penetration on big game.

say the round ball is like the bumblebee. The bumblebee should not be able to fly, or at least not very well, according to the theoretical assessments of experts. He has too much body mass for his wing area. And yet the bumblebee buzzes from flower to flower in ignorant bliss of his plight.

The round ball is the same way. It does lose velocity very rapidly due to its shape. A big-game muzzle-loader rifle may lose as much as half of its initial velocity over a range of only 100 yards. Yet, I have driven round lead balls completely through the chest cavity of a bull elk. Given the right rifle and sights, a patched round ball will print superbly tight groups. I made a fool of myself in national print early in my gunwriting career by lambasting the ball as a rather ridiculous missile. Fortunately, my ranting against the round ball was proved just that—pointless prattle—through using the ball in the field, for small and big game. Now I use the patched round ball for most of my shooting.

But that does not mean the conical is anything less than excellent in the muzzle-loader. I like the patched ball for its historical color, and it so happens that the ball is correct in those wonderful Pennsylvania long rifles I admire. Furthermore, the top-end loads in a round-ball rifle will render about 2,000 fps MV, and the top-end loads in the average conical shooter will yield about 1,500 fps MV. So trajectory for the two is similar, the ball starting out faster, but losing its velocity faster than the conical. Both show similar parabolas and I sight both in the same. Long range is out of the question with either.

Choose the ball or conical based upon appropriateness and accuracy. If you prefer a rifle which historically used the ball, pick the ball. If the rifle was a conical shooter, pick the conical. But most of all, use the one which is right in your rifle, and that is determined in part by rate of twist. A round ball requires very little RPS (revolutions per second) to stabilize it, while a conical demands much more RPS to keep it flying point-on. As an example, I have tested the excellent Navy Arms version of the Whitworth rifle. Here is a 45-caliber target-type rifle with a 1:20 rate of twist. Without doubt it was meant for the conical and it shoots elongated bullets in the 400- to 550-grain range beautifully. My custom 54 long rifle wears a 1:79 rate of twist. It uses the patched round ball.

THE PATCH

Just a bit of cloth, perhaps, but the patch is vital to round-ball accuracy. You will read that a main reason for using a patch on the ball is to seal off the bore, locking the hot gases behind the projectile. While the patch is not a gasket, it can detain, so to speak, the ball downbore so that obturation will prevail, upsetting the ball into the lands and grooves of the rifle barrel. So a patch does help, quite often, in achieving a higher muzzle velocity. But tests have shown clearly that an *unpatched,* but well-fitted, round ball will gain about the same MV as a patched round ball. Always use a patch!

The patch does have some very important values and the muzzle-loader shooter should understand them. First, the patch translates the value from the rifling to the ball, since the ball itself does not actually touch the rifling. The patch, then, is vital to accuracy. Second, the patch takes up the *windage* in the bore. Windage is the gap between the ball and the interior of the rifle bore. Third, the patch serves to *hold* the patched ball down upon the powder charge. This is advantageous for several reasons, one being safety. If the projectile gets loose and works upbore, it could present a problem, even bulging the barrel itself. The patch holds the ball down on the powder where it belongs.

Fourth, the patch keeps pressure upon the powder charge. Many experts agree that black powder burns more uniformly when compressed. Fifth, the patch can prevent leading of the bore. Since the muzzle-loader is a relatively low-velocity rifle, such leading would be minor anyway, but there will be no leading in the ball shooter because the lead ball never even *touches* the bore, the patch preventing such contact. Sixth, the patch holds the lube. A patch is lubed with various products, and these products are retained by the cloth patch. So the simple cloth patch has many functions apart from any possible value as a gasket.

Use good commercial patches. Or buy some pure Irish linen in a fabric shop. The cloth will have sizing, a sort of starch, in it. Wash to get rid of that sizing. Use a fabric softener in the rinse. Then you can precut your patches to the correct size and lube

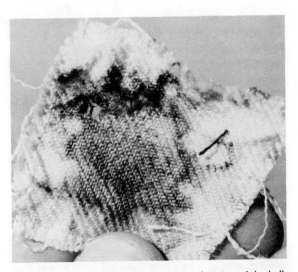

The patch is very important to the proper function of the ball-shooting rifle. It must hold up to the ravages of the black-powder charge, or be backed by hornet-nesting material as described in the text.

them ahead of time. There are three kinds of lubes, liquid, cream, and grease. In my small bores, I use a liquid, such as Falkenberry Juice or Old Slickum. The burning of black powder is incomplete. As much as 57 percent of the fuel remains behind as solids, mostly salts, and the liquid lube breaks these solids down. The small bore does not burn much powder, so the lube on the cloth patch is generally enough for sufficient fouling removal to allow several shots before a real bore swabbing is needed.

A grease is good on the patch, for it tends to stay on for a long time, rather than drying out. But greases do little to break down black-powder fouling. On the other hand, a cream-style lube, such as Wonder Lube, also stays with the patch, and it *does* attack black-powder fouling.

After firing the rifle, the patch will be located downrange, maybe 10 to 20 yards away. Pick up the spent patch. If it is torn, cut, or blown out, there may be some problems which need correcting. A cut patch usually means the rifling sliced it. A blown patch can be caused by several factors. Check the section on loading methods on p. 123.

BLACK-POWDER ACCURACY

It is safe to say that black-powder rifle accuracy is very similar to modern rifle accuracy. Given the right sights and proper bore, the muzzle-loader will keep right up with the newfangled cartridge rifle. But the muzzle-loader usually requires careful load-

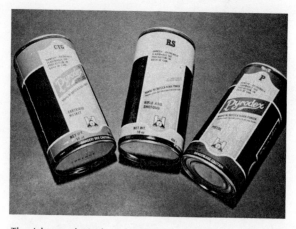

The right powder in the right charge is essential to muzzle-loader rifle accuracy, as is the proper granulation. Pyrodex, the replica black powder, comes in three granulations—CTG for cartridges, RS for larger-bore rifles and shotguns, and P for pistols and small-bore rifles with light charges.

ing and tuning to do so. Even a lube switch can sometimes make a difference. In firing the conical, it is customary to apply a bit of lube to the base of the projectile before loading it downbore. In one particular rifle a slight accuracy advantage was noted when a tiny cardboard disk was run down on the powder, and then the lubed missile rammed down after it. It is not within the scope of this book to go into details on black-powder accuracy; however, it must be pointed out that the early statement about intricacies of muzzle-loading is true. Hundreds of separate factors can be at work simultaneously.

The Right Powder and the Right Charge

The only right powders for a muzzle-loader are black powder (true black powder) or Pyrodex, a replica black powder. Accidents have occurred when other powders have been used. To date, there are no other correct fuels for the muzzle-loader, though chemists have been working to develop different muzzle-loader powders. Black powder is not simply dark-colored powder. It is true black powder and says so on the can. It is a mixture of carbon, saltpeter, and sulfur. It comes in granulations.

The granulations are generally Fg, FFg, FFFg, and FFFFg. Fg is good in a large-bore shotgun, but has little application in the usual muzzle-loading rifle of our day. FFg is very good in the big bores, from 45 and up, especially in full-throttle loads. FFFg is fine for the small-bore rifle, and it is also valuable for loads in the big bores, depending upon manufacturer's dictates. And FFFFg is pan powder, used to prime the pan of the flintlock rifle. Use these granulations precisely, for pressures vary between the various granulations. Fg is the most coarse. FFFFg the most finely ground. Do not mix them. Use these powders as they were intended to be used.

How much powder? That is always the big question the beginning muzzle-loader fan wants to know. First, consult the manual which came with your rifle. The gunmaker is responsible for telling you how much powder the rifle should use. Do not exceed that recommendation. It was once thought that black powder could never achieve more than 25,000-psi (pounds per square inch) pressure. But that error was betrayed many years ago. In the nineteenth century the United States Navy proved that 100,000 psi could be generated with black powder, and the same proof was given by Noble and Abel in England. Do not overload any powder, and this includes black powder.

LOADING METHODS

Here are some steps to follow in loading the black-powder rifle. They are derived from many years of experimentation, and though they are quite simple, they may be vital to accuracy as well as safe shooting practices.

Loading the Patched-Ball Rifle

1. Insure that the rifle is clean, with a dry bore, no oil present.

2. Pop a cap on the nipple. Point the muzzle at a lightweight object, such as a leaf. The leaf should be blown out of the way if the channel is clear from nipple to breech. If the leaf does not move, check for dirt or oil in the rifle.

3. Pour the correct powder charge downbore.

4. If a heavy hunting charge is used, run a couple of layers of hornet-nesting material down upon the powder charge. This is accomplished by using the off-end of the ramrod to seat these layers right on the powder charge. The hornet-nesting material will prevent patch burnout or blowout. Yet, it will not catch fire itself.

5. Run the patched ball down, using the short starter first and then the ramrod or loading rod. Insure that the lubricated patch and the ball remain firmly on the powder charge until fired away.

6. If a conical is used, be sure to lube it, and also check to see that it remains down upon the powder charge.

7. Cap the rifle and fire. A percussion cap can be detonated through excessive pressure or percussion. Therefore, I prefer a capper, a device which holds and dispenses the cap, rather than forcing it on with one's fingers.

Loading the Flintlock Rifle

1. Insure that the rifle is clean, with a clear touchhole.

2. Dryfire for a spark. Insure that the frizzen is clean and greasefree and the flint lined up to scrape against that frizzen. The flint actually scrapes off bits of hot metal when it strikes, but it can't do so readily when the frizzen is dirty or greasy.

3. Insert a blockage into the touchhole. I use a common pipe cleaner or a touchhole pick. The touchhole is blocked for a very good reason. We do *not* want powder in it. The idea is to set off a charge of FFFFg powder in the pan, the spark jumping through the clean touchhole and into the main charge in the breech. If there is powder in the touchhole, the touchhole becomes a fuse. That powder must burn out of the way before the spark can reach the powder charge in the breech.

4. Pour the carefully measured powder charge home, while leaving the blockage in the touchhole.

5. Seat the projectile as above.

6. After the projectile is firmly seated, carefully remove the touchhole blockage.

7. Now prime the pan. Do *not* fill the pan full of FFFFg powder. Carefully install about a third of a pan full of powder, making sure that the pan powder remains to the outside of the pan, not up against the touchhole. Remember that the idea is to convey a clear spark from the pan *through* the touchhole. A full pan of powder can almost defeat that purpose, sometimes actually pushing the pan cover aside and making a general open flame instead of a directed flame.

BALLISTICS

The small bores burn very little powder for good ballistics. For example, my long-barreled, 36-caliber Hatfield Squirrel Rifle uses 20 grains of FFFg for a muzzle velocity of about 1,470 fps. A charge of 30 grains of the same powder in the same rifle pushes the 65-grain lead pill at about 1,800 fps MV. And 40 grains of FFFg achieves close to 2,025 fps MV. At close range, that 36-caliber rifle has 22-Magnum power. My 54-caliber ball shooter drives its 230-grain lead missile at 2,000 fps MV, yielding a muzzle energy of over 2,000 foot-pounds.

Ballistic force in black-powder shooting varies widely. There was one black-powder rifle which shoved a huge 4-bore missile at modest velocity, creating far more energy than a 458 Winchester elephant rifle. In fact, the rifle was more powerful than any modern elephant rifle normally encountered, even the 600 Nitro Express. However, the muzzle-loader is mainly a short-range tool by modern standards and the frontloaders we carry today are not nearly as powerful as today's modern-cartridge, big-game rifles. They should be used within their range limitations. I prefer 75-yard shots for my own big-game hunting, for example, and I call 125 yards my maximum range. Part of this range limitation is due to rainbow trajectory.

Trajectory and Sight-In

I start off at very close range in sighting the muzzle-loading rifle, usually about 13 yards, because this distance often puts the missile back on target at 75 or 80 yards and only a little low at 100. Of course, the figures vary with ball size. The larger ball retains its initial velocity better than the smaller ball. Here are some sight-in clues. The reader can see why I call 125 yards my maximum range with either a ball-shooting rifle or a conical shooter, for the ball or conical has dropped by about a half foot at that distance, making certain projectile placement questionable.

32 caliber to 36 caliber (small game loads, 1,500 fps range)

25 yards	50 yards	75 yards
+ 1"	0	− 2"

38 caliber to 40 caliber (2,000 fps MV range)

25 yards	50 yards	75 yards
+ .5"	0	− 1"

45 caliber to 54 caliber (2,000 fps MV range for round ball, 1,500 fps MV for conical)

13 yards	50 yards	100 yards	125 yards
0	+ 1"	− 1"	− 6"

The sight-in for the 45- to 54-caliber range is for the round ball at 2,000 fps MV and the conical at about 1,500 fps MV because these muzzle velocities are possible and because the ball, losing its velocity more rapidly than the conical, but starting out faster, describes about the same parabola as the conical. One can see that the little round ball in the 32- to 36-caliber class gives splendid small-game trajectory even when it is very lightly loaded.

The use of black-powder accessories is vital to the sport of muzzle-loader-rifle shooting. However, a brief account of these tools will appear in the chapter on accessories. Also, black-powder rifles require a good cleanup due to fouling. That subject will be handled in the maintenance chapter. However, this brush with the old-time rifle should include a little commentary on the myths that have clung to the sport like lampreys to sharks. Many

are the old wives' tales in black-powder shooting and I doubt that a single gunwriter has avoided repeating some of them. They usually sound too good to be true—often because they are not. But they certainly are alive and well and they blow back and forth like winds in the canyon.

BLACK-POWDER MYTHS

It takes little imagination to guess that in those pre-science days of muzzle-loading, shooters were in need of guidelines, and as they tried various methods, some of them seemed to work all right—at times—and for some shooters. These ideas became chiseled in granite and the granite tablets were handed down from on high. They are still handed down to this hour. Here are four of them.

Shoot over Snow to Test Your Load

For a while, I really thought this one worked. It seemed like such a sensible idea. You grabbed your favorite smokepole and poured a modest charge downbore. Then you fired her over a clean snowpatch. After shooting, you looked around for flecks of unburned powder. The theory was this: If the load was just right, the powder would be consumed. In fact, there is an optimum point in the bore past which more powder does less work, so the basis of this myth seemed solid. You upped the load and checked again. And again. And finally, when you saw a lot of unburned powder lying on the clean snow, you knew you had gone too far, so you backtracked to that last load and were satisfied.

The trouble is, black powder does not burn completely in the first place. It does not go from solid to

This big bear was harvested by the author using a muzzle-loader.

gaseous state the way smokeless powder does. So of course there were black flecks on the snow. And furthermore, Fg would leave more sign in the snow than FFFg, but all of this proved little. If a person wishes to shoot over snow, he certainly has my blessings. But if he thinks he is going to prove how good his load is by doing so, well, it's not likely to happen.

Use One Grain of Powder for Each Caliber

Another lovely tale from the past, and a fairy tale it is. The idea was to use a powder charge commensurate with the bore of the rifle. A 32-caliber squirrel rifle would burn 32 grains of powder. A 54-caliber deer rifle would burn 54 grains of fuel. I have a 32-caliber squirrel rifle which gains over 2,000 fps MV using 30 grains of FFFg. Why would I want to use 32 grains? Furthermore, the rifle man-

ages 22 Long Rifle MV with only 10 grains of powder. Saying that an optimum load is 32 grains for the 32 rifle is ludicrous. And 54 grains in a 54 is fine for target work, but my own 54 is granted a lot more powder than that, up to 120 grains or more of FFg for 2,000 fps MV. A load of only 54 grains would be pitiful for big-game hunting. And wrong! Ignore this folly. It is naught but an old wives' tale.

Cover a Ball with Powder

Here, you put a ball in the palm of your hand. Then you pour powder over the ball. The amount of powder it takes to cover the ball is the amount of powder to use in your load. Hold out your hand. Put a ball in it. Cover the ball with powder. Do it again. If you come up with the same amount, call it luck. I tried this, just for the fun of it, and if I held my hand flat, I got a pretty healthy load in some instances, but I could cup my hand and the load would prove quite light. It's just nonsense, but if you look into enough black-powder literature, you may well find it there. I wouldn't be surprised if I mentioned it a time or two myself many years ago.

Listen for the Crack

Another one from the book of black-powder myths is the crack theory. The notion was this: Load the rifle with powder until it goes crack! instead of boom! Then you have achieved the speed of sound, about 1,100 fps MV, roughly speaking. In the first place, 1,100 fps MV is certainly nothing to get excited about. Most of my loads produce 1,200 and up just for plinking and my big-game, round-ball rifles pop the ball out at around 2,000 fps. In the second place, the slipstream behind the ball may achieve the speed of sound long before the ball does. So the ball may be going only 900 fps when the crack is heard, if you can hear it. I never could. Yes, I did try. Don't bother.

The world of black-powder shooting is deeply fascinating and replete with romance as well as lots of basic rifle learning for all of us. Mastering the muzzle-loader requires quite a bit of know-how. And it is a science, not a rule-of-thumb activity.

The serious black-powder shooter should venture to his library or bookstore and attach himself to a few texts, digesting them word for word. He may also wish to read monthly black-powder journals for more information. And he must always sift through the information he runs across with a probe, a probe of common sense and sound scientific questioning. The frontloading rifle embodies all that is exciting in shooting, but it is a far cry from the modern rifle. It must be treated differently, for it is a separate domain. And the muzzle-loader rifle must never be taken lightly. At first, the shooter may enjoy making smoke and stoking up his front-stuffer just for the experience of it all. But soon he will want to hit the target consistently or take game cleanly. And these are accomplished through learning, not through sorcery or guesswork.

The Varmint Rifle

13

COYOTES had put one sheepman out of business and were doing a fair job of depleting the flock of another when the government hunter/trapper was called in. He set his traps, which curtailed the raids of a few of the sheep-eating wild dogs, but the hunter couldn't catch the two big prairie wolves which were doing most of the damage. Over and over he found their tracks where they had sliced down several sheep, feeding on only a few of the carcasses. Finally, the professional hunter took a stand, literally. He posted himself in the rimrocks high above a buckpen where prize breeding stock was held. He waited for three days, hoping the two coyotes would show up. He also hoped that if they did, it would be light enough to shoot.

His rifle was a 270 Winchester firing 110-grain, Hornady hollow-point bullets exiting the muzzle at 3,300 feet per second. I know because I handloaded and chronographed the ammunition for him. The coyotes finally did approach the sheep pen and the hunter dropped both of them from long range, over 300 yards. Long range, that's the name of the varmint-shooting game. But when I was a young man, the most-used "varmint rifle" was the Model 94 Winchester 30-30, because it was the most-carried rifle. However, neither that trapper's 270, nor any 30-30, fits the category of varmint rifle now, in spite of the former's long-range potential and the latter's popularity.

Varmints are wild animals which wreak havoc upon livestock, crops, or game species. Nonhunters may not understand the game department's varmint classification; however, let one small mouse scurry across the kitchen floor and it will achieve varmint status immediately from most people, including nonhunters. Varmints have been and will continue to be dispatched by various control programs, and by riflemen. The latter have created a precision rifle designed specifically for long-range varmint shooting. The varmint rifle is usually a bolt-action or a single-shot model chambered for a high-intensity, high-velocity, flat-shooting cartridge of modest caliber. There are still countless varmints dispatched with 22-rimfire rifles, 30-30s, big-game arms, and even muzzle-loaders. However, that does not make any of them true varminters.

VARMINT CARTRIDGES

The list begins with 17 caliber and ends with 24 caliber. The 17 Remington and other 17s of similar ballistics propel tiny bullets in the 4,000-foot-per-second class, shooting flat enough to hit a varmint at 300 yards or more. Trappers who sometimes hunt for furs may select 17s because their lightweight bullets (25 grains usually) seldom ruin the valuable pelts of furbearing animals. Often, the bullet disrupts within completely, leaving no exit hole at all. Varmint hunters like the 17s because the bullet tends to disintegrate readily on impact, precluding ricochet. The 17s, however, do require very careful reloading, for tiny variations in powder charge can bring significant increases in chamber pressure.

At the other end of the varmint cartridge list are

Sometimes, the coyote will be taken incidentally by a rifleman who was in the area on other business, as was the case here.

The prairie dog tunnels into farmland and ranchland, wreaking havoc. Though cute to look at, the farmer and rancher find the prairie dog a problem.

the 24s. Why stop at 24 caliber? The magnificent 257 Weatherby Magnum, for example, will propel a 75-grain bullet at over 4,000 fps MV. Would it not be a varmint cartridge? No, because a varmint cartridge is one which allows repeated firing with modest recoil and muzzle blast, while the 257 Weatherby will flatten the ears of a brass mule. A logically defined cutoff point for varmint cartridges is caliber 24, despite the fact that varmints may be dispatched with calibers 25 and up. Here are some specific cartridges which meet the criteria of varmint round, flat shooting, mild recoil, frangible bullets which destruct on the landscape, modest muzzle blast, and low overall noise level.

17 Remington

This little cartridge shoots a light bullet, usually 25 grains in weight, as fast as 4,100 fps MV. Its

The 223 Remington is a popular varmint round. Here is the Federal factory load in 223 Remington using a 55-grain boattail, hollow-point bullet for explosiveness. *(Federal Cartridge Corp.)*

uniqueness has lured a number of varminters and its specific brand of performance has kept them. Light recoil, modest report, flat shooting, and minimal pelt damage on larger furbearing animals are some of its attributes. Comparatively rapid bore fouling, sensitivity to powder-charge variation, and modest delivered energy are its drawbacks. It's a fine 300-yard varmint round.

22 Hornet

Winchester did much for varminters when the company introduced the 22 Hornet. A modest range right for varmints, light recoil, and very mild report keep the Hornet alive today. It will fire a 50-grain bullet at about 2,800 fps MV, good enough for 200 yards, even 250 yards. Several beautiful, short-action rifles come in this caliber. Although the Hornet has been ballistically outstripped by many other rounds, it fits a specific niche, that of a mild-mannered, middle-range varminter.

218 Bee

A 1938 round which arrived eight years after the Hornet, the 218 has always been considered more powerful than its older brother. However, handload for handload, the Bee and the Hornet are nearly ballistic twins, both pushing the 50-grain pill at about 2,800. No rifles are chambered for the 218 Bee today, but there are still a great number of old functional ones around and that is why it's listed here. Factory ammunition is still available for the 218 Bee as are handloading components.

219 Zipper

Still factory-loaded, but no longer chambered, the 219 Zipper will drive the 50-grain bullet at 3,600 fps MV and it makes a good 300- to 350-yard varmint round for old, yet functional Zipper-chambered rifles.

222 Remington

One of the best varmint cartridges of all time, the 222 Remington is a good 300-yard performer. The 222 Remington Magnum and 223 Remington are considered ballistically superior to this little cartridge, but the chronograph shows a velocity increase of little more than 100 fps for either over the standard 222. The 222 Magnum and 223 are not listed below for that reason. In practical terms neither betters the 222 by a great margin. The 223, however, offers the advantage of good prices on military brass.

225 Winchester

Supposedly the successor of the 220 Swift, this round pushes the 50-grain bullet at about 3,800 fps MV. Its case is semirimmed, a good design for some single-shot actions. The 225 is a very good cartridge, but is ballistically bettered by the Swift.

224 Weatherby

A 50-grain bullet at 3,900 fps MV is the calling card for the 224 varmint round, and it is chambered in the famous Weatherby rifle. The belted case of this high-intensity cartridge is interesting, being the only cartridge of this size/design to offer a belt. It produces close to 220 Swift performance.

22-250 Remington

A 50-grain bullet screams away at 3,900-plus fps in this cartridge and the 22-250 is often considered the single best 22-caliber varmint cartridge of all because it has reasonably good case life as well as high ballistic delivery. While the 220 Swift lingers in the wings, the 22-250 occupies center stage in the world of varmint calibers.

220 Swift

Imagine the excitement. The year is 1935. Only forty years earlier, the amazing muzzle velocity of the 30-30 was news, being nearly 2,000 fps. The 30-06 is only 18 years old. Suddenly, the barely reached 3,000-fps realm is shattered by a little screamer capable of 4,000 fps with a 48-grain bullet. Most handloaders push the 50-grain pill at about 3,900 in the Swift today. Noisy, the Swift is not a popular farmyard pest rifle, even though its speedy bullet does fragment on contact with the ground. It shines where long-range, open-country varminting is the rule.

6mm Remington/243 Winchester

These ballistic 6mm twins were designed as compromise deer/varmint cartridges. Remington emphasized varmints by originally offering its 6mm as the 244 Remington with a rifling twist best suited to the lighter, shorter varmint bullet of 75 grains' weight. Less than exciting sales prompted Remington to reconsider, and the fine cartridge received a name change and a rifling twist alteration as well. Either the 243 Winchester or 6mm Remington will drive a 75-grain bullet at up to 3,600 fps MV for varmint hunting. Both are excellent for deer and antelope, too.

240 Weatherby

Very much like the twin 6mms above, the 240 Weatherby drives the 75-grain, 6mm bullet even faster, at 3,800 fps MV. The 240 Weatherby ends this list of varmint cartridges. After the 240, ballistics and consequent recoil, muzzle blast and report surpass the levels imposed by our varmint-round criteria.

THE VARMINTING GAME

The original idea of varmint-cartridge development was farshooting accuracy with sufficient power to dispatch varmints such as woodchucks of the East, rockchucks (hoary marmots) of the West, various ground-dwelling squirrels, prairie dogs, jackrabbits, coyotes, and others. However, varmint cartridges and rifles were so interesting to shooters that both gained status in target shooting. Handloaders improved upon varmint-round ballistics, and riflemakers improved upon varmint-rifle accuracy.

VARMINT HUNTING

Although the application of the varmint rifle has broadened into benchrest/target work for tight-group shooting, the rifle has maintained its function as a dispatcher of varmints. High velocity has been the passkey into the world of long-range varminting because the velocity allows flat trajectory. In varmint hunting, the shooter scans with binoculars or spotting scope for his quarry. Upon locating his target, the shooter must position himself for a shot. Commercial units, such as the Harris Bipod and Outers Varmint Rifle Rest, may be employed to help steady the rifle for a long shot.

Ranges of 200 to 300 yards are modest in varmint hunting. The really high-speed rounds have 400-yard-plus potential. The trajectory chart in Chapter 6 shows sight-in for varmint rounds and gives a clear illustration of bullet deviation from line of sight over long range. The master varminter can take advantage of this flat trajectory through shooting skill, of course, but also through accurate "doping" of the range. The 220 Swift, for example, can be sighted in to strike zero at 310 yards. By so sighting the Swift, the bullet drops only 8.5 inches at 400 yards. Larger varmints, such as the coyote, can be targeted with on-the-back sight picture at

400 yards; smaller varmints will require a modest holdover of the horizontal wire for a strike.

And then there is the wind. A key factor in wind-drift effect on a bullet is time of flight. The less elapsed time from muzzle to target, the better, for the wind has less opportunity to push against the bullet. Therefore, the varmint-class cartridge of the over-3,500-fps range does have a wind-deflection advantage over slower-moving projectiles. Bullet mass does play a role in wind drift as well. However, time of flight is more important than bullet mass.

For example, the little 22-caliber, 50-grain missile starting at 4,000 fps MV is drifted about 25.5 inches off course at 300 yards in a 30-mile-per-hour crosswind (per Sierra Bullets Reloading Manual data). But a 45-caliber, 300-grain bullet beginning at 1,500 fps MV, as from a 45-70 Government cartridge, will drift about 117.5 inches in the same crosswind at the same distance. Therefore, the varmint rifle has advantage not only in bullet drop at long range, but also in wind drift, contrary to the notion that such a small bullet would surely be blown off course easily. The fast bullet is still badly deflected from line of sight by the wind, to be sure (all bullets are), and a 30-mile-per-hour crosswind makes 300-yard varminting very inconsistent; however, the expert shooter can estimate modest wind drift and zero in on long-range varmints in a breeze.

Varminting can make pest control effective. However, this skill/sport has several other features. Practice is one. Varminting, be it with a true varmint rifle or other shooting instrument, sharpens the shooting eye. The varminter learns to estimate bullet drop with greater accuracy by "doping the range," and he also learns a lot about wind drift by firing at far-off targets. Serious varmint shooters may pace the range after firing in order to see how well they guessed the distance from muzzle to target. Such practice makes for a better game shot, and this improvement is transferred from varmint to big game. Furthermore, the rifleman gains greater mastery of all aspects of marksmanship in the varminting arena, including rifle control and body management.

I have witnessed giant leaps forward in field-marksmanship improvement when a big-game hunter gives varmint hunting serious consideration. He simply learns more about big-bore rifles and rifle shooting by association with the varmint rifle. The experience can lessen a tendency to flinch, and

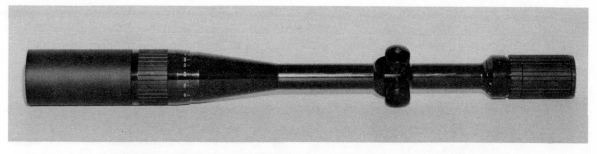

One of the best scopes for varmint shooting is the variable, allowing reasonably wide field of view for closer shots with extra magnification for the faraway shots. This is a Bausch & Lomb 6×–24× with sunshade and adjustable objective lens.

increase ability to lead running game. The varminter also gains speed in taking a good solid field stance, steadying the rifle for a well-aimed shot. Furthermore, the light-recoiling varmint rifle helps the marksman squeeze off without the twitch of an eyelash.

THE VARMINT SCOPE

The specialized varmint rifle created a need for a specialized varmint scope sight. Scope designers answered the need with numerous models, both in fixed and variable power. The long-range potential of the varmint rifle required greater-than-big-game hunting magnification, so varmint scopes became high-powered scopes. The target/varmint scope sights of the past, 10×, 20×, and more in magnification, were excellent, though field of view was greatly limited with these scopes.

I favor today's variable in the varmint field. In a test of long-range potential, a flat-shooting, bolt-action rifle was fitted with a Bausch & Lomb 6×–24× variable and results were very satisfying. The high-quality optics of this scope helped in clarifying the target, and the reasonably wide field of view at the lower setting allowed fast get-on-target potential. The adjustable objective lens, coupled with the thin center crosswires, made small-target hitting at long range more precise than it had been with the straight 10× scope that used to top that particular varmint rifle. And the built-in sunshade of the scope prevented lens flare.

Individual conditions call for specific hardware. Some varminters may prefer their 6×, 8×, 10×, or other fixed scopes. I found the modern high-quality variable in the 6×–24× range preferable to these. The reasonably wide field of view, 18 feet at

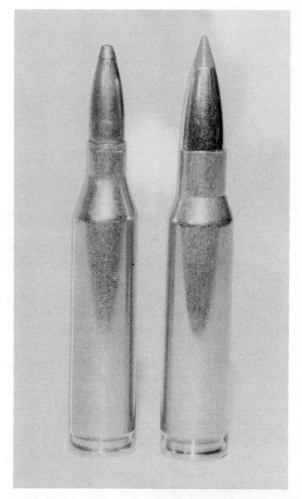

Varminting has promoted the creation of some very fine cartridges, many of which have been adopted by the arms companies for factory manufacture. Such a round is the 243 Winchester, left, which was developed by necking down its parent 308 Winchester cartridge (right) to 24 caliber.

6×, and high magnification combine in a scope which is useful on moving varmints at modest range, as well as for sedentary targets at long range. The above-mentioned 6×–24× B&L scope features all-steel target adjustments for precise reticle movement, which aids in sight-in and also in field variation of the setting for those who wish to make sight changes for various ranges.

THE VARMINT RIFLE AND THE WILDCAT ROUND

The varminter's quest has been for rifles of longer range and improved accuracy; however, the quest also led to some of the remarkable long-range cartridges we have today. Ammunition conceived on the drawing boards of wildcatters was sometimes adopted by the commercial ammo-crafters in original form or as modified wildcat rounds. Never satisfied, the wildcatters continued to neck brass down and to fireform cases.

Roy Weatherby's quest for higher velocity was prompted by his interest in shooting at long range, first with 30-06 brass and later with belted magnum cases. Weatherby experimented with dozens of different combinations of caliber, powder, and bullets. His wildcatting experiments culminated in the Weatherby line of high-velocity cartridges from 22 through 45 caliber. Improvements in smokeless powder, especially the addition of slower-burning progressive fuels, made the "necked down" round viable. Although still spoken of as "overbore capacity," many of the big-case/smaller-caliber rounds give very exciting performances. The long-range varmint cartridge gave rise to many big-game, long-range cartridges as well. While the ammo factories seemed slow to incorporate some of these advances, their engineers were looking and listening and an impressive number of the better factory cartridges we shoot today were born of the wildcat motivation for greater range with better accuracy.

Examples are not hard to find. The 225 Winchester is, for all intents and purposes, a 219 Ackley Improved Zipper wildcat. Ned Roberts's excellent 257, bearing his name, was born when he necked down 7 × 57 Mauser brass in order to achieve a lighter bullet of good sectional density at higher velocity. And the 257 Roberts was in turn necked down to create the 6mm Remington when the pro-

A high-grade varmint rifle, the Steyr Mannlicher Varmint Rifle available in various long-range calibers. *(Steyr)*

This Ruger Model 77 Varmint rifle is a typical varmint rifle. *(Sturm, Ruger Company)*

totype of that cartridge left the drawing board. The 308 Nato, later to be called the 308 Winchester, was necked down to 24 caliber and the 243 Winchester was born. The 250-3000 Savage was necked down to 22 caliber and we had the 22-250 round with a 28-degree shoulder.

Shooters interested in further wildcat investigation will find more on the subject in many sources, such as *Handbook for Shooters and Reloaders* by P. O. Ackley, Plaza Publishing, 1848 W. 2300 S., Salt Lake City, Utah. The specialized varmint rifle and its specialized cartridge helped to engender many changes in long-range shooting. Where will the trend take us in the future? To more accurate rifles and even better telescopic sights for those rifles and to further advances in bullets and cartridges. How about a 50-grain, 22-caliber bullet at 5,000 fps instead of 4,000? Not yet, but with continued powder improvement, we may see it happen.

An encounter with varmint rifles cracks the door open for a view into a fascinating adjunct of rifle shooting. The specialized varmint rifle and cartridge have promoted accuracy improvement, higher velocity, and flatter-shooting, long-range potential, along with many other rifle improvements (such as bolt-action rifle bedding) and cartridge improvements, all of which translate into improved marksmanship. Furthermore, the long-range varminter often becomes a better marksman in the big-game field for he comes to better understand exterior ballistics and garners a lot of experience in putting bullets on target with precision.

14

The Most Famous Sporting Rifle of All

A BOOK ON RIFLES and rifle shooting would be incomplete without the most famous sporting rifle of all time, the Winchester Model 94. You can't talk about American shooting without mention of the rifle that has sold about six million copies since its inception in 1894–95. Some shooters feel that the 94's fame grew from its chambering of the 30-30 cartridge, and others believe that the 30-30 cartridge gained fame because it was chambered in the 94; either way, 94s have reflected the light of campfires from South American jungles to Arctic tundra, and the 30-30 cartridge has gone up against every wild animal from bobcats to polar bears. If the 94 and the 30-30 round did not deliver the goods, shooters would have abandoned them a long time ago.

The Model 94, even with the 26-inch barrel, always handled smoothly and balanced like a rapier in the hands of an expert swordsman. Not too heavy, the 94 was easy to carry, the 20-inch-barreled carbine soon eclipsing the longer-barreled model in popularity, making the little lever gun even handier in tight situations.

Fast-pointing, strongly built, with sunrise/sunset reliability, the tough little lever-action 94 didn't let you down. When the lever was snapped down-up, a fresh round was fed home, and after firing, the empty case was shucked out smoother than a moss-covered stream rock. Fast follow-up shots were easy with the 94, too. The longer-barreled models had tubular magazines which packed up to nine rounds, making them ten-shot repeaters. The carbine fired seven times between reloadings. And the

30-30 was, as Warren Page of *Field & Stream* magazine used to say, a *balanced round*. That balance prompted its chambering not only in the 94, but in about three million Marlins and more than a few Savages.

Handy, reliable, sturdy, long-lasting, and not too expensive, the 94 became king of the eastern deer coverts, and was for a very long time of equal reign in the West. When I was growing up in Arizona, saying "Go get your deer rifle" was the same as saying "Go get your Model 94." All of this would be of historical interest only except for one fact— the Model 94 and its 30-30 round are still widely used in America, Canada, and Mexico. One snowy evening not long ago, I nudged up near the campfire with a group of brush hunters who were, as I was, in quest of white-tailed deer. Of the dozen riflemen gathered there, all but two were Model 94 shooters.

Today, the rifle of the West is a bolt-action model with a scope sight. The Model 94 30-30 still occupies a place in the gunrack, and the working rancher or cowboy may pack one into the field, but when hunting season arrives, even these on-the-land people turn to the more modern rifle for harvesting big game. There are western trappers and bear/lion hunters who pack 94s religiously these days, but all in all, the little lever gun has been replaced by the longer-range bolt-action model.

In the East, the 94 has fared better. However, there are plenty of fast-action semiautos in use in the East as well as slide-action rifles and, in spite of generally shorter-range shooting conditions, the

The most famous sporting rifle of all, with about six million produced, the Model 94 Winchester. Here is a cutaway view of the 94 showing its internal action workings.

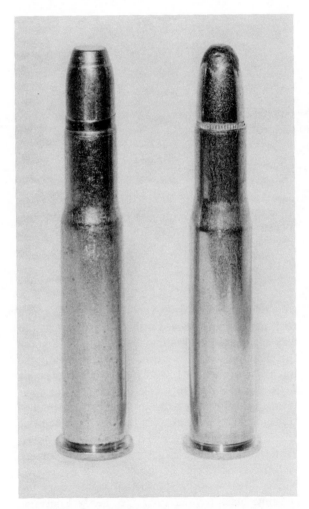

Although the 30-30 cartridge seems rather small compared with higher-powered rounds, it has made a great record for itself and is still used widely in both factory and reloaded form. On the left, a handloaded 30-30 round using a cast bullet. On the right, a factory cartridge.

Eastern hunter has found that he can also get opportunities at long range across meadows or from hill to hill. Therefore, the Pennsylvania venison seeker may have a bolt-action, scope-sighted rifle very much like the one carried by his Western counterpart.

Then why worry about the 94 today? Because every reader of this book knows what they are. He's either owned or at least fired a 94 30-30, and if not, chances are someday he will. Furthermore, the 94 is still in manufacture, and the modern Model 94 has been updated with a stronger action and more powerful cartridges. For the hunter who wants to carry history crooked in the elbow of his arm, while at the same time packing strong ballistic punch, the newer 94 is perfect.

The Model 1894 Winchester, later more simply called the Model 94, sprung from the fertile mind of famous gun inventor John Browning. The first models were chambered for black-powder cartridges, the 32-40 and 38-55. But in 1895 something happened to the Model 94 which shook the shooting world to its foundations. The Winchester 1894 rifle was given a nickel-steel barrel and two new *smokeless-powder* cartridges to go with it. These newborn rounds were the 30-30 and its little sister, the 25-35. The 30-30 was called the 30 WCF (Winchester Centerfire—or Central Fire). These were the first purely sporting smokeless cartridges in the world. The 8mm Lebel, a smokeless-powder *military* cartridge, preceded the 30-30 and the 25-35, as did another smokeless-powder number, the 30 U.S. Army, better known as the 30-40 Krag. France had the 8mm Lebel in 1886 and the 30-40 Krag was prevalent by 1892. But they were military rounds chambered in military rifles.

Sportsmen took to both smokeless-powder rounds in the reliable Browning-designed Model 94 the way black lab retrievers take to the water. Some sources note that both the 25-35 and the 30-30 were originally black-powder rounds. These shooters feel

Excellent factory 30-30 ammunition is common. Here is a breakdown of the Federal Premium load with the 170-grain Nosler Partition bullet. Note exposed lead at the base of the bullet. Fast bore time will not allow the lead to melt.

that the designations suggest a black-powder nature, for it was common to name a round according to its charge of black powder. For example, the 32-40 was about 32 caliber and it carried about 40 grains of black powder. The 38-55 was about 38 caliber and it was loaded with about 55 grains of black powder. However, the 25-35 and 30-30 were always smokeless-powder cartridges, as was the 30-40 Krag, which also carried the black-powder-type designation. The 30-30 was so called because it was a 30-caliber cartridge and it was loaded with about 30 grains of *smokeless* powder. Had the 30-30 been a black-powder round, it would have had the energy of a newborn puppy, being 30 caliber with only 30 grains of black powder. The 25-35 and 30-30 sisters were smokeless rounds from the start.

The 25-35 was a fair little cartridge, and a good

shot could reliably drop venison at modest range with just one cartridge. But it eventually went the way of the dodo bird as the 30-30 continued to take the shooting world by storm. Today, there's nothing exciting about a 160–165-grain bullet at about 1,970 fps MV, but in the latter part of the nineteenth century such ballistics and consequent flat trajectory were unheard of in the sporting rifle field. Black-powder cartridges had rainbow trajectories. Hitting a long-range target with them was for the well-practiced rifleman only.

The 30-30 was the shovel that helped bury the old-time black-powder cartridge. Teddy Roosevelt hunted with one on the plains and called it "an Ace." He could make sure hits at 200 yards with it. And he noted terrific penetration. We don't think about it now, but it was the 30-30 and similar early smokeless-powder rounds which led to high-velocity interest, whereby the additional bullet speed translated not only into flatter trajectory, but also into greater long-range delivery of energy.

Commercial ammunition was always exceptionally good for the 30-30. My recent tests with 30-30 ammo showed very low standard-deviation figures, indicating high quality. When Warren Page labeled the 30-30 balanced, he meant balanced in bullet weight versus velocity. His compiled data showed the everyday 30-30 with the 150-grain bullet to be one of the most reliable cartridges for dropping deer with one shot at modest range. Both bullet construction and striking velocity were excellent. Instead of fragmentation, bullets remained intact, penetrated well, created long wound channels, and yet opened up enough to disperse energy through the animal for a clean harvest. The 30-30 also has little recoil.

Today's 30-30 ammo is the best ever. The variety is broad, from Remington's Accelerator firing a 22-caliber, 55-grain bullet (the undersized bullet held by a plastic sabot) to Federal's Premium ammo with a 170-grain Nosler Partition bullet. Winchester's Silvertip is a reliable 30-30 bullet where deep penetration is desired, as is Remington's hollow-point Core-Lokt bullet. Federal's 170-grain bullet and Winchester's Power Point open up well, but cores remain wedded to jackets.

Hornady's Interlock bullet is another good one in the 30-30, as is Remington's Soft-Point Core-Lokt. The list goes on, from a 125-grain Sierra hollow-point load from Federal Cartridge Company to many 150-grain bullets from all of the manufacturers. The Canadian 30-30 hunter can buy Imperial ammunition with 150-grain and 170-grain bullets. These are not imported into the USA, so I've had no chance to test this ammo, but Canadian readers report it is very good. Having all of this excellent 30-30 ammunition available helps promote the round's efficiency on deer-sized game. The low-recoiling 30-30 is very easy to manage.

In spite of all its good factory ammunition, the 30-30 remains one of the most handloaded cartridges of all time. Detractors of the old round say that reloading does nothing for the 30-30 because it has such limited ballistic potential to begin with. But they are wrong. The 30-30 can be handloaded to mild 32-20 ballistics, making it an excellent wild turkey cartridge. Underloads for the 30-30 also make good small-game ammo. The 30-30 can be handloaded with a 150-grain bullet for about 2,500 fps MV for midrange deer hunting. So, as we can see, the 30-30 becomes an amazingly versatile cartridge through handloading.

Lyman's forty-sixth edition of *Reloading Handbook*, page 283, shows a 150-grain bullet backed by 39 grains of H-335 powder for a velocity of close to 2,600 fps. My personal 30-30 with 24-inch barrel gains close to 2,600 with only 37 grains of H-335. I have harvested antelope and deer at 200 yards and beyond with one shot each using this 150-grain-bullet load. I also have a pet short-range load for big game. Silvertip 190-grain bullets are pulled from new 303 Savage ammo, Winchester brand. Handloaded in the 30-30, the round becomes a fairly decent heavyweight contender for up-close work. My best load propels this 190-grain missile at close to 2,100 fps MV. The load, 25 grains of Rx-7 powder, was located in Lyman's forty-fifth edition manual. Pressure rating is listed at 36,400 CUP, okay in the 94 action.

The 130-grain Speer Flat-Point bullet departs the muzzle at over 2,600 fps using 37 grains of H-335 powder, this from the 20-inch barreled carbine. My tests have shown center-to-center groups of only .57 inch at 50 yards with this load. It's a good one for deer and antelope at ranges up to 200 yards. One hunting season I was on the Wyoming plains with my 30-30 and a variety of loads. A little 112-grain cast gas-check bullet, mold number 311316, was my small-game harvester, 13 grains of Unique powder rendering a MV of only 1,300 fps (22 Long Rifle speed). For antelope, my 30-30 fired a 150-grain bullet at almost 2,600 fps MV, and I had an additional deer tag which I filled on the riverbottom with a heavy-duty brush load, the 190-grain Silvertip at about 2,100 fps MV.

A renewed love affair with the 30-30 was born of necessity a few years ago. I found myself long-range-rifle rich, but brush-country-rifle poor. I needed a packaround model that would take a licking and keep on ticking. My earlier association with a 94 30-30 did not result in marriage. The rifle and I parted company after a bittersweet courting period when I was living in Arizona near the Mexican border. All my friends had 30-30s. So I got one, too. The deer thumbed their noses at me as I "snapshot" at them with the little carbine.

I used the rifle like a blackboard pointer. My mentors and peers knew better. They *aimed* and brought home the venison. As long as I pointed the 30-30 like a shotgun without true aiming picture, success eluded me. I missed several good bucks,

Nancy Fadala poses with a mule deer buck and the 30-30. The 30-30, properly handled, is
still a fine short- to medium-range deer taker.

blamed the saddle rifle for the failure, and traded her off for a bolt-action 270. I did get a fine buck immediately with the 270; however, the joke was on me. The range of the shot was a mere rock-tossing couple of dozen paces. The 30-30 would have served perfectly, if only I *aimed* it.

My new handmate rifle was another 30-30, a rugged little carbine. I had matured. I had learned to handle such a rifle and to aim it quickly, but with precision. Soon my freezer was rich with many different game animals, from tree squirrels and javelina to deer, all cleanly dropped with the brush rifle. A newfound passion for the old-time round brought me to the door of gunmaker Dale Storey. Dale and I sat around his fireplace for several evenings plotting a custom rifle based on the 94 action. The result was my Storey Conversion, with high-grade

American walnut stock, 24-inch Bauska octagon barrel, all fitted together tighter than a sledge-driven peg. Dale chambered the rifle for the 30-30 Improved, a blown-out case with sharp shoulder for better case life and handloading ease. Basic 30-30 loads were used.

The 94 stood in the middle of my shooting world. On the one end, there were my muzzle-loaders. In the middle the 30-30. And on the other end, the fast-stepping numbers, such as my 257 Weatherby Magnum. Low on recoil and high on efficient harvesting of game, the 30-30 worked hard for me, with pip-squeak loads for small game and turkeys, medium-velocity loads for longer range, and a 22-caliber, 55-grain bullet at 3,400 fps MV with factory Accelerator ammo for practice and pleasure shooting.

Sight-in was no problem. The 130-grain Speer bullet struck about 2.5 inches high at 100 yards for a zero of 200 yards. A 170-grain handload, without sight change, struck center at 150 yards (2,300 fps MV). The 190-grain bullet landed about three inches high at 100 and three inches low at 200 yards. The only negative aspect of 30-30 use was the preclusion of pointed projectiles, for a pointed bullet in the tubular magazine could set off the round in front of it through recoil. All the literature recommended only *single-loading* of pointed projectiles in the 94. I single-loaded the Speer 150-grain Mag-Tip bullet with excellent results. Following a recommendation in a *Rifle Magazine,* one, and only one, round was chambered in the magazine.

The 30-30 went where I went. Because it was handy, the 94 accounted for varmints, as well as deer, and I found the challenge of open-country hunting very rewarding where the 30-30 put considerable pronghorn antelope meat on our table.

Although I did not employ the 30-30 on game larger than deer, it has been a favorite of the Eskimo, who have killed many polar bears with 30-30s. Natives of Alaska dropped grizzlies with it, too. In Canada, grassroots hunters dropped not only bears but winter moose meat with the 30-30. However, we have many cartridges more correct for larger-than-deer hunting, and big-clawed bears especially are better handled with more than 30-30 authority.

John Kane, professional hunter/trapper of Colorado, has used his 94 30-30s to stop many stock-killing black bears and mountain lions, however. He finds the little rifle easy to pack, fast to shoot, and more than accurate enough for the work he does, with the exception of long-range coyote hunting, where he uses a flatter-shooting rifle. John has also used the 30-30 for considerable deer harvesting in Arizona and Colorado. So the 94 30-30, properly handled, can do a lot for today's shooter. The big

Professional hunter John Kane has used the 30-30 for many years as his mainstay bear and lion rifle. Here he is with a bear taken in Colorado with a Model 94 carbine in 30-30 caliber. John likes the factory load firing 170-grain bullets.

problem with the 94 is a tendency to snap-shoot with it rather than concentrate on careful aim. A fast second shot is nice. But it's only good following a carefully aimed first shot.

Learn to operate the 94 smoothly. Don't drop the buttstock from the shoulder after firing. Keep the rifle mounted and lever a new round home. Most of all, *aim.* If by snap-shooting you mean aiming rapidly, fine. If by snap-shooting, you mean upping the rifle and pointing it like a shotgun, forget it.

Over the years, the 94 has been an object of collection as well as shooting. Original Models 94 came in a variety of styles within the general design pattern. There were takedown versions, half-magazine models, long and short barrels, and dozens of sight variations. Custom-order 94s were also available. And there were many 94s which were called by other names. The Model 64 Deer Rifle, for example, was a 94 with a 24-inch round barrel and a semi-pistol grip stock. The Model 55 was a 94 with a button magazine of four-shot capacity.

There have also been many commemorative 94s over the years. The Winchester NRA Centennial Rifle honoring that organization is one, as is the Oliver Winchester rifle, which memorializes the man who helped launch the company. The Chief Crazy Horse commemorative rifle bears a medallion in the stock with logos of the United Sioux Tribes. The Model 94 Antlered Game commemorative rifle honors American deer, elk, moose, and caribou, species which have been harvested with 94s over the years.

The Model 94 has also been a movie star, appearing in hundreds of pictures. True, the similar Model 92 is often used in films because of more prevalent blank ammo for it; however, the 94 has seen action in many films, Westerns and otherwise. It was labeled the "cowboy rifle" because of its association with trail riders of Western films, but the Mounties have carried 94s in a number of movies and so have other policemen of the silver screen, and those in real life.

The modern Model 94 has a stronger action than the original model. This added strength allows for cartridges such as the 307 Winchester, a round similar to, but not as powerful as, the 308. The factory-loaded 307 propels a 150-grain bullet at about 2,600 fps MV, about like my 30-30 handload, and a 180-grain bullet at 2,375, which is greater in muzzle energy than any of my 30-30 handloads. The 375 Winchester round, which is similar to the 38-55 Winchester but *not* interchangeable with it, shoots a 200-grain bullet at 2,100 fps MV and a 250-grain bullet at 1,850.

The 356 Winchester, a smaller rimmed version of the 358 Winchester round, fires a 200-grain bullet at 2,350 fps MV and a 250-grain bullet at 2,025 fps. I'd harbor no feelings of inadequacy in using the latter for elk in the black timber, nor for any other species of North American game at close range. The interesting 7-30 Waters is another modern round for the updated Model 94. A slim 24-inch barrel with full-length magazine denotes the special 7-30 Waters rifle. The cartridge is closely based on a 7mm-30-30 wildcat created by Ken Waters and it fires a 120-grain bullet at an advertised velocity of 2,700 fps; however, my chronograph shows Federal ammo delivering 2,750 fps. The 7-30 offers light recoil and sufficient deer-dropping ballistics.

A little Model 94 Trapper with 16-inch barrel can be purchased in 45 Colt caliber (often erroneously called the 45 Long Colt round). This is a light, fast, handy short rifle for use in thick cover. Muzzle velocity with a 255-grain bullet is about 1,000 fps. The same style 94 comes in 30-30 caliber as well, and my tests show that factory ammo ballistics out of the 16-inch barrel drop by only 100 to 150 fps, approximately, with the short barrel.

One of the many Model 94 commemorative rifles is this Chief Crazy Horse model. It honors the Sioux Indian tribes. *(USRA)*

The 30-30 Model 94 was back in my gunrack. Along brush-filled creeks it cleanly harvested white-tailed deer. It was at home in a saddle scabbard in high timber country. It was ideal for toting around in everyday shooting situations which did not require long-range specialty rifles. Its middle-of-the-road characteristics provided a different challenge, one between the muzzle-loader and the far-shooting rifle.

In the high lonesome country some seasons back, my four-wheel-drive vehicle came to a halt. I set up camp. It was a simple but sound camp, a pitched tent, plenty of firewood, a rock bluff as a reflector for my fire, with water trickling down a nearby rock-strewn creek. The first afternoon was spent building the camp and laying in a supply of wood. In the morning, I checked the two deer tags in my shirt pocket, loaded my day pack with provisions, slipped it over the pack frame, and took off.

I slapped the stock of the 30-30. "When will I give you a name?" I asked. Many 94s got names. There was Little Eva, a Depression rifle that fed a family, Novia, a Mexican bear hunter's pet, and Turkey Track, a border-country carbine that brought venison to the *rancho* many times. I loaded

the rifle and struck out. Before the day ended, I had one of my two deer harvested and a brace of mountain grouse for my evening meal, and next day my second deer tag was filled. The birds were cleanly taken with 30-30 underloads and both deer dropped as if the earth had been pulled from beneath their feet. The 30-30 had done it again.

Most popular sporting rifle and round in the world, the 94/30-30 combo has earned its own niche in American shooting. So when you see one of those mundane, everyday, common 30-30s at your hunting campfire, don't stick your nose in the air. That rifle will deliver the goods in the hands of a shooter who knows how to handle it. Just remember that the hunter carrying that 94 has probably learned its ways, and through learning them has overcome the rifle's shortcomings and increased the rifle's advantages. He'll likely bring in the venison with the rifle before camp breaks.

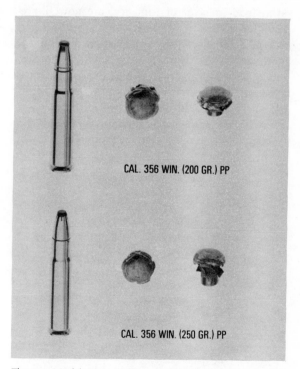

CAL. 356 WIN. (200 GR.) PP

CAL. 356 WIN. (250 GR.) PP

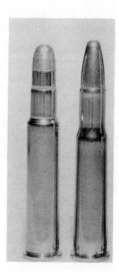

The author has found the 30-30 Improved, left, a good round. Rifles so chambered still allow the shooting of standard factory ammo in the Improved chamber. In fact, that's how the Improved round is made, by fireforming.

The new Model 94 Angle-Eject rifle has a stronger action than the old 94, hence some high-powered rounds are now chambered, such as this 356 Winchester cartridge using 200- and 250-grain bullets. *(USRA)*

15

The Hunting Rifleman

IN WINTER, bucks recently in rut, having forsaken food in favor of romance, are now ill-prepared for the cold and snow. Quite a number perish. Small game suffers the same cycle. Even in the Southwest, where winters are not bitter, the seasonal cycles are at work. While the grade-school notion is that the "balance of nature" is a straight line, in fact, it is an up-down world of feast and famine. Most small-game populations rise and fall by large numbers. One year the cottontails may be

The cottontail is a rifleman's harvest. Here, Gene Thompson collected a rabbit with the author's Hatfield 36-caliber Squirrel Rifle (flintlock). Most riflemen use the 22 rimfire for rabbits, but a frontloader works well too.

thicker than summer moths round a nighttime lantern. And the next seeing even a few bunnies could prove a problem.

Hunting has little to no effect on many small-game and upland-bird populations as long as it's done in the proper time frame and within the rules and regulations of bag limits. As for big game, most herd animals can withstand an annual decrease of 40 percent because births will replenish that number annually. In other words, a 40-percent cutback of a deer herd each year will usually result in stability of the herd numbers. Naturally, that 40 percent includes normal attrition, so game departments try to set tag limits to include all aspects of population dynamics. Allow a deer herd to go unharvested and, though it may flourish for a time, it will most likely crash one day, for the animals will deplete their own food supply, and once that forage is gone, few wild creatures survive.

And so there is the annual hunting season. It is a harvest. Nothing more, nothing less. It is the use of a renewable resource and is much like crop management. Some of the animals are taken and used for table fare. And of course some of the population is left behind for procreation of the species. Hunting rules and regulations are predicated on biological study. The right times for harvest are selected. And the right bag limits. These regulations are devised by biologists. Game managers are not infallible. But they generally do know what they are doing.

We hunt with shotguns also, of course. Upland birds are most often bagged with the scattergun.

The little Thompson/Center Cherokee rifle is a good muzzle-loader for rabbit and squirrel hunting. *(Thompson/Center)*

Waterfowl is a shotgun harvest. Sometimes cottontails are brought to bag with the smoothbore, too, and a charge of shot, as are wild turkeys. The handgun has made great strides in the world of hunting as well. Large-bore sidearms of very good power have been used to harvest just about every type of small and big game we have. Even Tembo, the mighty elephant, has been dropped with the one-hand gun, revolvers with plenty of potency and strongly constructed bullets. But most big-game hunting, a great deal of small-game hunting, and even a bit of bird hunting are accomplished with the rifle.

SMALL GAME

The Cottontail Rabbit

The cottontail is ubiquitous. It is the number-one small-game animal in North America, and is harvested by riflemen just about everywhere on the continent. Where the cottontail is not prevalent, one of his cousins usually is. I hunted cottontail rabbits around Fairbanks, Alaska. And even farther north, the snowshoe rabbit was a source of high-protein food which we enjoyed. If a hunter will study the game laws of his state, he will usually find some form of edible rabbit available.

Most of all, I like to hunt the cottontail or one of his equally edible cousins with a rifle. The cottontail, including the "brush rabbit," or pygmy rabbit, or whatever species may be in your area, often has a burrow or den. Even in the desert regions, this rabbit may dart into a cholla clump or other "housing" unit. The snowshoe, which is a hare and not a rabbit, though the distinction for our purposes is not important, may use a "form," a kind of shelter, but where I've hunted these hares—call them rab-

bits if you like—they depended on a fleet dart for cover as an evasive tactic.

Rabbits are prevalent on farms and ranches, as well as in wilderness settings. And a hunter finds his quarry by searching out sign in the form of droppings. A close look at low browse plants may also reveal a lot of cutting back, nipping off of leaves and even stems, evidence of rabbits at work. And in winter, there may be actual trails in the snow cut by rabbits going to feeding areas. I've even *trailed* rabbits in fresh snow. And I have used binoculars to locate rabbits sitting by their dens.

Mostly, rabbits are taken by slow-pacing an area. When I lived in Yuma, Arizona, we bagged a lot of bunnies by padding along the dusty roads of a canal bank, hoping to spot a rabbit before it took off for its burrow. Along fence lines, in brush piles, wood-

Bob Hirsch, Arizona outdoor writer, poses with a tree squirrel bagged on the San Carlos Apache Indian Reservation in Arizona.

piles, and even junkpiles, rabbits like to hang out. They may use an old pipe for a quick burrow hideout, too. In early morning and later afternoon, the rabbits may be feeding and away from the burrow, making them easier to locate. Ideally, the rifle shot will be taken at close range, and at a stationary target. But running rabbits can be brought to bag, too.

The Rifles

The high-velocity precision air rifle of excellent accuracy is more than adequate for cottontails. These rifles offer plenty of penetration for both head and chest shots, but the former is preferred. I don't think the air rifle is right for running shots. If the pellet does not strike the vitals, the rabbit might get away. Stick to sitting shots for air-power rabbit hunting.

Where I live, the 22 Short hollow-point is just about perfect among the 22-rimfire loads. Most of my shots are close, in the 20-yard range, and that quiet little Short does perfect work. A chest strike with the 22 Short hollow-point is also effective for close range.

Of course, some rifles won't handle the 22 Short. Then the Long Rifle is put into play. I have such rifles, one an old Targeteer. I use solid bullets of standard velocity and go for head shots with this rifle. If running shots are the rule, use the 22 Long Rifle hollow-point or one of the hyper-velocity, 22-rimfire loads for added impact if you think the bullet might miss the vitals. These hollow-point bullets do destroy meat. I use them seldom, much preferring the smaller hollow-point of the Short, which offers sufficient impact with well-placed bullets. But locales differ. If your rabbits are usually on the run, consider the Long Rifle hollow-point.

Although there's no doubt that the 22 rimfire is the king for riflemen cottontail hunters, you'll never know how enjoyable it is to bag a limit of bunnies with a muzzle-loader until you try it. One of my favorite cottontail rifles is a flintlock Hatfield in 36 caliber. Actually, 32 caliber is enough, but not all squirrel rifles are offered in 32 caliber. You may have to settle for 36. Don't worry about using a lot of powder unless your rabbits are on the run. A 32 using a mere 10 grains of FFFg will drop a rabbit, and a 36 with 15 or 20 grains of the same powder will do likewise. But if running shots are the rule, speed the ball up for higher impact in case the vitals are missed.

Food

All kinds of good dishes can be made with cottontail or snowshoe meat. A simple one is fried rabbit. I field-dress my bunnies within moments of the harvest, placing the carcass in a plastic bag after it has cooled and then into my game bag. At home, the meat is sectioned. Then it is marinated overnight in a mixture of milk, eggs, paprika, garlic powder, and pepper. Use only enough of the milk to cover and a single egg will do for a couple of rabbits, maybe up to four depending on size.

Put a couple of cups of flour into a small paper bag, such as a brown lunch bag. Drop the meat, which has soaked in the marinade, into the bag and shake. This coats the pieces. Then fry in your skillet until golden brown. Medium heat is best. Delicious. And good for you. Rabbit meat is a high protein source. My book, *The Complete Guide to Game Care and Cookery,* goes into the details of a vinegar-water soak to insure perfectly clean and white rabbit meat, this prior to marination. And should you run into some older, tougher rabbits, a fifteen-minute workout in a pressure cooker will tenderize the meat.

The Squirrel

Nothing can compete with the rabbit in numbers. But the tree squirrel is the number-two small-game animal in the land. The squirrel has managed to thrive where man has left a bit of habitat for him. Timber cutting can remove his home, and as the winter goes, so goes the squirrel population in many regions. There are five major groups of squirrels in America: fox, gray, red, flying squirrel, and tassel eared. Arizona has the greatest variety of tree squirrels—three races of tassel eared, four of fox, and two of red.

The squirrel is mostly solitary, except for mating season. Usually silent, except for the chattering alarm call, the squirrel goes about his business by day. He stores but little food and does not hibernate in winter. Most active in the morning, the bushytail likes good weather. Rain and wind drive him indoors. Good hearing and sight make the squirrel a wary customer. He can be hunted, however, by walking the woods at a modest pace, looking for squirrels mostly on the ground.

If a squirrel is sighted, the hunter hurries after it. The bushytail will scurry up a tree. Partners can work around the tree trying to spot the squirrel on high. Binoculars are not only useful, but practically essential where I hunt. The trees are tall and full-limbed and a little squirrel among that much cover is not easy to find. Binoculars isolate and magnify bits of the treetops until the squirrel is located, if ever he is. While I do very little shooting at running rabbits, I do no shooting at all at running squirrels.

The Rifles

The best rifle for squirrel shooting is the rifle which allows the hunter to place his bullet in a very small target at modest range. If I had to select one and only one rifle for my own squirrel hunting, it would have to be a 22 rimfire, preferably scoped. The 22 Short hollow-point has worked well for me, but most squirrel hunters like the Long Rifle, especially in the hollow-point version. Squirrels can be tough, and if the head shot is missed, the hollow-point Long Rifle round will do a bit better job than the solid bullet. The only shot I try for is the head, however. Usually, it's head shot or miss on my squirrels.

A good shot with a scoped air rifle of high velocity and super accuracy can take tree squirrels regularly. But the pellet is easily deflected and a mere leaf may send it off target. The air rifle, good as it is today, is not going to beat the 22 rimfire for squirreling. However, there are, no doubt, certain areas and conditions which offer excellent air-rifle squirrel hunting. The muzzle-loaders are great for bushytails. Use the same rifle you would carry for rabbits.

Food

Squirrel stew is famous fare in many parts of the country, but the bushytail can also be fried. Get the hide off quickly. It's tough work if you wait. At home, fill a pan with cold water, drop in a tablespoon of salt and a fourth cup of vinegar and soak the squirrel meat a couple of hours, rinsing in cold water and patting the meat dry with a paper towel. Then hot-fry some salt pork cubes in a little lard. Remove the cubes. Flour the squirrel pieces in a brown paper sack, mixing some onion salt, thyme, and pepper with the flour. Brown the floured squirrel parts nicely in the rendered grease from the salt pork. Use a pressure cooker to cut cooking time. Drop the fried squirrel into the pressure cooker, just covering with water and two cans of broth, either beef or chicken. Ladle in a couple of tablespoons of the salk pork drippings. Strain this liquid

if it is loaded with bits of cooked flour from the squirrel meat. Cook for twenty minutes in the pressure cooker.

Let the pressure cooker cool and open it. Add a half cup of dry Sherry, along with a fistful of freshly chopped parsley. Let it cook again for ten minutes. Cool and open the pressure cooker. Now you can add the vegetables you like—include carrots, diced potatoes, mushrooms, even green beans. Pressure-cook again for about four minutes. You have a good squirrel stew and it wasn't that much trouble.

There are other small-game animals, such as the armadillo, raccoon, opposum, muskrat, and beaver. But the mainstay game animals of the small-game class are the rabbit and the squirrel. The other species of this set are more esoteric and not as well distributed. They fall outside of our scope, but most of them are indeed a rifleman's harvest, and they are legitimately hunted in many locales.

Mountain Grouse

The Western states, northwestern Canada, reaches of Alaska, and many other areas hold bird populations which are legal fare for the rifleman. I have grown to enjoy such hunting and its rewarding table fare, but most outdoorsmen will seldom encounter these delicious edibles. Often, they are taken incidental to big game along the big-game trails of the high mountains. Just remember that the rifle scope sight is mounted above the bore. We usually think of holding low at close targets because the bullet is on the rise when it leaves the muzzle, since the muzzle is pointed upward to take advantage of the parabola of the bullet. But these grouse may be taken at only a few *feet*. Then, the idea is to hold the crosswire a bit above the head for a head shot. I've gotten my grouse by simple walking and looking, especially at dawn or dusk.

When I hunt mountain grouse as a main harvest, I prefer a 22-rimfire rifle or an air rifle. Either will drop the grouse nicely. A solid bullet is used in the 22 rimfire. Should the bullet hit body instead of head, the meat will not be so spoiled as it is with a hollow-point strike. These grouse are prepared in various ways. Use the marinade mentioned for rabbit, for example, and flour-coat the meat. I bone the breast meat out with a fish fillet knife and wash it. The fillets fry up golden brown. I've also eaten the birds on the spit, done over the coals of a campfire, lacing them with condiments and basting with butter to keep the meat from going dry.

The wild turkey is a rifleman's prime game, and a potential feast for the table as well.

The Wild Turkey

A challenge with any firearm is the wild turkey, not because he is especially intelligent—birds are not geniuses—but because he is very wary, has keen senses, and, of course, lives where he can hide extremely well. The wild turkey is that proverbial needle in a haystack. But the wild turkey is the largest of our game birds and in many ways is considered big game. He is definitely rifle-worthy and I seldom use other than the long arm to bag this bird.

There are quite a number of wild turkeys in America and the number is growing. The bird has been introduced in many areas and reestablished where he was rousted from his home. Texas boasts something like 400,000 birds, Alabama 300,000, Mississippi 80,000, Arkansas 20,000, Wyoming about 17,000, and roughly the same for Arizona. Other states have huntable numbers, too. There are many ways of hunting this magnificent bird from still-hunting (which means slowly moving through the woods, not staying still) to stumpsitting, which does mean staying still, on stand, to gaining high vantage points and actually looking for the birds through binoculars. Where I hunt, the latter works

fairly well, for the birds weave in and out along the stream bottomlands like a needle pulling thread behind it.

Look for sign; turkeys leave plenty. Big tracks decorate the sandy places or muddy water edges. J-shaped droppings note the male, while amorphous blobs denote the female bird. A feather or two on the trail is a telltale sign and sometimes a hunter will find a roosting tree used by the birds. And there are dusting areas, roundish places in the ground where the birds have been rubbing. You can call them, too. This works best in springtime when the mating season is in full swing.

The Rifles

In the West, the rifle is often the same big-game tool used for deer or even elk. This means that other than head shots are out, for a solid smack with a 270 Winchester will certainly ruin the meat of this tasty bird. The handloader can prepare squibs (underloads) for wild turkeys, loads which shoot low-velocity bullets that won't spoil meat too badly. Still, the head/neck shot is preferred, and a very difficult shot it is. I am against the use of the big-game rifle for wild turkey hunting, even though it is legal in many areas and accepted practice.

Perhaps some of the older, now obsolete, rounds and rifles were really the best turkey-hunting medicine. The 25-rimfire to 32-rimfire class pushed bullets of 80 to 100 grains at very modest velocity. In most settings, these rounds were quite right for the wild turkey—good bullet weight, but not explosive. The 25-20 and 32-20 were often called upon to harvest the turks, too, and they could be all right with the low-velocity load. Today, the cartridge often called upon for wild turkey harvesting is the 22 Winchester Rimfire Magnum, a lot more punch than a 22 Long Rifle, but without quite the explosiveness of the faster rounds, such as the 22 Hornet, for example.

Since the 22 WMR is offered with a full-metal-jacket bullet, and since that bullet is legal in some areas (check your local game laws before using the FMJ), the 22 WMR stands tall as a turkey taker. I have harvested most of my birds with a black-powder rifle, usually in the 36-caliber piece, but also 32. Either will drop these birds swiftly, neatly, and without too much blowup. Any round balls in the 32 through 38 class will do, actually. But with the 32 and 36, load up to 1,800 fps or so. The wild turkey is tough. While you do not want to waste the meat, neither do you want to wound a bird.

Aim for the head if you are good enough, and if the shot presents itself. With the 32 and 36 ball, I generally take the bird in the pinion area, where the wing joins the body. This hit does not spoil much meat, and it does put the bird down quickly. Birds going straight away can be dropped with a low hit without taking breast meat out. But do quickly get up to the fallen bird and administer the coup de grace if the low back hit does not put the bird away instantly.

Food

Cook the wild turkey as you would a domestic bird, but with a couple of very important differences. Spices are the same. Cooking time may be several hours. And forget higher temperatures. Run the oven at 250° F and keep the bird in thirty minutes per pound. The meat should be falling off the bone when the turkey is done correctly. Remember that the wild bird is not as fatty as the pen-raised product. I suggest a covered pan, using aluminum foil to insure that the steam is kept in on the meat. Cooking bags are also very good. Add moisture by dropping in two cans of broth, either beef or chicken, along with a half cup of Sherry, any kind.

JAVELINA

In a class by itself, this small wild pig or peccary lives in parts of Arizona, Texas, New Mexico and Mexico. A musk hog, the javelina field dresses at 30 to 40 pounds, generally. It is hunted on a permit basis in Arizona and New Mexico, with more open hunting allowed in Texas and Mexico. In Arizona, the Indian reservations offer javelina hunts separate from those in the rest of the state. Therefore, it is possible, on a permit basis, to harvest more than one animal annually in that state.

The pig roots about and makes excavations in the soil. His sign is easy to spot. He also bites hunks out of cacti of various types, including the prickly pear, perhaps his favorite food. Rooting wild onions and other tubers, chewing up plants, and in general leaving notice of his feeding habits, this little animal is often located through his gastronomic calling cards. I have found, by far, the most harvests by looking for sign and then using the binoculars to locate the porkers. Search around water holes, of course. As with wild turkeys, a watering site can be a good starting point in eventually locating these

The javelina of the Southwest (collared peccary) is another rifleman's harvest. This one was taken on the San Carlos Apache Indian Reservation in Arizona on a hunt with Game Department Director Charles Aday. The author used his Storey Conversion Model 94 30-30.

desert ghosts. Then stalk in close and take your shot. These javelina see poorly, so you can get close if you watch the wind and insure that your boots don't stomp on anything that will scream out a message of your coming.

The Rifles

I have bagged these wild pigs with everything from the 222 Remington to big 30-caliber rifles used for the experience only. If I had to pick one rifle to hunt javelina, it would be the 30-30 lever-action. This rugged little rifle and more than adequate round are just right for javelina. Long shots are not necessary. Spot the hogs and then stalk in for one well-placed shot. A 30-30 with any reasonable load will drop a javelina with one shot. Some hunters use a 22 WMR on javelina. Up close, this is enough gun. Muzzle-loaders 40 caliber and up are fine, too.

Food

Not noted as the best table fare, part of the problem with javelina meat is the removal of the musk sac located on the animal's back. Hunters have been told for longer than I have been on the planet that you simply must hack this musk sac out for the meat to be fit to eat. Just about the opposite is true. When you cut the sac out, the musk can spread to the meat. Simply skin the animal. The sac will come off with the hide, *intact*. There is no mess, no musk, and a lot better chance for good meat this way. Skin soon and place the carcass in a game bag away from the hide.

A decent javelina meal is the simple roast. A whole haunch is the usual portion for a meal for five. Wash the meat. Place it in the roaster. Then splash on some Worcestershire sauce and soy sauce. Be generous. Sprinkle garlic powder on the meat next, along with a handful of ground oregano leaves. Plop a quart of water into the roaster and at least three or four beef bouillon cubes. Cook covered at only 225° F for four hours, then open up the roaster and reverse the meat so the other side can soak up some of the good broth. Keep the meat moist. Don't let the water cook off, for it will be a fine gravy soon. After turning the roast, drop a cup of Sherry or Port in the pan. Cover and cook a couple more hours. The slow cooking for a long while makes an already tender piece of meat even more tender. The meat, light in color and fine-grained, will be good if the musk was kept away from it.

DEER

The white-tailed deer is the most prevalent big-game trophy in America, and the mule deer is also heavily harvested all over the West. Deer are hunted in heavy brush and thick wood and also in the high mountains where a shot across a canyon may be the only shot a hunter will get. In some parts of the country, deer are hunted from a stand. The hunter simply takes a good spot, sometimes by a trail or natural pass, and he plants his posterior there and stays still, waiting for a buck to saunter by.

The drive is very successful in some places, whereby hunters are again posted at strategic spots while other sportsmen beat the brush in an effort to push deer toward those in wait. Without this method, some areas would see a poor harvest, for the hunter alone on foot would have little chance of getting a clear shot. Sometimes still-hunting pushes a buck out of its lair and a running shot is the only shot. Other times, the still-hunter will spot a buck in the distance, allowing for a closeup stalk with wind in the face and boots quietly picking out the places on the trail devoid of twigs and other noisy giveaways.

Most of my deer hunting has been in the West where we have both white-tailed deer and mule deer. The white-tails generally prefer the riverbottoms and creek bottoms, where there is plenty of growth. The mule deer are prevalent in the open terrain, and way up in the forest as well. I've taken mule deer on barren deserts, on seemingly more barren badlands, along high trails in the mountain where sheep were only a short distance above, and in various other settings.

Mostly, I've gotten my bucks as I've gotten my javelina: through a lot of high-lookout glasswork. The rules of good glassing are rather simple: Get a good glass to begin with, one of top quality and high definition, such as the B&L Elite I carry, expensive, but cheap in the long run when hunting trips cost a lot and the hunter wants to harvest his quarry. Glass from a rest. Don't stand up the way most posed photographs show, the binoculars pinched in hand like a little opera glass. Get steady. You'll see a lot more that way.

And then don't look for a deer. Look for a part of a deer. I have seen many mule deer by locating the white rump patch in the distance. And I have found white-tails, especially the clever Coues deer of Arizona, by locating no more than a glint of an eye or the bony shine of an antler tip. Sometimes you will spot a deer, big and sassy, feeding, usually, on an early morning or late evening pasture, but take pains with the binoculars. It is a fine tool for location of game, but don't use it haphazardly.

The Rifle

For brush and woods hunting I'd as soon tote a simple 30-30 as anything else, but I practice with my 30-30 and I feel comfortable with it. If a sportsman has little practice time, he's best off with a rifle like the 30-30, 307 Winchester, 35 Remington—any of these, but with a low-power scope. Many rifles of these calibers wear scopes just fine. A 2 ×–7 × is sometimes selected by brush hunters. Then the 2 × setting can be used for the up-close work, but if a buck is spotted across a meadow, the higher magnification can pull the picture in for a clear view.

Out West, or wherever the shots tend to be a bit long, certainly more than 100 yards and usually in the 200-yard-plus range, the bolt-action rifle has achieved highest status. Any of the high-intensity, long-range rounds will serve for deer in these rifles. But a big high-mountain mule deer can indeed be *very* large. While the 6mm family will most definitely take these deer at modest ranges, and while the 25s are equally successful, if not more successful here, I think the power of the 7 × 57 and up is more correct for those across-the-canyon shots.

One of my hunting friends has turned to the 7mm Remington Magnum for his serious long-range mule deer hunting in high country. He's taken a large number of very big bucks with various calibers and he always returns to the Big 7 as a surefire meatmaker at long range. He uses bullets of 160 grains' weight shoved out at about 3,100 to 3,150 fps MV with H-870 powder, a favorite load of mine also. When this bullet connects "over yonder," the buck usually folds instantly. The 270 Winchester is very popular for mule deer in the mountains, as is the 30-06 Springfield. I have always been a 270 fan. You can't go wrong with one and it has ample power for deer hunting. That it is better than the 30-06, however, is not accurate, not in terms of delivered power, even at longer ranges. My handloads push a 130-grain bullet at 3,100 fps MV from the 270 and a 165-grain bullet at a flat 3,000 fps MV from the 30-06. At 300 yards from the muzzle, the 270 has about 1,600 foot-pounds of energy remaining. But the 30-06 has about 1,950 foot-pounds remaining at 300 yards, with the above starting velocity and the 165-grain bullet. These are facts taken from the Skyscreens of the Oehler chronograph actually set up at 300 yards.

Deer are also fair game for the muzzle-loader, of course, and I've taken many with mine. My favorite deer-hunting frontloader is a 54 caliber firing the patched round ball, but I've harvested bucks with 50-caliber ball, too. And there is nothing wrong with conicals either. Anything in the 50 to 54 class seems to me quite adequate for deer. But get close. That 30-06 load spoken of above has more energy at 300 yards than some pretty hefty 50- and 54-caliber muzzle-loaders at 50 yards.

Food

You can do anything with a good venison steak that you can do with a good beefsteak, even cook it over coals, provided that you keep the meat from drying out by basting with butter as it broils. Don't overcook. That tends to toughen the meat. Low in cholesterol, game meat is recommended by some doctors whose patients should refrain from eating too much fat. A deer will be fat in the fall, but the meat is not marbled. The fat does not run throughout the muscle of the animal. Field care is vital to venison, as it is to all meat. Get the buck skinned soon, cooled, kept cool, and clean at all times.

Slice the deer steaks a bit thinner than you might your favorite beef cuts, maybe up to a half-inch thick. Pound the meat a little bit with a meat hammer, mostly to shape it. I've yet to run into much tough venison and we harvest quite a number of deer annually, my family of five hunters having at least ten tags. Sprinkle lemon and pepper condiment and a trace of garlic powder over the steaks and then quick-fry them in half lard, half margarine, or in rendered beef fat. This little bit of fat won't bother the cholesterol watchers. Blot the cooked meat on paper towels until the juices cease to flow freely.

BLACK BEAR

I like the black bear. His meat is good when properly prepared and he is an awful lot of animal. The black bear is often classed as a clown. Maybe so, but blackies have killed men. A matchup of black bear against a sumo wrestler would be like a fight between a pit bull and a poodle, with the sumo wrestler being the poodle. Never underestimate a black bear as a harvestable game animal.

Most blackies are taken incidentally by deer and

elk hunters. However, those who wish to hunt the black bear with still-hunting methods may certainly do so. I have taken a couple of black bear by still-hunting. But odds are against the hunter using this method. Bears are often hunted with dogs and horses or over baits. Some people think both ways are unsporting. I am not going to philosophize on the matter; however, keeping up with a pack of dogs in the mountains takes strength and stamina. Tree limbs are spiteful arms trying to tear the rider from his horse or rip his eyes. Often, the bear is never even seen, in spite of it being treed by the dogs. As for baits, that is another matter of opinion. Bait a bear and you may be deemed an unfair hunter. Set out decoys for ducks (bait) and you are not violating any code.

Nancy Fadala got this big antelope buck in Wyoming, where she used her Frank Wells custom rifle in caliber 6mm-222 and an 80-grain Speer bullet.

The Rifle

For the few hunters who will take to the bear country in the spring of the year, or even in the fall, and who may try for bruins across canyons, the rounds spoken of for long-range mountain mule deer hunting apply, including the 270 and 30-06. The horseman following dogs needs no more than a 30-30 to get the job done. In fact, many professional bear hunters have relied on this caliber. Hunting in brush/woods where shots are close, even the still-hunter may rely on the 30-30, a 35 Remington, or 375 Winchester—any of these mediums.

Food

Roast black bear as you would the javelina. Bear meat should be cooked all the way through, and the slow-roast javelina recipe is a good one for black bear meat. Also, though bear fat is prevalent on an animal, and often rendered as some of the finest cooking grease there is, the meat is not as heavily marbled as beef and the cook should insure that the roast remains moist as it cooks slowly.

ANTELOPE ON THE PLAINS

The pronghorn antelope is a major game animal in parts of the West. Wyoming is the number-one pronghorn state, and it is not unlikely for 50,000, 60,000, or even more annual tags to be issued. Antelope are hunted primarily by covering the country while glassing frequently. Spotting scopes are used to sort out the really nice trophy bucks from the standard animals. And, of course, a stalk follows the finding. Stalks on the open spaces are not always that easy, but can usually be managed if the hunter will use the lay of the land to his advantage. Antelope can, as one old hunter put it, spot you at a distance of a mile or two and count the cartridges in your belt loop. They can see amazingly well, so a stalk means staying out of sight.

Remember that an antelope changes character toward the latter part of the day. A very jumpy buck that could not be approached closer than 400 yards at noon may provide a muzzle-loader shot at dusk. And these prairie goats like their food and water. They feed much of the day and a watering hole is usually not too far from their favorite haunts. The hunter should stick it out all day, taking a lunch with him rather than returning to camp at noon. While deer hunting is generally very slow in midday, the feeding and watering antelope are still up and about and may be spotted readily.

The Rifle

I hunt pronghorns with three distinct groups of rifles. When I want a real challenge, I go with a muzzle-loader, and my current 54 and an older 50 have brought me some fairly nice trophies. It takes more stalking, getting closer than you ever need to with a modern rifle. But hunting pronghorns with a smoke-belcher is great sport. The 50s and 54s in ball shooters are my favorites because they "carry up" better at longer ranges. At 125 yards, for instance, the ball from a 50 or 54 will go through the chest cavity of a 'lope, which is not that large, the ball often ending up under the hide on the off-side. Naturally, the conical-shooters are also good in the

A dweller of the open spaces, the antelope is generally dropped at longer range than deer or other big game. This nice buck was stalked for a close camera shot, however, by using the lay of the land to cover the approach of the cameraman.

field. I've seen a 45-caliber Whitworth do the job on the plains.

My second group is led by the 30-30, a middle-of-the-road approach. My custom 30-30 and I have partnered on the plains many times and I feel very confident in a strike if I can close to within 200 yards, even 225 yards or so of a buck. And the third group is mastered by the real long-range rounds. My personal favorite is the 257 Weatherby Magnum with a handloaded bullet of 100 grains darting out at over 3,600 fps MV. But a whole range of rounds will also work well on the flats, including those of the 6mm clan, the 25s, such as the 250 Savage and 257 Roberts, and all the rest up to the big 30-caliber magnums. A cartridge of 30-06 or larger power is certainly not needed for such game, but these rounds do serve well anyway. A 30-06 can be handloaded with a 150-grain bullet at 3,100 fps, for example, making it quite workable in the flatlands. The 270 is also highly admired for antelope.

Food

Antelope meat is very fragile. In my book *Complete Guide to Game Care and Cookery,* I talk about aging. Do not age antelope meat. Get the hide off soon, and package the meat as soon as possible after it has cooled. Double wrapping is called for, as freezer gases tend to invade the delicate meat. I use a plastic wrap on the meat followed by a good grade of paper freezer wrap. Tasty antelope burger is made by spicing cubed meat with a light dose of paprika, pepper, and a trace of garlic powder, then grinding. Also dash a few splashes of Worcestershire and soy sauces on the meat. Mix thoroughly with 10 to 15 percent beef fat, fresh from the butcher, and grind. The meat is good for broiling over coals.

Another good recipe calls for larding. This simply means poking holes deeply into a large roast and inserting fat. I use a fish fillet knife to make the holes. Into these long channels, slices of fresh beef fat are pushed. Season to taste, as with pepper, paprika, garlic salt, onion salt, and herbs and spices you would normally use on a beef roast. Then install this big hunk of larded meat over the coals, especially if you happen to have an electric rotisserie. Cook about medium. Don't overcook. The beef fat keeps the meat moist and adds that familiar flavor. This recipe delivers a product much like the standing rib beef roast.

SHEEP AND GOATS

Both of these species are hunted on a lottery basis in most areas and the average hunter will never find himself in the high country after either one. Furthermore, a hunter who finally does draw a tag for either is well advised to hire a professional guide. The cost may be significant before the ram or billy is taken back to camp, but trying to hunt these high-mountain dwellers on a shoestring can be risky in more ways than one.

As for rifles, any of the 270/30-06 class will work out well. The 7mm Remington Magnum through the 300 Weatherby Magnum are also quite fine for these animals. Sometimes shooting is from a great distance, sometimes not. The mountain men of the Far West ate plenty of sheep meat and they had only muzzle-loaders to harvest them with. Of course, the sheep were also in greater number in

Largest of the deer family is the moose, of which there are three types in North America, the Shiras (smallest), the Canadian, and the very large Alaska-Yukon moose.

those days. The once-in-a-lifetime sheep hunter usually carries a long-range rifle, scope-sighted and carefully sighted-in. Sheep have also been taken in recent times with the bow and arrow, muzzle-loader, and handgun. If you have the time and faith in your ability, all of these tools will work well.

Goat is considered tough and stringy by some. I have tried it and while it was not bad, it is not my favorite. The sheep, on the other hand, is a treat, especially the ribs cooked over coals.

LARGER THAN DEER— ELK AND MOOSE

The elk is the more tenacious of the two, but the moose is larger. The moose is a very important game animal in various parts of the globe, and when I lived in Alaska, dropping a moose before the long winter set in was like winning a grocery store sweepstakes. Both of these animals require some pretty careful hunting, the elk because it thrives in wilderness areas, and the moose because of its size. You do not simply shoot either and pack it back to the car in an afternoon unless you have horsepower working for you, and I do mean a horse.

Successful elk hunters watch the weather. When the high country gets pasted by storms, these hunters head for favorite places where the migrating elk herds may be encountered. Often, these hunters are horsemen, but certainly not always. They do not shy away from rough country, for elk can negotiate a blowdown of thick timber the way a cat traverses its own backyard, and just as quietly, too. The elk hunter does not shy away from the roughest part of the mountain. He glasses across the slopes. Walks or rides his horse a lot. And he definitely watches the weather patterns.

The moose hunter who scouts the haunts of this huge deer before season, locating where the big boys are hanging out, can usually do well when the season opens. Moose are not terribly crafty, but despite their huge size, they can be difficult to locate in so vast an environment. So knowing that a moose is working the willows in a certain canyon before the season opens gives a hunter a good chance to relocate that animal.

The Rifle
Once upon a time a circus elephant had to be dispatched and the only tool handy was a gun

chambered for the 22-rimfire round. However, the elephant was killed with a well-placed missile from that rimfire. I tell this tale because rifles for elk and moose are somewhat the same way. If you get close enough, a 25-35 or even smaller round will drop either the elk or the moose with one well-placed shot. In fact, through the years, the 30-30 has taken plenty of both and can do so today in the hands of a good hunter who is also a cool shot.

But if I were to choose a rifle dedicated only to elk and moose hunting, and if I wanted a no-nonsense tool for harvesting these large fellows, the smallest I'd use would be the 270 Winchester. The 30-06, especially with good handloads of 165- to 180-grain bullets, the former at 3,000 fps MV, the latter at about 2,800, will drop moose and elk nicely, and a 300 Magnum is even better. A lot of hunters feel that the 338 Winchester is ideal for either animal. The old 348 Winchester, with at least the 200-grain bullet and preferably the 250-grain bullet, was considered superb on this size game.

Most Western hunters carry their deer rifles when they go after elk or moose, these being the 30-06 Springfield, 270 Winchester, and the 7mm Remington Magnum, with the 308 Winchester also well represented. A bullet from any of these, well placed in the chest cavity, will cleanly claim an elk or moose. I've taken elk with the 7mm Magnum, and also, from close range only, a 54-caliber muzzleloader. I have a special frontloader for elk, caliber 54, 1:34 rate of twist, heavy 1⅛-inch barrel (across the flats), firing the Buffalo Bullet Company 460-grain missile at more than 1,700 fps MV. It's muzzle energy is just short of 3,000 foot-pounds.

Food

Elk meat and moose meat are both delicious. The previously mentioned venison recipes work well with either meat. Roast moose or elk is fine. Elk or moose steaks are a treat, too. And don't forget larded roast over coals. Both also offer excellent burger meat. Use the recipe given under antelope above. Any recipe that calls for a cut of beef can be served up with a cut of elk or moose. I've eaten both and can't decide which is better.

DANGEROUS GAME

The American sportsman is not likely to encounter a lot of dangerous beasties roaming the woods and brushlands. To overly concern oneself about

the danger of wild animals in the outback is, then, fairly foolish. To consider all American game harmless is far more foolish. A very short time ago, a visitor to Yellowstone Park decided to lay hands on a buffalo (American bison more properly). He died for it. The buff simply looked up, took one quick dash with a horn, and killed the man. The bison is the largest of the four-footed animals in this country, bigger than a moose or a grizzly. A herd bull can go as much as three thousand pounds on the hoof.

And a bison can outrun the fastest olympic track star who ever lived. In fact, the bison can also leap a six-foot fence without a run. I've seen this myself. There is very little bison hunting going on these days, though a few free-roaming animals are still legally encountered. However, I start with him because of so much misunderstanding. The bison is but one of the dangerous-to-man game animals walking around. A mountain lion grabbed a boy in British Columbia and tried to carry him off. A moose put a fellow in the hospital. So respect all game.

Although animals from deer to elk have taken after two-legged as well as four-legged hunters, there are only a couple of animals which we consider dangerous in North America from the standpoint of an out and out charge during the hunting season. A moose may come for you, as suggested, and a downed deer can kick you senseless. But a grizzly may actually charge and attack just because you have invaded his territory. Most of us will never see a grizzly in the wild, of course, and darn few of us will hunt one. But for those who do, the 338 Winchester, 350 Norma Magnum, and similar rounds do make sense. Polar bears have also caught and killed men.

Again, we should remember the circus elephant being killed by a 22 rimfire, for the grizzly has been dropped by many small arms. Furthermore, the careful shot with a repeater is more than a match for a bear. But just for the record, let's call the 338 and its cousins, the 8mm Remington Magnum, 350 Norma, and others, fairly proper grizzly medicine. A guide friend of mine who makes a good part of his living hunting coastal grizzlies uses a 375 H&H Magnum and other Alaskan guides have gone to a 458 for backup.

African game hunting is a bit different. It was the Indian hunter who said that when you set forth to hunt a rabbit be prepared to meet a tiger, and the rule applies in Africa as well. Actually, the 7mm

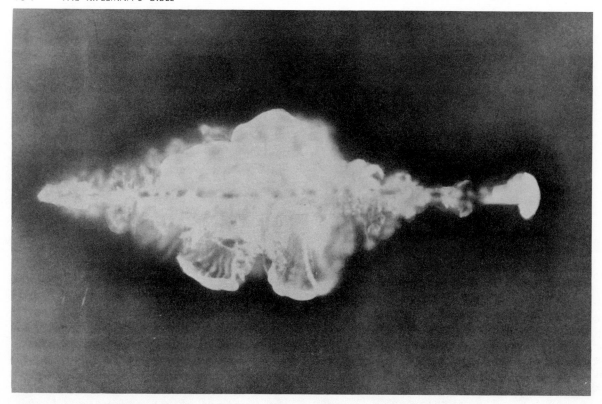

Wound channels vary with many factors, including the construction of the bullet and its arrival energy. This Sierra bullet demonstrates the great shock wave attending the high-velocity projectile. Note the "mushrooming" effect in the gelatin test block.

Magnum is ample for most of the game encountered in Africa, but I saw a Cape buffalo absorb seven shots from a 416 Rigby and 375 H&H Magnum before toppling and can attest that many of the African species are tough and willing to come at you without much provocation.

In Africa, the 375 H&H is considered a medium. Even the 416 Rigby with its 400-grain bullet is no powerhouse over there. The 458 Winchester has become very popular and well thought of for elephant, buffalo, and rhino when the latter can be hunted. Dangerous African game is hunted with big bores firing heavy bullets, usually at modest velocity. The professional hunters I met there had little use for high velocity without bullet weight, and the "solid," or full-metal-jacket bullet, is a standard on many dangerous beasts, certainly the rhino, buffalo, and elephant. The latter was deemed the most dangerous game in Africa by five of six professional hunters I asked. But all said the buffalo was a very

close second and the sixth man put the buff first, the elephant second.

While we may not encounter much dangerous game on our continent, it is still worthwhile to have a knowledge of ballistics for "stopping power." And it seems that where stopping power is sought, the larger, strongly constructed bullets are preferred over lesser ones at any speed. Penetration, of course, is vital here. And when you see a 400-grain 416 bullet of full-metal-jacket design turned into splinters on a cape buff you understand why true full-patch bullets of terrific strength are sought after.

Under the supervision of game biologists, seasons are set and limits to go with the seasons. The limits are realistically based on the laws of population dynamics, and no species is going to be "shot out" these days. Habitat loss remains the big threat. Remove the natural vegetation, cultivate the earth, and most homes for game are gone for good. Fly

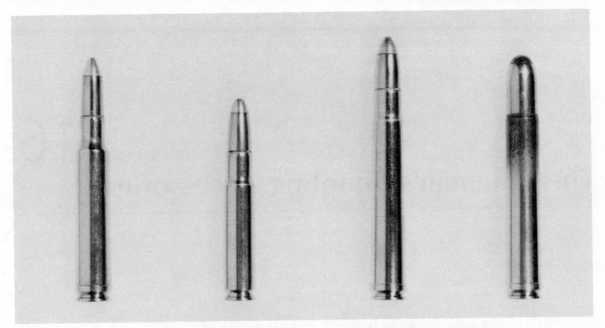

A few cartridges considered useful on larger-than-deer game are, from the left, the 338 Winchester Magnum, the 358 Winchester, the 375 H&H, and the 458 Winchester. The 338 has been widely used in Alaska for big bears and moose. The 358 is more at home in timber country on elk and similar game at medium range, and is also used for deer harvesting. The 375 H&H is considered an "all-around" caliber in Africa and has been used by grizzly bear guides in Alaska. The big 458 Winchester is much used in Africa on game up to the size of elephants, but has also seen service in Alaska, where a few grizzly bear guides use them.

over the Wyoming-Nebraska border. In Wyoming, where alkali soil has curtailed much cultivation, antelope herds abound. In Nebraska you are more likely to encounter "herds" of wheat. But it's also nice to enjoy the other harvest, the wild harvest, game animals small to large, well managed in the field and well prepared for the table, cleanly dropped by riflemen who have studied not only their long arms, but also their hunting methods, honing both to razor sharpness.

16

The Rifleman's Shooting Accessories

SHOOTING without proper accessories is like digging a canal with a garden spade. You can do it, but it's certainly not going to be easy. Shooting accessories enhance safety, efficiency, marksmanship, and longevity of the rifle. Rifleman's tools range from the practical to the collectible. There are so many hundreds of incidental shooting items that an entire text could be devoted to them. Our scope is more focused.

THE SHOOTING BENCH

Sight-in from the prone position with a tightly rolled blanket beneath the forearm of the rifle is technically sound, as are other methods of securing the rifle. However, the major function of the benchrest is to remove as many human variables as possible, such as the unsteadying effects of heartbeat, breathing, and body tremor. A machine rest is practical under laboratory conditions, but most riflemen will not have access to such an elaborate system. Instead, two basic types of benchrest are used, stationary and portable. The stationary unit is, of course, the more stable. However, there are many excellent portable rests, such as Cabela's, which can be carried collapsed into the field and set up in moments.

The ideal benchrest offers sufficient support to fully steady the firearm, but it does much more. It is designed to accommodate the individual shooter. Seat height must allow his feet to rest firmly on the ground. The bench should suit both right-handed and left-handed riflemen, especially if it is a permanent unit at a public rifle range. The surface of the bench should be smooth, splinter-free, and strong enough to support the rifle, accessories, and the normal pressures exerted upon the bench during shooting.

Accessories for the shooting bench are sandbags or other forms of support upon which the fore end of the rifle is rested. There are also adjustable rests which serve the same purpose. The latter can be

The benchrest is a very important shooting accessory, allowing a more precise assessment of rifle accuracy and sight-in. *(Kenn Oberrecht)*

altered to suit the stature and shooting style of the individual rifleman. Often left out of the benchrest picture is sufficient support for the elbow. When firing a high-power rifle, the elbow of the shooting hand may be scraped over the surface of the bench, which is disconcerting. A pad under the elbow prevents injury and increases shooting stability.

All tenets of good shooting are observed at the bench, including body control and trigger squeeze. The shooter who has walked to the butts and back to the bench should wait until his breathing is under control before he attempts further grouping. The forearm of the rifle should be rested, not in the palm of the hand, nor on a hard object, but upon a stationary pad, such as the sandbag. Sight-in, resighting before the hunting season, checking the accuracy of a load, making a check of bullet trajectory by shooting at various ranges, rifle accuracy— all of these and more are accomplished from the rigidity of a solid benchrest. For these reasons, a proper benchrest is a must for the rifleman.

RIFLE BIPOD

The buffalo runners (hunters) of the last century knew very well that in order to consistently score hits at long range, some means of rifle rest was necessary. An offhand shot was not going to deliver hit after hit, even on the huge shaggies of the plains, not when the range was often 300 yards and farther. Even from the prone shooting position, human error was still as unpredictable as a wild bird. The famous crossed sticks of the baffalo runners came into being. The crossed sticks, with rifle resting at their juncture, pinched the fore end and controlled it. The lower ends of the sticks dug into the earth as legs, the legs of a bipod, as it were.

Today, the bipod has come of age. The now-famous Harris unit, such as the High Rest model, attaches to the forearm of the rifle. The unit collapses against the fore end of the stock, out of the way until needed, and then it snaps into play neatly, offering the shooter a rocksteady rest. In over twenty years of manufacturing, fewer than one out of one thousand Harris bipods have been returned to the factory. This brand of reliability has made the bipod a well-respected accessory for riflemen. Long-range varminting, big-game hunting in plains and mountains, or just plain shooting, the modern metallic version of the cross stick is a big aid in putting the bullet on the money.

TARGETS

Also essential accessories are the various targets riflemen shoot at. There are official targets for formal matches. These targets bear the exact dimensions required for a given event and set of rules. The sight-in target is different from these in that it is designed to help the shooter aim at a very specific bull's-eye which can be readily seen and concentrated upon. The sight-in target usually has a grid with one-inch squares so that the shooter can readily see how many inches off the desired point of aim the group has struck. Bull's-eye size and even shape may vary target to target, too. So do colors. Targ Dots, for example, are bright blaze orange stick-on bull's-eyes which are used as aiming points. An adhesive back allows the shooter to attach these dots on blank paper or over any target for a bright aiming point.

Targets vary with the need of the shooter. They also vary with the rifle. Targets for a 30-caliber, high-power rifle may be all wrong for a 22-rimfire rifle, for example. Air rifles require special targets, too, especially for 10-meter shooting, where the range is very close but the bull's-eye very small. Targets are not always paper. The metal cutouts of the *silueta* game come in various sizes, from the official units for formal big-bore matches to minia-

This is the Harris bipod, which may be adjusted in various ways and which offers excellent field-shooting stability to the rifle.

ture chickens, javelina, turkeys, and sheep for 22-rimfire and air-rifle shooting. There are also swinging targets, gongs, and other "animated" units, both commercial and homemade. Air-rifle and 22-rimfire shooting may be accomplished in close quarters with special shooting traps made for the purpose of capturing projectiles. The pellet trap, for example, allows safe indoor practice when set up properly.

THE SHOOTING BOX

My personal shooting box arrived when I took up the sport of muzzle-loading. I needed a container for the many tools and accessories which attend frontloader firing—cleaning hardware, extra powder, ball, caps, solvents, patches, and other paraphernalia. An old hinged box, made of wood with a sturdy top, came to the rescue. I soon found out that such a box was a boon to modern rifle shooting as well as to muzzle-loading. I purchased a wooden container from Winchester and turned that into my modern shooting box. The shooting box is a time-saver which prevents the frustration of having to look all over for needed supplies.

When I go shooting, I grab the intended rifle and ammo, the appropriate shooting box, muzzle-loader or modern, and head for the range. I know that when I reach my destination I will have targets, a screwdriver which fits the scope sight for adjustments, or the micrometer sight for the same purpose, another set of screwdrivers for the bolts and screws of the rifle itself, notebook and paper for jotting down shooting results, a set of allen wrenches, bore brushes, pull-through cleaning cable, breakdown cleaning rod, scissors, knife, and so forth.

THE BULLET BOX

Another useful accessory for the rifleman-hunter is the bullet box, which may range from a sophisticated compartmentalized unit to a simple cardboard container. The former is made of wood and different materials are installed in each compartment, such as clay, water balloons, wet newspapers, backed at the end by large department store catalogs in some instances. The cardboard version need be no more than a container filled with wet compacted newspapers or damp sawdust. Either style of box is used to trap fired bullets.

The rifleman can pretest the effect of his hunting bullets with such a box. A bullet that fragments in the box will normally come apart on game. A bullet which holds together in the box will normally remain intact on game. Reliability of such test boxes is high and the shooter can enter the big-game field

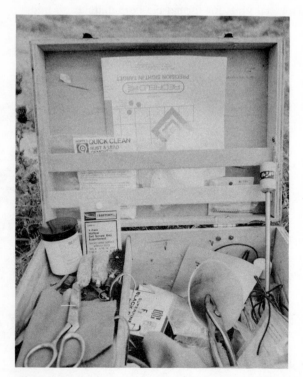

Anything from ammo to earplugs will fit neatly into a shooting box such as this one.

The cleaning kit offers a compact rifle-care package.

with a very good idea of bullet performance. In order to gain valid data from the bullet box, the rifleman must shoot from various ranges for various arrival velocities—or handload his ammo to the normal terminal velocities he's interested in testing for.

MAINTENANCE ACCESSORIES

Cleaning kits are a good purchase because they contain everything a shooter will need to keep his rifle maintained, from cleaning rod and bore brushes to solvents and protective chemicals. On the other hand, serious full-scale maintenance usually requires more than the basic cleaning kit. For example, I have a sturdy one-piece cleaning rod (not jointed) for home use which would be unwieldy on an outing. I have a pull-through cleaning cable for rifles, such as many lever-action models, which do not allow access to the breech for cleaning. A small jointed rod will always be found in my backpack on any shooting trip. This rod can be used to expel a stuck case, as well as clear the bore of fouling or dampness from foul weather.

Cleaning jags and tips should fit the bore just right. If oversize, the tip will not accommodate a sufficiently thick patch without getting stuck in the bore. If undersize, the tip may become damaged in the rifle bore, or even break off. Cleaning kits are offered in various calibers with proper-sized cleaning rods. Kits may be listed as 22 caliber or 30 caliber, or they may encompass more than one caliber size, such as 24–25 caliber. Even though the 22-caliber rod will fit all larger calibers, use the correct rod size for the caliber of your rifle.

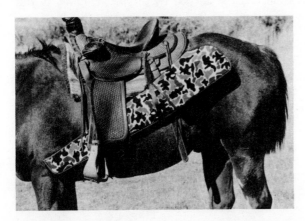

The Uncle Mike's nylon scabbard is a modern model at a modest price. *(Michaels of Oregon)*

For rifle cleanup at home, the one-piece, nonjointed cleaning rod is often the best choice. It's sturdy and will take more strain than most jointed rods. A one-piece rod will often allow the use of tighter patches without the rod bending or breaking. On the other hand, the jointed rod fits neatly into a kit or shooting box. I use both kinds, a one-piece rod for home rifle cleanup and a jointed one for travel and rifle range. Soft, clean rags are also a part of the maintenance kit, as are cleaning patches, either commercial or home-cut.

CHEMICALS FOR MAINTENANCE

There are dozens of modern chemicals used in rifle maintenance. Modern solvents do a wonderful job of reducing bore fouling to a softened mass that can be wiped from the bore with cleaning patches on the end of a rod. Shooters Choice, for example, is known to remove stubborn powder, lead, and bullet jacket fouling, as is Gold Medallion, another premium bore cleaner and conditioner. WD-40 and similar sprays help preserve rifle barrels, too. There are high-grade oils such as Accraguard and Accralube which wed with the metal for the same preserving purpose. And stock preservatives from oils to creams keep the wood in good order. Modern chemicals make cleanup and maintenance easy.

GUN CASES

A very important accessory for the rifleman is the gun case, which may be soft or hard. The soft case offers a lot of protection from scratches and abuse of the elements. If a rifle is always carried in a safe place in the vehicle, the soft case is very workable, taking up less space than the hard case. But if the rifle is going to ride in the back of a pickup truck, or in an airplane or train baggage compartment, the hard case is the only choice. Hard plastic cases are good and they are not expensive. Metal cases will take more of a beating, but they also cost more than plastic.

SCABBARDS

The saddle scabbard was widely used to pack the rifle on a horse, just as the pickup truck rack is used today. However, quite a number of modern riflemen know the value of the scabbard and a shooter can still buy various models, from the modern-style Uncle Mike's nylon unit to handmade leather types. Popularity of the snowmobile and ATV (all-terrain vehicle) has given the scabbard new reason for being, as has a new love affair with the mountain bicycle. You can ride a bicycle of this sort into some very out-of-the-way places and a scabbard is a good way to tote your rifle along.

The scabbard is also useful for camp protection of the rifle, allowing its quick retrieval without unzipping a soft case or unlatching a hard one. Also, horses are still used in hunting, especially out West where a number of sportsmen use the pony to carry them over the mountains. Fine-tooled leather scabbards are seen here, some of them beautifully handmade rifle protectors custom-built to fit a given rifle. The nylon scabbard is also increasingly popular on the side of a horse. It's very functional, even water-resistant.

THE GUN SAFE

The gun safe is a fortress against home theft of your rifles. Not to say that the professional burglar might not be able to crack a gun safe; he probably will be able to. However, an amateur is not going to easily invade the modern gun safe. Of course, there are many different models of varying sophistication and weight. Those of heavy-duty construction and advanced design are definitely going to thwart the thief who does not have safecracking tools with him.

THE SLING AND CARRYING STRAP

Except for my muzzle-loaders and a few 22 rifles, the bulk of my long arms wear a strap of some sort, mainly for ease in carrying, but also for stability in shooting. A sling is an adjustable strap attached to the rifle for aiming support. Target shooters slide an arm through their slings, and their scores immediately improve. Most of us use either the sling or strap less formally, rarely in the "military style." The carrying strap is wrapped around the left arm for a right-handed shooter. This process does not offer full-fledged military sling support, but I believe it helps in steadying the rifle. Such use of the carrying strap for shooting stability is called the "hasty sling" method.

This rifle is carried with sling attached to a pack frame hook. The rifle is out of the way, and the sling does not cut into the shoulder.

I prefer a one-inch strap to wider ones because on my outback treks I carry a pack frame. On the frame, I have installed a hook on the upper vertical strut. The rifle strap or sling attaches over this hook and the rifle is immediately out of my way, though I can still snatch it off the hook very quickly when I need to take a shot. The side of the pack frame is covered with sheepskin to protect the rifle stock from being scratched by the metal frame. A rifle strap is an essential part of the big-game long arm, be it full-fledged sling or simple carrying unit.

CARTRIDGE HOLDERS AND POUCHES

You can stuff your rifle cartridges into shirt or pants pockets, coat pockets, vest pockets, even packsack pockets, and none of these methods of toting shooting fodder is either wrong or outmoded. But an accessory I'd not think of being without is an ammo carrier, especially of the folding type. A round or two in a shirt pocket is all right, but I don't like the tinkling and jingling of metallic

An Uncle Mike's ammo pouch holds eight rounds of big-game ammunition in the field. Ammo is easy to get to and not likely to get lost.

belt. For more ammo, carry two carriers, one on each side. On long treks into the backwoods, extra ammo can be carried in the packsack.

OPTICS

A beginning shooter may fail to note that binoculars and scopes with good optics are essential accessories to help him fully appreciate this sport. First awareness may come when a rifle scope is attached to the firearm, giving longer potential range and a clearer sight picture. At the range, the rifleman grows tired of walking from bench to target and back. He buys a spotting scope. The high-power scope allows him to immediately assess the group on target—both in center-to-center excellence and placement—and to make adjustments from the bench.

In the field, binoculars can make all the difference between a successful outdoor adventure and a flop. Especially in open areas, mostly in the West, but also in the East, hunters often locate big-game

shooting materials as I trailwalk. There are **many** better ways to carry ammunition.

For example, the Uncle Mike's Sidekick Double Speedlock Pouch, though made for the revolver, works perfectly for the clips of my Ruger Model 77-22 rifle. Two of these double-pouched units will hold four 77-22 clips. That's forty rounds of 22 Long Rifle ammo. Another clip in the rifle gives ten more shots, so with the pouches and one loaded clip (empty chamber on rifle), I can tote a full fifty-box of 22-rimfire ammo on an outing. No reloading of clips is necessary for most sessions. Shoot. Switch clips. Shoot ten more times.

A folding ammo carrier on the belt is by far my favorite means of packing big-game rifle ammo. The little folding pouch does not pinch, remains out of the way until needed, holds at least eight big-game rounds (and up to ten, twelve, or more, depending upon cartridge and carrier size), is easy to reach, easy to extract rounds from, and fast-handling. The loop-style holder attaches to your pants

Dale Storey uses a B&L spotting scope, attached to a rifle stock to scan the distance.

animals which never would have been seen without the aid of the glasses. It's not a simple matter of peering through the binoculars, for a specific technique is necessary to really *find* game with these optical instruments. But with practice, it can be done, and it is done all the time.

The new lightweight, compact spotting scopes are also beneficial in the field, as well as on the shooting range. Backpacking hunters will find that these scopes, coupled with their ultralight tripods, are highly useful in big, open terrain where viewing across canyons is prevalent. This optical field aid is also a rifleman's friend in many other ways—enjoyment of animal watching, finding a hunter friend on the other hill, even locating a distant camp, road, or structure.

THE CHRONOGRAPH

No longer a device strictly for the shooting laboratory, the chronograph has entered the world of the everyday rifleman. Modest prices for superlative machines are now the rule. A chronograph tells a lot more than velocity. It indicates ammo quality as well, which is very important to handloader and factory-ammunition user alike. I have used a chronograph in building pet loads. All of my black-powder loads are chronograph-tested. I compared velocity with powder charge in the individual muzzleloader until the right balance was reached, ceasing to add fuel which gave more recoil and smoke, but not much more projectile speed.

Recently, using the Oehler Skyscreen system, I've been able to record remaining velocity data up to 300 yards from the muzzle of the rifle. I learned, for example, that loads in the 7mm Remington Magnum were delivering very high remaining energy at 300 yards from the muzzle. H-870 powder coupled with the Hornady 162-grain bullet allowed a remaining velocity of 2,640 fps at 300 yards in one test for an energy of 2,508 foot-pounds, more than some big-game rounds deliver at the muzzle.

The chronograph has also revealed other interesting facts. For a long time, I believed that the smashback of the bullet tip, due to the projectile hitting the atmosphere at the rifle's muzzle, probably took a very significant toll on downrange ballistics. I know from tests with full-metal-jacket bullets and bullets with very hard points, such as the Rem-

ington Bronze Point or Nosler Ballistic Tip, that bullet weight/caliber for bullet weight/caliber, the hard-points do deliver more remaining velocity than the soft-points. But the differences are not enough to worry about in the hunting field, for the soft-points of Spitzer or Spire profile *still* hold up extremely well over long range. They are not sufficiently blunted by the atmosphere to give them round-nose performance.

The chronograph can be purchased by the individual rifleman, or, at the very least, the shooting club (with cost being spread among the members). A public shooting range could set up a chronograph and charge a shooter for the privilege of chronographing his rifle, thereby paying for the machine in short order. There are very good chronographs offered in the $300 range, machines that give digital readout of highest recorded velocity, lowest recorded velocity, average recorded velocity, extreme spread, and standard deviation of the string.

BLACK-POWDER-SHOOTING ACCESSORIES

The Shooting Bag

Called a possibles bag by most shooters, this container is made, generally, but not always, to slip over the shoulder. It's often a leather outfit, and it

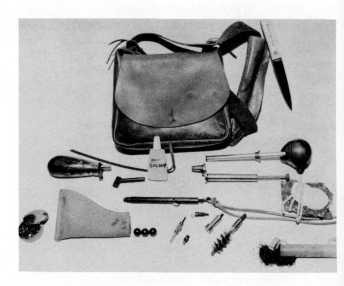

The black-powder shooter's pouch, known as a "possibles bag," can be filled with all the essentials necessary in field shooting.

can be plain or ornate depending on the shooter's wishes. I prefer to set up a shooting bag for each of my muzzle-loading rifles. Then I can grab a rifle and its appropriate shooting bag and head for the range or field knowing that I have everything necessary to fire that rifle. My own shooting bags contain everything from ball and powder to spare nipples, prelubed patches, various tools, capper, powder measure, powder flask (small one), cleaning solvent, and short starters.

The Possibles Bag

The possibles bag or sack is any container which includes a variety of items necessary to the black-powder shooter/hunter. These things may be tools of various types or extra clothing. The mountain man's possibles sack sometimes contained extra lead (galena) for round-ball manufacture, a bullet mold, spare wiping stick, tobacco, and so forth. The possibles bag is a relative to the shooting box mentioned above.

Powder Measure

Black powder may be loaded accurately in bulk measure by volume. This is why a simple powder measure is viable. An adjustable powder measure allows load alteration on the spot and is very popular with black-powder shooters today. However, the preset, nonadjustable measure is also excellent, generally sized to contain a load which has proved accurate in a given rifle. These measures are basically tubes with a ring soldered on the closed end. A leather thong through the ring allows easy carrying of the measure.

Powder Flask

I am inclined to carry a small powder flask in my shooting bag as my extra supply of black powder. For example, in the shooting bag that attends my favorite 54-caliber rifle, I have a tiny powder flask from which I pour charges into a nonadjustable powder measure. The flask holds sufficient powder for several recharges, plenty for hunting purposes. The powder is safe from moisture and spillage in the flask.

Speedloader

Every big-game hunter who carries a muzzle-loader should avail himself of some sort of speedloader, homemade or commercial. The commercial models, such as Butler Creek's, Winchester Sutler's, or Leding Loader, are well designed and well constructed. The speedloader gives a fast second shot. The unit contains a premeasured powder charge and the appropriate projectile and patch system. After the first shot is away, the rifleman puts the speedloader into action for that quick second shot. I make it a practice to load again after firing in the field, even when I know my first shot found its mark. Hold the muzzle of the rifle away from the face when reloading, of course, as is always advised.

Pan Primer

This is a small powder container which holds FFFFg black powder. A trickle of FFFFg is directed from this container directly into the pan of the flintlock rifle. The pan primer is perfect for concentrating the charge away from the touchhole and to prevent powder spillage.

Nipple Wrench

Whether for cleanup or checking for a clear channel from nipple vent to breech, a nipple wrench is indispensible for removal of the percussion rifle's nipple. Pliers and other pinching tools may damage nipples. Insure that the nipple wrench you have is the correct fit for the specific nipple size.

Wiping Stick/Loading Rod/Cleaning Rod

The modern wiping stick, once no more than a long ramrod, is now a loading/cleaning rod. The rod drives the projectile downmuzzle onto the powder charge in the breech. It also serves to hold a jag and a cleaning patch for in-between-shot bore wiping, as well as aftershooting cleanup. The tip of the rod accepts many tools, such as worms or screws which can extract a stuck patch or stuck ball. After seating a load downbore, the loading rod can be marked where it makes contact with the muzzle of the rifle. This mark should meet the muzzle at the same place for subsequent loadings. The mark acts as a guide, showing the shooter whether his rifle is loaded, unloaded, or perhaps short-started with a gap of air between missile and powder charge, an unwanted condition.

The Short Starter

Tests have shown that tightly fitted projectiles generally deliver greater accuracy than loosely fitted ones. In order to start a tight-ball/patch combination, however, a device is needed. That tool is the short starter, essentially a very short ramrod with a tiny stub projection and a longer rod, both incorporated on a single ball. The stub gets the projectile started into the muzzle and the longer rod section drives the missile a few inches into the bore, where the loading rod or ramrod can take over for full seating onto the powder charge.

Worms, Screws, and Jags

A simple but useful black-powder tool, the worm is a corkscrew-like tool which is used to extract a stuck patch from the bore of the muzzle-loader. Its sharp tines are twisted into the patch, capturing it for extraction. The screw is just that, what appears to be a wood screw without a head. The shank of the screw is threaded and this threaded section screws into the tip of the ramrod or loading rod. Then the rod, with screw in place, is pushed downbore to expel a stuck projectile. The screw digs deeply into the lead projectile, and a strong pull on the rod brings the stuck ball upbarrel. Jags are of many types and styles, but all do essentially the same work. They screw into the tip of the loading rod. The face of the jag is used to force the missile downbore. And the jag also holds a cleaning patch tightly, delivering it downbore and back up to the muzzle in cleaning.

Cappers

In-line cappers and magazine cappers are the two main types. Both are used to dispense percussion caps. They are handy because the shooter doesn't have to fumble for a cap and they place the cap directly on the nipple of the rifle without the rifleman's fingers having to pinch the cap in place on the cone of the nipple.

The Powder Horn

As much art form as utilitarian muzzle-loader tool, the powder horn, usually made of cow horn, serves to hold a supply of black powder. It is a nonsparking container, strong, waterproof, and it can be shaped to fit around the shooter's waist if carried on a thong around his neck. The funnel-like end of the horn makes powder pouring easy and spillproof.

Any list of shooting accessories must be abridged, for it can stretch as far as the imagination of the shooter himself. You can call a hat a shooting device, for it shades the eyes. A scope sunshade keeps light rays out of the objective lens of the telescopic rifle sight, so it's another accessory. There are shooting glasses, hearing protectors, shooting jackets, and more. My lightweight hiking staff, called a Moses Stick, is also a shooting rest. While not all-inclusive, this compilation covers many important accoutrements for the rifleman—tools of convenience, safety, and even necessity.

The list of shooting accessories grows and grows. There are now many video tapes for shooters who want to learn more about their sport. There are also computer programs for shooters who wish to enhance their knowledge. Such a program is the "Windbag" from the George Brothers Ballistic Software Specialist Company. Operating with Lotus 1-2-3 and Symphony, the program deals with exterior ballistics. Some shooters use the computer to store shooting data as well, calling up ballistic results of handloads, various sight-in data, as well as wind drift and other figures.

17

Maintaining Your Rifle

RIFLES ARE EXTREMELY reliable and durable tools. I recently hunted with a Winchester Model 1894 30-30 rifle which was manufactured *circa* 1899 and it proved to be as worthy as it had been the day after it left the Winchester plant last century. The key to such longevity, however, and continued reliability, is *maintenance*. A rifle with moving parts is a machine, and a machine is subject to wear. Bore friction will take a toll on the rifling. Metal-to-metal friction will wear the action. And in the past, corrosive primers and hygroscopic powder —which attract and hold moisture from the atmosphere—promoted pitting and rust.

Corrosive primers are gone. And smokeless powder allows a great many shots before a thorough bore scrubbing is necessary. Of course, the modern black-powder user still faces the drawbacks of that fuel, but even he gains maintenance relief with the use of modern solvents. Keeping a rifle in like-new condition is no longer much of a trick. You need a few tools and chemicals, and you have to know how to use both. Here is how to keep your rifle in near-new condition.

CLEAN BORES AND ACCURACY

Confusion concerning the cleanliness of a rifle bore and consequent accuracy delivered from that bore is still with us. Shooters on one side of the argument insist that the bore should be scrubbed clean only occasionally, and not after every shooting session. They contend that noncorrosive primers and modern smokeless powders do not demand a rigid bore-cleaning schedule, and that overcleaning of the bore is abusive. Shooters on the other side of the argument say that after firing a rifle, the bore should be swabbed free of fouling, with attention to the action and stock after every shooting session.

The basis for the confusion may rest with the old practice of "dressing the bore." Tests in shooting shotgun slugs showed that a squeaky-clean bore did nothing to promote projectile accuracy. In fact, a shotgun bore with powder residue dressing its walls showed improved grouping of slugs over a shiny bore. In black-powder days, the same phenomenon was discovered, and many riflemen fired a shot prior to a match to dress the bore with a coating of carbon and powder residue. Only one warmup shot was taken, of course, and as the match progressed, *excessive* fouling was removed in order to promote continued accuracy.

This important subject has a middle ground. Dressing the bore was not and is not the same as fouling the bore. Fouling cakes the rifling, which prevents proper association between the projectile and the lands and grooves. My own accuracy/ clean-bore tests indicate that the clean bore delivers better accuracy than the dirty bore in modern rifles, and that if a prematch shot is fired in the muzzle-loader, it should be followed with a swiping of the bore with a dry cleaning patch before the next ball is sent downrange.

Furthermore, tests indicate that old rifles with neglected bores can often be made to shoot far truer after a sound bore scrubbing. However, a clean *but* oily bore in either modern or muzzle-loading rifles tended to change point of impact and in some cases reduced accuracy. The upshot of the whole dirty bore versus clean-bore problem boils down to this: The best practice is to clean the bore after a shooting session if the rifle is not going back to the range within a week or two, and always after shooting sessions in which a large amount of ammo has been fired, more than twenty rounds in the big bore or one hundred rounds in the rimfire. The clean rifle bore is given a light coating of protective oil. But prior to firing the rifle, the bore is *dried* and rendered as oil and grease free as possible by using a clean patch.

TOOLS FOR RIFLE MAINTENANCE

The previous chapter on shooting accessories made brief mention of the rifle cleaning kit and attendant maintenance tools. Without these tools, the bore and action of the rifle, as well as the outer metalwork and wood, cannot be properly maintained. Rifle maintenance is easier than hitting the floor with your hat. But you need tools and know-how. Resting in front of me is an Outers Rifle Cleaning Kit, calibers 243–25. It includes a sectioned aluminum cleaning rod, a phosphorous bore brush, a slotted cleaning tip, a jag, nitro solvent,

The cleaning jag—this one is for the muzzle-loader—is used to guide a patch through the bore, and retract that patch from the bore as well. The properly sized jag will retain the cleaning patch while delivering solvent to the rifling.

gun oil, cleaning patches, and instructions, all in one plastic storage case.

The rod is correctly sized for 24- to 25-caliber bores. The cleaning tip and jag are also correctly sized for these bores. So are the patches. The cleaning rod is a driver unit only, its function being to deliver and retrieve a patch or bristle brush. The patch holds cleaning and preserving agents, also acting as a sponge to remove fouling as well as to deposit chemicals. The patch is held by the slotted cleaning tip, or pushed through from breech to muzzle by the jag. And the bristle brush gets down into the grooves of the rifling for removal of powder and metal-jacket fouling.

The jag, the screw-in unit without a slot, allows a clean patch to be shoved through the bore without the return of the patch (with any consequent dirt that may adhere) being drawn back through the bore. In the black-powder rifle, the jag is made to grab the patch so that the patch will be drawn back from breech to muzzle. The only advantage of the jag in modern rifle cleanup occurs when a shooter wants the patch to fall free at the muzzle, rather than returning through the bore.

An old toothbrush can be used to remove dirt from hard-to-get-at places, such as the checkering of the stock. Cotton swabs and pipe cleaners make good dust and dirt removers, too, and can be used to deliver grease to an action. Screwdrivers are essential, but they must fit the bolt and screw heads properly or both will be ruined. Clean, soft cloth can also be considered a tool here for its many obvious uses. And cleaning patches, cut by the shooter or commercial, are necessary items for maintenance.

CHEMICALS FOR RIFLE MAINTENANCE

Cleaning and preserving chemicals prolong rifle life. Solvents break down leftover gunk and metal fouling from primer detonation, powder burning, and the passing of the bullet through the bore. Acids left behind by our fingers are also attacked by solvents, as are other foreign substances, dust and dirt mainly. Preserving chemicals are introduced to the cleaned firearm to protect against wear caused by friction and to help thwart rust. Solvents and preserving chemicals have to be used wisely. A drop of oil in the action, for example, is a good idea. Dousing the action in oil is a terrible idea.

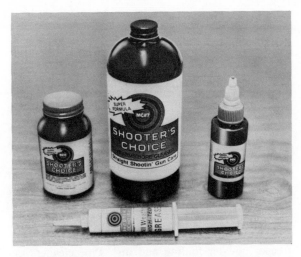

Modern chemicals are the best ever in removing fouling and preventing rust. Shooter's Choice grease has a very low freezing point and is recommended for cold weather shooting. *(Venco)*

Excess grease and oil collect dirt and defy the very reason for using these agents in the first place, to create a film between moving metal parts and to form a protective shield against humidity. In one test, bullets grouped six inches off of sight-in because of an oily bore.

Furthermore, it's been shown that damage can occur to the rifling if a bullet has to force its way down an oily bore. The oil is compressed by the bullet. Look at the oil dent in a resized cartridge case, which is caused by excessive lubrication in the resize die, and you get a good idea of how much hydraulic force can be applied by a liquid or grease under pressure.

For everyday cleanup, chemicals, such as Outers solvent, work very well, either in liquid or spray form. I routinely clean my rifles with this type of solvent. However, every few sessions a heavy-duty solvent is necessary to remove stubborn powder and metal fouling. J-B Cleaning Compound, for example, aids in the removal of lead, bullet-jacket metal, and powder residue, as do other hardworking cleaning agents, such as Shooter's Choice and Gold Medallion.

Silicone water and stain repellents, such as Outers Water Shed, WD-40, and RIG 2, are also useful in removing various types of metal fouling in the bore and on outer barrel and action. Sometimes a metal degreaser, such as Outers Crud Cutter, can be used to get rid of all previous chemical preservatives before reapplying a fresh coating. Another chemical which can be named in the preserving role is a cold blue, such as Birchwood Casey's Super Blue. Shiny metal parts can be touched up with this blue, not only for cosmetic reasons, but to restore the protection that blues provide metal. Modern technology has also given the rifleman Accralube and Accraguard as metal preservatives, as well as Shooter's Choice All Weather High-Tech Grease.

THE CLEANING PROCESS FOR THE MODERN RIFLE

Powder burners, from 17 caliber up, shooting smokeless powder, require basically the same cleaning regimen and maintenance steps. Can the sequence be altered? Of course it can. However, the following system works well and will keep rifles properly maintained. Here is a walk-through of rifle cleanup steps.

1. Be certain that the rifle is *unloaded.* Pull the bolt from the action and look into the breech, if possible, to insure that no round is in the chamber. Check the magazine for a cartridge, too. Though this step may seem painfully basic, it's never wrong to remind oneself that safety comes first.

2. Clean the rifle from the breech if possible. Cleaning from the muzzle can cause damage to the crown, which in turn may reduce the accuracy of the firearm. The rifling at the crown of the muzzle makes last contact with the bullet and has much to do with the missile's guidance. It's been said that more 22-rimfire rifles have been worn out by cleaning than by shooting, and a major reason for the statement is cleaning from the muzzle. Avoid it.

If the rifle must be cleaned from the muzzle, however, because of design, there is a way to prevent damage. Use a cleaning rod with a muzzle protector attached to it. The muzzle protector is a funnel-like metal unit which rides on the shaft of the cleaning rod. Its cone-shaped section enters the muzzle of the rifle and keeps the cleaning rod *centered* at all times, preventing scraping of the crown of the muzzle or the bore of the barrel.

In this second step, cleaning from the breech when possible, a solvent-soaked patch is run through the bore at least ten times from breech to muzzle and back. Old newspapers piled on the floor beneath the muzzle catch and hold excess solvent.

3. After the solvent-soaked patch has been run through the bore, a dry patch is used to sop up leftover solvent. At this juncture, it's wise to look into the bore. Use a bore light or hold the rifle up to a light source. If the bore is bright and shiny at this

The bolt of this Marlin rifle has been removed in order to allow the cleaning rod passage through the breech.

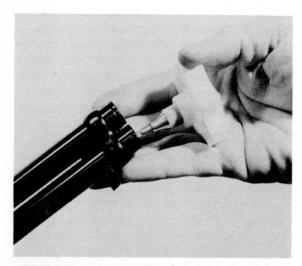

If the rifle cannot be cleaned from the breech, the pull-through cable can be used to safeguard the rifling at the crown of the muzzle.

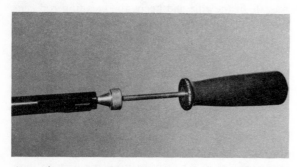

A muzzle protector. This cone-shaped device fits into the muzzle, keeping the cleaning rod centered in the bore and preventing the rod from scraping the rifling at the crown of the muzzle.

point, with no visible powder residue, lead, or metal fouling streaks, it can be considered clean enough for step four. If fouling shows, one of the heavy-duty chemicals mentioned here may be necessary for further bore cleaning.

4. The clean, dried bore is now treated to a light film of preserving oil or grease. On a clean patch, apply a small amount of either oil or grease and run this patch through the bore a few swipes only. And remember that this trace of preserving chemical should be wiped free with a single clean patch before the next shooting session. For long periods of nonuse, the application of bore grease or oil can be heavier.

5. Using a toothbrush, the action is scrubbed free of powder fouling and dirt. Pipe cleaners or cotton swabs may also be used to reach out-of-the-way places. The bolt may be disassembled occasionally for a thorough cleaning, a procedure which is usually described in the rifle's instruction booklet.

6. A light oil or grease is now applied to the action, bolt, and rails. Wipe the follower (the metal bar beneath the cartridge in the magazine) with a soft rag and lightly oil its surface, too.

7. Using a clean cloth, wipe the outer metal parts free of dust, dirt, and fingerprints. A touch of solvent may be needed. A trace of gun grease should be applied to these metal parts now.

8. The stock is now wiped down with a clean cloth. A touch of pure, inedible linseed oil on the cloth will help remove fingerprints and dirt, as will an application of other woodwork products, such as Wood Love or other commercial substances. Do not leave the stock coated with any of these products, for they may hold dust. Wipe the stock lightly with a clean cloth before putting the rifle away.

9. Store the rifle in a dry place. Arguments concerning muzzle-up or muzzle-down storage techniques have resulted in more heat than light and are inconclusive. Store either way, as necessary. If the rifle is to be stored for a long time, several months or more, it's wise to check it now and then to insure that it remains rust-free.

HEAVY-DUTY CLEANUP

Every third or fourth cleaning session, it's wise to do a little extra maintenance. The steps above are followed. However, the bristle brush is also put into action. Doused with solvent, the brush is run through the bore several passes. This action will loosen fouling. One of the heavy-duty bore cleaners can be used to attack stubborn debris. Extreme bore fouling should be attended to with a lead-removal package. These kits are available at the gun shop, with instructions for their use. Finally, in severe cases, the rifle may have to see the gun doctor, for a gunsmith can dismantle the piece fully, secure the barrel in a vise, and thereby really get rid of the worst fouling.

MAINTAINING THE AIR RIFLE

Shooters sometimes get the idea that powderless rifles couldn't require much cleanup because there is no burning powder to contend with. Consequent neglect may ruin a fine air rifle. Air rifles do get dirty. Minor lead deposits occur in the bore and so does ordinary dirt buildup. Friction-reducing oils applied to the workings of the air gun are forced through the bore at high speed. These oils become deposited on the metal and should be cleaned and replaced with fresh preservative. Furthermore, break-open air rifles are cocked by hand and hands can leave oils and acids on the barrel metal. Inside and out, the air rifle must be cleaned.

Do not use standard oils in the workings of air rifles, even if they are gun oils. The air rifle requires its own special lubricant. If a standard oil is used, it could gum up the inner workings of the rifle. Air rifles do require lubricant, however. The spring-piston design, for example, must have its piston oiled periodically. I go by the number of pellets fired. When a box of five hundred pellets is exhausted, the piston receives a drop of oil. Smoke emitted from the muzzle should last for only a few shots. If the rifle smokes for a number of shots, that indicates that too much oil was used in the piston area.

An example of a special air-rifle oil is Dri-Slide, a molybdenum disulfide–base oil which leaves a dry film on the metal. Remember to shake the can before use to distribute the elements in the oil. And don't use too much. A very little bit of this oil suffices. This lubricant dries in seconds, leaving a nonstick film which does not retain dust or dirt particles. A single application lasts a long time and the 500-shot piston-lube rule is viable.

Buy a true air-rifle cleaning kit. Finding a 17-caliber cleaning rod is difficult in the first place, but even for the 20- and 22-caliber air rifle, the proper kit is the best choice because it contains special, properly sized, air-rifle maintenance tools. My air-rifle kit, from RWS, has a high-quality, three-piece rod, a threaded bore-swab unit, a bristle brush, nylon brush, and a corkscrew-like jag which is used to run a patch through the bore.

The properly cared for air rifle will last a very long time. Stock, barrel, and outer metalwork are cleaned much as described for the powder-burning rifle above. Working parts are treated with the special air-gun oil. Incidentally, some experts feel that under high pressure standard oils could actually ignite in today's air rifles. Therefore, the use of special air-gun oil may serve safety as well as maintenance.

CLEANING THE MUZZLE-LOADING RIFLE

I know some would-be black-powder shooters who have given up the sport before really getting into it because they had to clean the frontloaders after each shooting session, and even during a shooting session. This is too bad, because the muzzle-loader can offer some of the most relaxing, enjoyable, and challenging shooting of any long arm. However, I can understand the reluctance to get up to one's elbows in hot water and rotten-egg-smelling fouling as a passport to black-powder shooting.

For a number of years, I went by the book concerning the proper cleanup of the muzzle-loader. In fact, I even passed on methods many times, warning shooters that if they did not put plenty of hot water through those frontstuffers the rifles would soon fall apart from decay. Then a letter arrived at my door. It was written by William Large, who had made rifle barrels, especially muzzle-loader barrels, for about fifty years at that time. The barrels of Mr. Large had won many, many contests. It was a nice letter, a cordial letter, but it also contained a plea.

Mr. Large wanted me to stop telling people to run hot water, or any water at all, into their muzzle-loader barrels. "I never touch water to a barrel and haven't for years," this master barrelmaker told me. I was so imbued with hot-water cleanup that I simply had to try William Large's suggestion in an experiment before telling it to the public. So I got a brand-new 50-caliber muzzle-loader and used it as my laboratory rat. In fact, I more than used it. I abused it. My pattern was to shoot the rifle at least five times with full-throttle loads, setting it aside for a minimum of twenty-four hours before trying the no-water cleanup.

This muzzle-loader has a cleanout screw at the bolster. By removing the screw, the area can be flushed clean or cleared of fouling with solvent-soaked pipe cleaners.

Naturally, we must clean our muzzle-loaders as soon after shooting as possible, but I ignored this because I wanted to see what would happen to the bore using the no-water cleanup method even when the bore was abused by allowing the fouling to cake up. I hasten to add that the humidity where I live is very low. The results of my minor experiment with the 50-caliber rifle would have been quite different, I think, had I been living in a high-humidity area.

However, after one full year of no-water cleaning, the muzzle-loader barrel was just fine. I had it pulled from the breech plug and studied it carefully for signs of pitting or other damage. There was none. After that, I used the no-water cleanup on all my black-powder rifles. Several years have passed and my muzzle-loaders are completely intact and in good shape. I still feel that an occasional hot-water cleanup might be called for if a shooter lives in a high-humidity area, but thus far I can report that the method about to be outlined here has worked for me.

The shooting is a lot more fun without having the dread of water cleaning on your mind. The fuss and mess are mostly gone, and I save time. The following steps have been laid out after considerable trial and error. If the shooter feels that he would like an annual or semiannual cleanup of his muzzle-loaders using the old hot-water routine, I won't argue. But the following method will keep black-powder rifles in good shape. Remember to clean between volleys at the range and to use liquid lubes or special creams which attack fouling in the bore. These make later cleanup easier. Excess crud in the bore can raise bore pressures.

NO-WATER CLEANUP

1. Using a solvent-soaked patch, soak the bore for at least five minutes. In this first step, I employ any good lube, such as Falkenberry Juice or Old Grizz, allowing the lube to do its work.

2. After a few minutes of soaking, run a few more solvent-soaked patches down the bore to loosen the fouling.

3. Sop up excess solvent in the bore by using several drying patches.

4. Use another solvent-soaked patch in the bore. Wait a few minutes, allowing the solvent to penetrate and to break down the fouling.

5. Repeat step 3.

6. Using patches from which the solvent has been wrung out so they are not sopping wet, see how clean the bore is according to how dark the patch is after being run up and down the bore a few times. This step indicates how much progress has been made. Sometimes the patch will emerge fairly white at this stage. Often, it will not. Either way, the next step is still vital because it will get down into the grooves of the rifling.

7. Attach a bristle brush to your cleaning rod. These brushes are available in black-powder-bore sizes. A good bore fit is necessary because the whole idea here is to work the bristles down into the grooves of the rifling, loosening up whatever may lurk there. There is a tool which scrapes the bottom of the breech, a jag-like instrument with a sharp edge. It works in scraping the breech area, and may be put into service here.

If the use of a dry bristle brush seems to dislodge a lot of black fouling, which you can detect by holding the rifle boredown and smacking the side of the barrel, it may be well to pour a bit of solvent into the bore, allowing the bristle brush to work the solvent right into the grooves of the rifling. This will usually get the stubborn salts worked free so they can be removed.

8. Now remove the cleanout screw if your muzzle-loader has one. Also remove the nipple. The reason for waiting until this step for their removal is simple. Solvent will have worked into the threads at this juncture and both cleanout screw and nipple will be easier to extract now.

9. A pipe cleaner drenched in solvent will remove fouling lurking in the cleanout-screw threads, nipple threads, and nipple-seat area.

10. Using a toothbrush dipped in solvent, scrub out the lock area and the hammer nose cup. The toothbrush will get rid of this exterior fouling easily.

11. A dry pipe cleaner and soft rag will sop up the lube left over in these areas. Wipe well.

12. Using a good grease-type lube on the tip of a pipe cleaner, apply a film on the nipple threads, nipple seat, and cleanout-screw threads.

13. By running a clean patch downbore, any lube or grease which entered the breech area through the cleanout screw channel or the nipple channel can be picked up.

14. Spray a good light application of WD-40, Tri-Lube, or similar product on the lock plate and on all metal surfaces. Wipe down, but do leave a trace of this protective oil on the metal.

15. Apply a light lube in the bore. But be certain to remove this when you next head for the shooting range.

EXTRA PROTECTION

Every now and then, I do a special bore-cleaning job on my muzzle-loaders, but again without water. This cleanup uses Shooter's Choice, a solvent popular with modern riflemen. Here are some simple steps in using Shooter's Choice:

1. Using a soppy patch, wet the bore with the product.

2. Work a bronze brush, soaked with Shooter's Choice, through the bore.

3. Use solvent-soaked patches again, two or three of them. The idea is to pick up any fouling dislodged by the previous bronze-brush passes.

4. Dry the bore with clean patches.

5. Apply a light coating of protective oil, such as Accraguard, which is a high-quality metal saver.

If the bore still looks dark and dirty after this, block the nipple channel with a toothpick and fill the bore with Shooter's Choice. Leave the rifle overnight. In the morning, pour the solvent out and bristle-brush the bore to release the gunk which has been softened and displaced by the solvent. Then dry the bore. This should free stubborn fouling. Always remember that shooting with an oily bore

may send the projectile off the mark, so no matter the method used to clean the bore, be sure to wipe any protective oils away before shooting the rifle again.

ROUTINE MAINTENANCE

Here are a few tips which may help your rifle last several lifetimes.

1. Never bring your rifle into a closed area, such as a small tent, uncovered. If it's raining and you want to protect the rifle in your shelter, insure that it is dry and well covered before bringing it inside. Keep it away from your body. If possible, leave it in a protected area outdoors so that it will not be subjected to a drastic change in temperature that would make the metal "sweat."

2. Keep rifles cased in transit, unless they are secure in a gun rack in the vehicle. Sights get banged around easily, and contact with other items being carried in the vehicle can scratch a nice stock.

3. Keep screws and bolts snug. When they get loose, the recoil of the rifle can actually damage parts of the bedding.

4. Do not dry-fire rifles which have exposed hammers. In fact, refrain from dry-firing any rifle unless a snap cap or similar device is in place to protect the firing pin and the bolt face.

5. Do not fire your rifle in rapid succession, especially if it has one of the high-intensity cartridge chamberings. As the steel heats up through successive firings, it tends to erode more easily. Throats in some rifles are damaged because of repeated firing without a little cool-off period between shots or volleys. In benchrest shooting, I fire five rounds, but no more, allowing the bore to cool totally before loading up again.

Rifle maintenance is not such a difficult job. Even the muzzle-loader can be well cared for with minimum effort. The process sounds rather long and tedious, but it isn't. Modern ammunition has made rifle care very simple. Creation of good hardware for maintenance has added to that simplicity. And the chemistry of rifle cleanup has further decreased the labor and time required to keep a nice rifle nice. Even smokepole fouling succumbs to the solvent formulas of the day. So there is no excuse for allowing a good rifle to decay. A little elbow grease, a maintenance routine, and a few tools and chemicals are all a rifleman needs to keep his firearms in like-new condition.

18

Shooting Safety

THE BEST RIFLEMAN is extremely safety conscious. Sport shooting has enjoyed an enviable record of safety over the years, and when we say that the bathtub is more dangerous than the shooting range, that's factual, not metaphorical. Shooting safety is guided by common sense and a set of rules. This important chapter deals with those rules.

GUN HANDLING

The basic precept for safe shooting is gun-handling methods. One deer season I was on the trail with a good friend and his young son. My friend wanted his boy to follow the shooting tradition. This was the lad's first time out with a rifle. He certainly kept us on our toes. The muzzle of his rifle was like the eye of a Cyclops, and that eye always seemed to be looking for somebody. When the boy was tracking behind, I'd look back to see his rifle muzzle staring at me. When he led the way, a ploy I used to keep him in front where I could watch him, he assumed the soldier's over-the-shoulder carry and the eye of the muzzle was again staring at me.

The boy was unaware of gun safety. His rifle handling was poor because he lacked common sense in the field and he was unfamiliar with the rules. And something else—he wasn't interested in being there. His lack of interest led to a poor attitude about his rifle. The rules of gun handling are as simple as they are vital. The muzzle's direction is controlled *at all times*. In showing a rifle to someone, make a habit of opening the action first and maintaining

the muzzle in a safe direction at all times, even though you know the rifle is empty.

In the loading process, direct the muzzle either toward the sky or toward the ground. The former is often preferred when the rifleman is surrounded by other people. The same is true of unloading the rifle. And if the rifle's not in use, leave it alone. Don't handle it. A shooter waiting his turn to fire may inadvertently allow the muzzle of his rifle to wander, something it can't do if it remains in the rifle rack until it's time to load and fire it. Gun handling is also a matter of rifle function. Amazingly, some shooters fumble with their rifles, unsure of exactly how to load and unload them. I watched a fellow trying to install a clip into his semiauto rifle. He became frustrated from lack of success and the more frustrated he got, the more the muzzle waved around.

EXTREME RANGE OF AMMUNITION

Know how far your rifle will shoot. Since a backstop is paramount to any shooting, this note may seem superfluous. However, knowing the range of ammo brings respect for the rifle and sounds a definite warning against shooting when the destination of the bullet cannot be determined. Ammunition boxes may state extreme range. Take these figures as serious warnings. They are not exaggerated. It's difficult to say just how far a bullet will fly under a given set of physical circumstances; however, the

Extreme range warnings, such as this 1¹/₂ mile extreme-range statement, are to be respected. Also note the words "Keep out of reach of children" on the box, another sound piece of advice.

Never fire at anything on the horizon, such as these deer. You can never be sure of the bullet's final destination when there is no backstop. Pass this shot up.

common 22 LR will travel over a mile when the muzzle is held at about a 45-degree angle. Even a blunt-nosed bullet from a 30-30 will more than double that distance. And streamlined bullets from high-power rifles will cruise three miles, sometimes farther.

The upshot of this extreme-range knowledge is this—never fire at anything on the horizon. One hunting season a magnificent buck walked up a hillside and by the time I got a good look at him, he was silhouetted against an orange sundown like a painting. I was tempted, you bet, but my forefinger never entered the trigger guard. I stalked for a safe shot. Never got it. I didn't get that buck, but neither did I have to wonder where the bullet went after it missed or passed through the game.

Another aspect of knowing extreme range is the understanding it gives of ballistic potential. Some shooters seem to believe, for example, that the little air rifle allows relaxed safety measures. After all, it's only an air rifle. Shooting a modern air rifle with a 100-yard range, however, changes that opinion. Its ability to zip a pellet that far should convince anyone that the air rifle is no toy and must be used within the framework of all safety precautions.

Understand ammo force and teach these facts to beginners when you play the role of instructor. I start my newcomers by filling ordinary beverage cans with water, then shooting these cans with 22 LR hollow-point ammo. The young would-be riflemen gain a healthy and immediate respect for the potential of the "lowly" 22-rimfire round when they see the cans burst wide open and flatten out,

spraying water into the air. Help the shooter understand that shock waves attend the bullet, and that these are powerful forces. We see them at work when a bullet penetrates game, leaving an exit hole far larger than the bullet's expanded diameter. For example, a teacup-sized exit hole delivered by a 30-06 demonstrates the magnitude of these forces. No 30-06 bullet, no matter how flattened, becomes the size of a teacup. Something other than the *direct* force of the bullet made the large hole.

RICOCHET

In Western films one noteworthy sound effect is the bullet ricocheting into space. Whang! Whew! Away it goes. In the movies that sound is make-believe. In real life, that's a noise you never want to hear. It means that a bullet has glanced off of the earth or an object and is now freewheeling through the air. Bullets bounce off many things, hardpan earth, rocks, smooth surfaces, such as water in a pond, and so forth. Angles of approach make a big difference in ricochet. Once, a companion and I were shooting into a dirt cliff which collected fired bullets nicely. A visitor to our little "test range" shot at the same dirt bank, but from the oblique. Whine! His bullet's ricochet made my hair stand on end.

Bullet construction and terminal velocity can also work for or against the ricochet. A farmer had a pest problem in his pasture and he wanted a couple of local riflemen to help him with it. But he

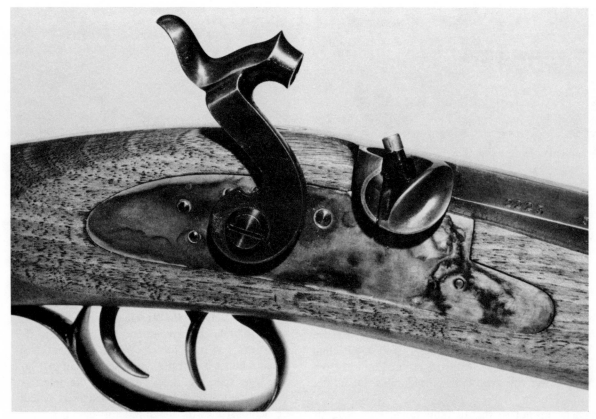

Treat every rifle as if it were loaded. In firing percussion caps to clear the nipple, aim the rifle in a safe direction. A capped muzzle-loader must always be considered fully loaded.

demanded that they shoot only 22-rimfire ammo, not the 22 centerfires they proposed to use. The former were nice and quiet. The latter were noisy. He was right about the extreme range of the 22 rimfire versus the extreme range of the 22 centerfire, but he was wrong about safety. The 22-caliber rimfire bullet would deflect if it struck a hard surface in his pasture. The soft-jacketed 22-centerfire bullet would self-destruct upon hitting the earth at high speed. Under those shooting circumstances, the high-speed, fragile bullet was safer than the lead bullet at low velocity.

THE UNLOADED RIFLE

Treat every rifle as if it were loaded at all times. No matter how positive you may be about a rifle's unloaded condition, assume it to be loaded anyway and *check it.* Control the direction of the muzzle always, even if the bolt is removed from a rifle.

Inspection of the rifle should include *looking* into the chamber when possible, or thrusting a pinky finger inside to feel for a round. Unlikely as it is, a cartridge could be stuck in the chamber. Every time I unload a rifle I work the action several times, ending with a visual and/or pinky-finger inspection of the chamber. A friend of mine aimed his 22 rifle downrange and pulled the trigger. He thought the rifle was unloaded, but the result was a hole in the bull's-eye. A cartridge had been stuck in the chamber. His habit of never aiming a rifle, even one thought to be unloaded, toward anything he did not wish to shoot at prevented a possible accident. However, for safety's sake, just remember to treat every rifle as if it were loaded.

EYE AND EAR PROTECTION

In my early days of shooting, a plug of cotton stuffed in an ear was considered heavy-duty protection against hearing loss. An earful of cotton was better than nothing, but it wasn't then, and still isn't, true hearing protection. Good hearing protection can be obtained from a commercial earplug or earmuff, or a combination of the two. Years back, most shooters who wore glasses on the range did so because they couldn't see well without them, not because they wanted to protect their vision. Today, that situation has changed. I recently had a pair of eyeglasses made for me, clear lenses, no correction, of tempered safety glass (polycarbonate). Such glasses will ward off a jet of gas should a round go haywire in the rifle.

Shooting glasses, as offered by B&L or Bushnell, do the same thing and I also own these with shaded lenses, one pair yellow, one green. Ear and eye protection is not new in the world of shooting; however, the widespread acceptance of muffs and shooting glasses is a relatively modern concept, and a good one. Protect your sight and hearing as part of your rifle-shooting safety plan.

FIREARM CONDITION

"Try my rifle," the gentleman offered. I wanted to. It was a neat single-shot piece from years gone by. "It'll sort of sting your face once in a while," the man added, and I balked. The reason the little rifle would "sort of sting your face" was that it was sort of worn out in the breech lockup. Gas was escaping rearward. Problems of excessive wear or erosion are commonly found in very old firearms, though there are, of course, thousands of very sound and safe old guns, too. If in doubt concerning the mechanical worthiness of a rifle, have a gunsmith check it out, especially for headspacing problems. Excessive headspace can cause a burst case. Dirty guns can also be dangerous guns. A clean bore and action are necessary for safety. A filthy firearm can malfunction.

USE THE CORRECT AMMO

Every year in this country, somebody sticks the wrong ammo up the spout of a rifle and somehow makes it go off. Cartridge nomenclature is part of the problem and gunstore clerks sometimes need to study a little harder than they do, because I have personally been given some very poor ammunition advice by them. I heard one clerk trying to sell a

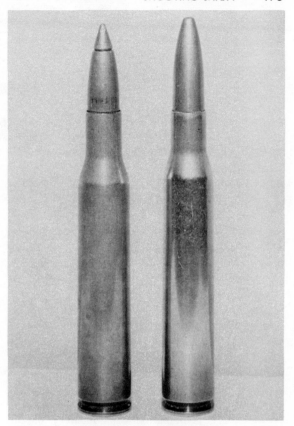

Certain cartridges look alike, even though they differ considerably in actual dimensions. The 270 Winchester and 280 Remington are similar-looking at a glance, but certainly not interchangeable.

fellow a box of 7mm Remington Magnum rounds for a 7mm Mauser. No real harm would have resulted here, since the big 7mm Magnum won't chamber in the much smaller 7mm Mauser; however, this is an example of caliber confusion. Despite the fact that most cartridge mixups are harmless, since the wrong round will rarely chamber, it's still very wise to promote a knowledge of cartridge designations so that any possible trouble is averted. On an experimental basis, some 270 Winchester ammo was fired in a 30-06 and no damage was done (that could be detected). Accuracy was nil, of course. Even so, let's keep the right ammo in the right rifle, just to be extra safe.

OVERLOADS

A friend of my son's was hunting with us a couple of years ago, firing his own handloads. I asked him what he was using and he named a bullet and

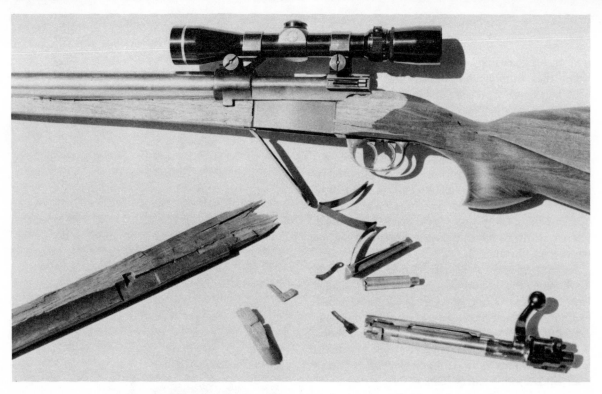

The shooter of this rifle decided to add more powder than was called for in the manual. The results are self-evident.

powder charge combination which memory told me was over maximum listing. I asked about it. "Oh, it's two or three grains over the book," the young man told me, "but the book probably has some leeway in it." Never handload this way. If a loading manual calls for X amount of powder in Y case with Z bullet, stay with that prescription. Always treat a maximum charge as just that, a maximum charge. While the action of your rifle may withstand high pressure, the cartridge case itself may not. Maximum loads are safe, of course, or they wouldn't be listed. But do not exceed them.

USING THE RIGHT POWDER

Amazingly, some shooters actually substitute one powder for another. This is glaringly wrong. If a handload calls for 57 grains of H-4831, use 57 grains of H-4831. You should not, for example, use 57 grains of IMR-4831 as a substitute powder. Adhere to every aspect of the powder's nomenclature. The 4831 part of the two powders above is not enough. The prefixes, H for Hodgdon's and IMR for Improved Military Rifle, have significance. A shooter should consult several handbooks in looking for a best load for his favorite rifle, of course,

since manuals differ, and some shooting houses arrive at a better given load for a specific rifle. But the loading manual remains the handloader's bible. And powder nomenclature indicates a specific set of burning characteristics.

MAKING BULLETS

Safety precautions are of the utmost importance in this hobby, which deals with molten lead, lead fumes and hot molds, and furnaces or melting pots. Wear protective clothing, shirt, gloves, and shoes as well as eyeglasses to guard against splashes of hot lead. Never cast bullets where any source of water, including rain, can hit the molten lead, for this may cause a "boilover." Keep kids away from the operation. Cast bullets in a ventilated area to avoid breathing fumes (lead is a toxic metal). Insure that your heat source is safe and not likely to catch your house on fire.

THE TUBULAR MAGAZINE

Never load a sharp-pointed bullet into a tubular magazine with one round behind another. The point of the bullet may set off the primer of the cartridge in front of it. Injury to rifle and shooter could result. In those rifles which have tubular magazines, use only blunt-nosed bullets, or load Spitzer- or Spire-point projectiles *one at a time only* (single-shot fashion). It has been recommended that the tubular magazine rifle may also be used as a two-shot system with one, and only one, round in the magazine plus the one in the chamber.

SAFETY ON THE RANGE

Public shooting ranges always have a set of safety rules underlying all firearm activity on the premises. The range officer is generally responsible for enforcing these rules. It is important to study the regulations at your range and know them. Usually, only single-shot shooting is allowed, for example, meaning that repeating rifles are loaded one shot at a time, no ammo in the magazine at all. Signals rule range movement, too, and no one is to step forward of the firing line without a given command from the range leader. Range rules are designed for everyone's safety. Follow them.

INCENDIARY AMMO

He set his own ranch on fire. The shooter had bargain-purchased a batch of 30-06 Army ammo. The only problem with the ammunition was its incendiary nature. Tracers can start fires. My friend started a small fire and the flames were quickly snuffed before they devoured much pastureland, but the result of misusing tracer ammo could have been much worse. Be sure to study the nature of any ammunition which was originally intended for military purpose. Some of this stuff can be dangerous in civilian rifle-shooting situations.

DANGEROUS UNDERLOADS

Overloads can cause trouble, but what about the opposite condition, the *underload?* It seems, at first glance, that using *less* powder would always result in a condition of lower pressure. Not always. Sometimes an underload can be dangerous. There are documented incidents of underloaded ammunition causing high pressures, specifically with the slower-burning fuels. For example, a light charge of

H-4831 in a 270 Winchester rifle badly damaged the rifle. Some researchers feel that when a slow-burning powder is used as an underload, the granules are *detonated* all at once, rather than being consumed *progressively* in the bore. The flash from the primer darts over the top of the powder in the partially filled case, making contact with all of the granules almost simultaneously, rather than igniting the charge from the head of the case first. Result—explosion. Such speculation may not be accurate; however, high-pressure underloads have happened.

When using squib (reduced) loads, follow the manual. Use the powder recommended, in the correct amount, with the right cartridge case, bullet, and primer. Squib loads are safe when the loading manual is their source. Furthermore, follow the manual's prescription concerning the bullet. For example, certain half-jacket bullets are *not* supposed to be fired at dramatically reduced muzzle velocity. An underload using these bullets could conceivably allow a stripping away of the jacket from the core within the bore of the rifle. Then the next bullet fired in the rifle has to ride over that jacket. Do not invent your own underloads. For safety's sake, follow the manual.

EXPERIMENTATION

Experimentation has been the cornerstone of shooting. I have considered experimenting a part of my job as a firearms author, learning and passing information on to readers. However, all tests have been conducted under the umbrella of laboratory-safe conditions. The shooter should let the professionals take the chances, I feel, if any chances must be taken. Do not create your own handloads. Let the ammo labs do that for you. They have the proper pressure-testing tools.

BORE OBSTRUCTIONS

A stripped bullet jacket is one kind of bore obstruction. There are many such obstructions and they can be dangerous. Mud and snow stuffed up a muzzle can destroy a rifle. If anything does become lodged in the bore, *never* try to shoot it out. If the obstruction cannot be expelled with a cleaning rod, take the rifle to a gunsmith for debreeching.

THE PELLET TRAP

Do not alter the pellet trap in any way. Do not substitute thin paper targets for heavy cardboard targets, for example, as bits of pellet lead may fly back through this paper from the inside of the trap. Wear eye protection in the basement range. A high-speed pellet can ricochet. It isn't always going fast enough to self-destruct.

STORING AMMO

Keep all ammunition stored away from the reach of children. Store it away from sources of heat or possible ignition. Heat may alter the character of powder. So may age. Therefore, watch out for old ammo. A while ago, I shot a few old 303 Savage rounds. A couple of them split at the neck and one was a near case-head separation. I quit using that ammo. Keep ammunition dry. Moisture may eventually invade the powder charge or damage the brass case.

POWDER STORAGE

Keep just enough gunpowder on hand for immediate reloading purposes. Store powder out of reach of young hands, heat, or moisture. Keep the fuel in its original container, sealed. Never transfer powder to a glass container, which could break. Glass allows light penetration, which may alter the nature of the powder. Never fool around with powder. While modern gunpowder is not going to "blow up" from a minor bump, it may detonate from heavy percussion. One shooter found this out when he was in the process of showing his neighbor that you couldn't detonate a bit of smokeless powder with a hammer blow. He smacked a tiny quantity of powder with the hammer. It responded with a boom!

RAPID FIRE

The benchrest shooter had been at it for hours. He was using loads which had been fired in his particular rifle for years. Nothing could possibly go wrong with them. Something did go wrong. It wasn't terribly serious, but upon ejecting a fired case, the primer fell out when the case smacked the benchtop, indicating a hot load or an old, worn-out case. The case was new. The load had been tried many times before with no ill result. However, rapid fire had heated the barrel and the cartridge case had been heated, in turn, in the chamber, altering the reaction of the powder to ignition. Rapid fire as play is a foolish practice. The only place for rapid fire is during a special target session under controlled conditions.

THE SAFETY OF THE RIFLE

Treat every rifle as if it were loaded. Good rule. But to extend that advice add "Treat every rifle as if it were always off safety." Safeties work. However, they are mechanical devices and, as such, can fail. Furthermore, certain so-called safeties are really no such thing. The half-cock position of some exposed hammer rifles, for example, is not a true safety. It is not a blockage of the sear. Occasionally, the half-cock notch may become worn. Check this condition with an *unloaded* rifle by setting it on half-cock, then trying to push the hammer forward with your thumb. If you can push the hammer off the half-cock notch, bring the rifle to a gunsmith immediately for repairs.

PRIMERS

For some strange reason, shooters sometimes treat primers as if they were *not* explosive devices. They are. Here are some good rules to follow in primer management. Nine of them were developed by a leading component manufacturer. I added the tenth.

1. Keep primers away from children.

2. Never smoke near primers.

3. Remember that *heat or percussion* may cause a primer to go off, even though they are made to explode by percussion.

4. Wear safety glasses when handling primers.

5. Never force a primer to fit. If the primer will not seat, stop and find out why, but never try to bully it into the pocket.

6. Keep primers in their original packaging. Removal to other containers may alter identification.

7. Work with a minimum of primers. Never pile primers in a bunch. Should one go off, the entire batch may do likewise. Primers have been known to fly through the air at high speed after detonation.

8. Do not decap a live primer from a cartridge case.

9. Never attempt to seat a primer deeper into a loaded round.

10. Store primers in a cool place. Keep your supply of primers in a larger container, such as an army ammo can with a seal.

SAFETY AND THE GUN SAFE

The gun safe was developed to thwart thieves. However, it is also an excellent means of keeping firearms out of the hands of children.

BLACK-POWDER SAFETY

Most of the above safety principles pertain to muzzle-loading as well as modern rifles. However, the frontloader fan should be aware of a few other measures which promote the safety of his sport:

1. Never smoke around black powder (or any other powder). Black powder ignites very easily. A spark from a match, flame from a cigarette lighter, or ash from a cigarette, cigar, or pipe could cause a can of black powder to burst into flame.

2. Keep black powder covered at all times for the reasons mentioned above, and also to avoid possible contamination from any outside source.

3. Never hurry. While it's true that I use a speedloader to gain a fast second shot in the field, it's equally true that I keep the muzzle away from my face when reloading just in case a spark lingers downbore. Allow the frontloader to rest a moment between shots.

4. Never overload the muzzle-loader, any more than you would overload modern ammo. Black powder can produce dangerously high pressures.

5. Never fire a separated ball/charge. Keep projectile and powder together as a unit until fired away. A spaced load may bulge or burst a barrel.

6. Treat percussion caps much as you would treat modern primers, for they have a similar nature. Never expose to undue heat or pressure. Never force a percussion cap onto a nipple.

7. Aim the muzzle away from your face when loading, and in a safe direction.

8. Use only black powder or Pyrodex in your muzzle-loader. No other powder is correct at this time. There are developments toward other safe fuels, but as this is written, *only* the two powders listed above are muzzle-loader-correct. There are many dark-looking powders. They may look black, but only true black powder is right for a frontloader. Modern smokeless powders may destroy a muzzle-loader and could badly injure the shooter.

9. Watch out for old muzzle-loaders. Some appear to be shootable, but the metal may be fatigued and they can be dangerous to fire. Bring any questionable original frontloader to a qualified black-powder gunsmith for inspection. Have him fire it under safe test conditions, preferably by remote control. Some valuable old-time muzzle-loaders are ruined by firing them. They are best left for admiration only.

10. Shoot quality muzzle-loaders only. There are still a few junkers around. They can usually be spotted by their poor workmanship.

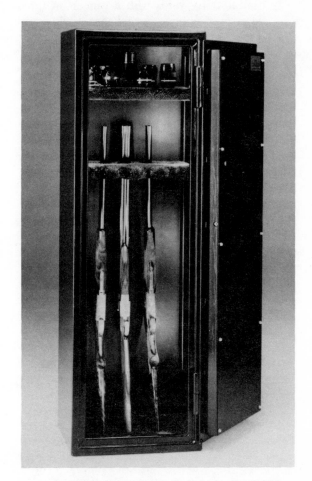

Use a gun safe to keep firearms out of the hands of children. *(Browning Arms)*

11. Be informed. Black-powder shooting is an intricate endeavor. It is not a simple pastime in which any haphazard method will work. The art of muzzle-loading is old, but the sport is still a science. Understand black powder and frontloaders before embarking on their use.

Never become so familiar with your firearms that you lose respect for them. Let your familiarity with rifles breed more respect for them, rather than less. Millions of rounds of ammo are fired annually in this very safe sport. Adherence to basic safety rules will keep the record a good one.

> Never meddle with old unloaded firearms; they are the most deadly and unerring things that have ever been created by man. You don't have to have a rest; you don't have to have any sights on the gun; you don't have to take aim, even. You just pick out a relative and bang away at him. A youth, who can't hit a cathedral at thirty yards with a cannon in three-quarters of an hour, can take up an old empty musket and bag his grandmother every time, at a hundred.
>
> MARK TWAIN

Load with the muzzle away from the face.

Glossary

SHOOTING TERMS have been a part of our culture from the beginning of America. These words and phrases have sifted down from the shooting field to the avenues of everyday speech. We say, "He's a straight shooter," meaning he is honest. "He missed the mark that time," meaning he didn't get it right. He sold the farm "lock, stock, and barrel," meaning *all* of it. "Don't go off half cocked." That says, "Wait until you have the facts before you act," and it comes from the problem of the rifle slipping the half-cock notch and firing prematurely. "The project was just a flash in the pan." That one comes from the flintlock muzzle-loader world, where the FFFFg pan powder went woosh!, but the rifle did not go off, and it translates, "It got off to a fast start, but fizzled out right away." This glossary, however, is a practical word guide to the language of shooting, with emphasis on the rifle, of course.

ACCOUTREMENT
Also spelled accouterment. Originally was the equipment carried by a soldier, and included everything except his firearm. However, the word has broader meaning in shooting today, and it suggests all of the accessories which attend the sport of shooting.

ACTION
The mechanism by which the rifle is loaded and fired, also covering the withdrawal and expulsion of the fired round.

BALL
Originally, the missile, regardless of shape. Hence, to this day we say "round ball," which seems redundant, but it is still correct to say "conical ball"; therefore, round ball is an acceptable term. Also used today to denote military ammo using a full-metal-jacket bullet or "ball ammo."

BALLISTIC COEFFICIENT
Noted as C, this term is a mathematical ratio between the bullet's sectional density and its coefficient of form, a construct originally designed around a "standard" bullet form.

BALLISTICS
The study of projectiles in motion, to include many aspects, such as extreme range and trajectory, as well as energy ratings from muzzle to termination of flight. Exterior (also external) ballistics treats the bullet after it leaves the muzzle. Interior or internal ballistics deals with the bullet in the rifle from primer detonation to bore travel.

BEARING SURFACE
The portion of the bullet which makes contact with the bore is the bearing surface of the bullet. Bearing surface is related to pressure and other aspects of interior ballistics.

BEDDING
For our purposes, the mortise in the rifle stock which contains the barrel and action of the rifle.

BELTED CASE
The cartridge case which has a band ahead of the extractor groove is a *belted case*. The band or belt is generally a feature of the so-called *magnum* cartridge. The band is used as the headspace gauge in the belted round. Also, the wise reloader uses the belt as a gauge to measure pressure, miking the belt after one firing and then miking again after consequent loads to inspect for further expansion. Expansion across the belt indicates a condition of high pressure (as well as possible brass fatigue).

BOATTAIL BULLET
Also boat-tail, or BT. A bullet with a tapered heel. The shape of the boattail bullet aids its flight in the atmosphere, and boattails will usually show a higher retained velocity at long range over flatbase bullets of the same caliber and weight, all other things, such as profile, being equal. However, in many practical aspects, the boattail is

not a distinct advantage, such as in the short- to modest-range hunting rifle.

BORE

The hole in the barrel through which the bullet passes.

BORE DIAMETER

Generally, a measurement from rifling land to the exact opposite rifling land. A 30-06 would have a 30/100-inch bore size, land to land. The diameter from bottom of groove to bottom of opposite groove may be .308 inch, and the actual diameter of the 30-06 bullet would be .308 to match groove-to-groove distance in the bore.

BORE SIGHTING

A means of matching the sight picture with the alignment of the bore. This is accomplished by securing the rifle, looking through the bore, "aiming the bore" at a target, and then adjusting the sights until they are "looking" in the same place. In addition, a bore sighter (also called a collimator) may be used, which is an optical device that attaches to the muzzle of the rifle. Again, the sights are adjusted to match the direction the bore is pointing to. Bore sighting aids in getting that first shot "on the paper." By firing first rounds from an unsighted rifle at very close range, much the same advantage is realized.

BREECH

That portion of the rifle barrel which will contain the load, be that load a cartridge or, in the case of a muzzle-loader, a powder charge and projectile.

BREECH PRESSURE

The force of the expanding powder gases as bled off and measured at the breech. Now most often read as CUP or LUP, Copper Units of Pressure or Lead Units of Pressure. Also measured as psi, pounds per square inch. That is, pounds of pressure rated per square inch.

BULLET

From the French *boulette,* or small ball, the term is now used to denote any projectile fired from a rifle. The "round bullet" is a term seldom used. The term cylindro-conoidal bullet is also seldom used. Generally, the term "bullet" refers to the elongated missile, while ball often represents the spherical missile.

BULL PUP RIFLE

A bolt-action rifle which has been shortened by moving the action back into the buttstock region of the rifle.

CALIBER

A measurement in fractions of an inch or in millimeters referring to either bore size of the rifle or diameter of the bullet. A 30-caliber bullet is usually .308 inch in diameter, a size which matches the groove-to-groove distance in the bore. A 7mm bullet is .284 inch in diameter. Very crudely, we may multiply by 4 in order to convert from millimeter to caliber. For example a 6mm bullet is about 24 caliber, a 7mm bullet about 28 caliber. Although it is a habit to list a caliber as .30, .30 is 30/100 of one caliber and not 30 caliber. Loosely, we also refer to

caliber as the cartridge. "He owns a 30-30 caliber rifle." While this is not technically correct, it is accepted in shooting-language usage.

CANNELURE

Usually the indentation on the shank of a bullet. This groove is used to help hold the bullet in the mouth of the case. The neck of the case crimps into the cannelure. The cannelure may also aid in holding core and jacket of bullet together following bullet impact.

CARBINE

Simply, a short rifle. The Model 94 carbine, for example, wears the 20-inch barrel, while the original rifle had a 26-inch barrel. It is not incorrect to call a short-barreled rifle a rifle, however. But when a reference to "carbine" is made, one knows that a shorter rifle is being spoken of.

CAST BULLET

A projectile which has been prepared by pouring molten lead into a mold to form the missile. Most modern cast bullets are molded from an alloy, generally of lead, tin, and antimony, and in various proportions to alter the hardness of the finished product. Care must be taken to follow the proper alloy formulas for various applications. Very hard bullets may raise pressures in certain firearms. As for casting black-powder bullets, "pure" lead is preferred, that is, lead which has been cleaned, with impurities skimmed from its molten surface.

CHAMBER

The rearward portion of the barrel which has been reamed, using a specific reamer to create a specific cartridge dimension. The cartridge itself fits into this section of the barrel for firing, held there by the breech. That portion which lies ahead of the neck portion of the chamber is called the leade or throat. Free-bored chambers have more leade than standard chambers.

CHRONOGRAPH

A device used to calculate the velocity of a projectile. Modern chronographs also allow the gathering of other data, such as standard deviation from the mean velocity, extreme spread, highest velocity in the string, lowest velocity in the string, and an average velocity, rather than one simple velocity statement.

CREEP, TRIGGER

The slack which must be taken up before the trigger disengages the sear is called creep. A military-type or two-stage trigger may have intentional slack and this slack is not generally referred to as creep, whereas a trigger which is supposed to activate directly following pressure from the pad of the finger but which has slack is known as a trigger with creep in it.

CROWN, MUZZLE

The very last portion of the muzzle of the rifle, sometimes indented or recessed to protect the rifling.

CUP

Copper Units of Pressure, whereby a copper pellet is crushed to a specific point. The more the pellet is deformed, the higher the pressure in the rifle chamber. Used for pressure ratings *above* 10,000 units. Not directly related to psi, but used in the same manner, to denote pressure.

DRAM

A weight of 27.34 grains. Archaic: drachm. Latter also an apothecary weight of 60 grains. In shooting, consider a drachm or dram to be 27.34 grains.

DRY-FIRE

To fire the rifle without ammo, as in practice. Insure that no damage is done during dry-firing by using a snap cap to protect the firing pin, bolt face, etc.

DUPLEX LOAD

The duplex load uses two different powders in one cartridge case, or two different granulations of powder in a muzzle-loader. Also a practice of using a small charge of smokeless powder underneath a black-powder charge. *Not recommended.*

EJECTOR

Device, generally spring-loaded, which expels the cartridge or the fired cartridge case from the action.

EXTRACTOR

Device which pulls the cartridge or the fired cartridge case from the breech.

FIREFORMING

The expansion of a cartridge case, upon firing in the chamber, to a dimension different from the original. For example, a standard 30-30 round fired in the 30-30 Improved chamber expands the walls of the case so that they are much straighter, also creating a sharper shoulder.

FRIZZEN

The pivoting metal bar associated with the lock of a flintlock firearm upon which the flint scrapes to produce sparks.

GAS CHECK

A metal cup which fits the base of the cast bullet. The gas check allows for less erosion of the bullet base. It is used where higher velocity is desired. Low-velocity, low-powder loads may be fired with plain base, or nongas-check cast bullets.

GLASS BEDDING

The use of a synthetic substance to form a barrel channel and/or a seat in the stock for the action. New compounds are stronger than ever, and easier to use. Also good for repair and strengthening of specific areas of the stock.

GROUP

Two or more shots fired at the same target with the same rifle, usually measured from the center of one bullet hole to the center of the farthest bullet hole from it.

HALF JACKET

A bullet of swaged lead which has a partial jacket of thin copper covering the bearing surface only.

HANGFIRE

A delay in ignition. Unlike a misfire, the hangfire does go off; however, the rifle does not fire immediately. Associated primarily with muzzle-loaders, especially flintlocks, but can occur in a cartridge as well.

HEADSPACE

That distance as measured from the bolt face of the rifle to that point in the chamber where forward progress of the cartridge is halted. In a rimmed cartridge, this distance is taken from the bolt face to the end of the rim itself. In a belted magnum, the belt is used to gauge headspace. On a rimless cartridge, the shoulder is used to mark headspace distance. Gauges are used by the gunsmith to check the headspace in a rifle. These are Go and No-Go gauges, sometimes a "field gauge" as well. The Go gauge should allow the bolt to close down easily. The bolt should not close on a No-Go gauge. It will close snugly on a field gauge. If the bolt of the action (and this applies to lever-action, semiauto, and pump guns, as well as bolt-action rifles) *will* close on a No-Go gauge, that indicates excessive headspace and the condition must be corrected.

JACKETED BULLET

Consisting of the lead core and an outer metal covering, the outer covering being the jacket. Jackets are of various thicknesses and designs and often are partially responsible for the degree of deformation the bullet takes upon striking its target.

KENTUCKY WINDAGE

Used today to denote the guesstimated altering of the sight picture in order to hit a target. For example, a shooter may hold off-target for wind deflection. Although windage refers to lateral movement, the term now also applies to holding high or low on a target.

KEYHOLING

Loss of bullet stabilization, causing the bullet to tumble end over end, all gyroscopic effect in keeping the bullet point-on having been dissipated.

KINETIC ENERGY

For shooting purposes, the energy of the bullet in motion, computed by Newtonian methods, as described in the text.

LOCK TIME

In modern terminology, the elapsed time from the release of the sear due to activation of the trigger to the actual impact of the firing pin upon the primer. A fast lock time is desirable.

LUP

Lead Units of Pressure. A counterpart of CUP, Copper Units of Pressure. Again, a pellet is deformed in a crusher activated by a piston, which in turn has been activated by the generation of gases in the chamber area of the rifle. The amount of deformation is calculated and transformed into a number. LUP is used for those ratings of 10,000 and below. Recall that CUP was used in ratings higher than 10,000 units.

MAGAZINE

That part of the rifle which contains the ammunition in storage, ready to be transferred into the breech.

MIDRANGE TRAJECTORY

MRT is the highest point in the parabola that the bullet reaches from muzzle to point of impact at the target. Since the bullet must arc upward from the muzzle in order to strike a distant target, it does climb above the line of sight. How high it must climb to reach a given distance is the MRT.

MINUTE OF ANGLE

Specifically, one sixtieth of one degree, but for shooting purposes a minute of angle consists of an inch at 100 yards, two inches at 200 yards, three at 300, and so forth. A rifle capable of minute-of-angle accuracy will group its bullets into an inch center to center at 100 yards, two inches center to center at 200, three at 300, etc.

MISFIRE

In the misfire, as opposed to the hangfire, the round does not go off at all after the trigger is pulled. Sometimes a dead primer is the cause. In muzzle-loaders, misfires often result from lack of flame reaching the main charge in the breech.

MUSKET

This term has changed meaning over the years. Originally, the musket was simply a smoothbore rifle and over the years it has been associated with a military smoothbore. However, the term has been used to describe long-barreled rifles with barrel bands. Its specific meaning has broadened over the years.

MUZZLE BLAST

The violent expulsion of powder gases emitted at the muzzle of the rifle.

MUZZLE PROTECTOR

A device which generally slips onto the shaft of the cleaning rod, its function being to keep the rod centered in the rifle bore so that the rifling, especially at the muzzle, is not scraped.

NIPPLE

The metal cone upon which the percussion cap rests on the rifle. The nipple allows the fire from the cap to be directed into a channel which leads to the main charge of powder in the breech of the muzzle-loader.

OBTURATION

Expansion of the projectile in the bore due to reaction of gas pressure and inertia of the bullet. Also used to designate the expansion of the cartridge case as gases exert pressures which force the case to meet with the walls of the chamber. Also known as "bullet upset" in internal ballistics.

OGIVE

The part of the bullet forward of the bearing surface of the shank.

OIL DENT

In reloading, the dent which appears in a cartridge case due to excessive lubrication being trapped between the case and the walls of the resize die.

PARTITION BULLET

A bullet which has a band between the rear and forward parts of the projectile. This band prevents mushrooming of the projectile past a given point. It also prevents separation of bullet core from bullet jacket upon impact and during penetration of the missile.

PERCUSSION CAP

A small metal cup which contains fulminate. It is sensitive to the blow from the hammer of the rifle. When the hammer falls on the cap, the contents ignite, sending a flame through the vent in the nipple and from there through a channel to the main charge in the breech. Associated with the percussion or caplock rifle.

PITTING

The deterioration of the metal of a rifle due to rust. Used rifles may have "pitted bores," meaning the bore is pockmarked with erosion caused by metal deterioration.

PRESSURE

Resulting thrust from expanding gases emanating from the burning powder charge. Without such pressure, the bullet would not be driven from the rifle bore.

PRESSURE CURVE

A graphic line showing the variation in pressure from ignition until the bullet clears the muzzle; usually in time versus pressure, and read with an oscilloscope.

RECOIL

Recoil is a phenomenon explained by Newton's Third Law of Motion—every action has an opposite and equal reaction. If the rifle and the bullet were of the same mass, both would gain the same velocity after firing. Since the rifle is far heavier than the bullet, it is the bullet which speeds away from the rifle. However, the rifle does come back toward the shooter, "kicking" him. The attributes of recoil include, aside from rifle weight, the weight of the powder charge, weight of the bullet, and velocity of the bullet.

RIFLING

Grooves cut into the bore of the rifle at an angle (there were straight grooves in some bores of long ago) which, in turn, leave a raised rib of metal in the bore called a land. The grooves are the channels, with the lands being the "ridges" which actually engrave the bullet, thereby guiding it. The actual pitch of the rifling is geared according to the mass of the projectile and its sectional density, as well as other factors. The pitch of the rifling is commonly referred to as "twist," and listed thus: 1:10, one turn in 10 inches of bore. The result of twist is RPS, revolutions per second, of the bullet rotation, and it is that bullet rotation which gives it the gyroscopic ability to remain point-on in flight. RPS is a function of *rate* of twist and exit velocity of the bullet and not of barrel length per se.

RIMFIRE

A cartridge with the priming mixture distributed around the rim of the case. The 22 rimfire is a good example.

REGULATED BARRELS

A double-barreled rifle whose bores are adjusted so that point of impact for both barrels is the same.

SAAMI

The Sporting Arms and Ammunition Manufacturer's Institute, an organization responsible for the standardization of measurements in the industry, including chamber dimensions and other important specifications in shooting.

SABOT

From the French, this term was used to denote a wooden shoe. In early shooting, the sabot was wooden. Today, the sabot is plastic. It is a heavy-duty device which fits around a bullet. Specifically, the sabot is used in modern ammo in order to fire a 22-caliber bullet from a 30-caliber bore. It can, and may, be used for many other calibers as well. Remington Accelerator 30-30, 308, and 30-06 caliber ammo uses the sabot, all three firing a 55-grain, 22-caliber bullet. The plastic sabot simply falls away from the bullet and the bullet speeds to the target. It is a good way of turning a larger-bore rifle into one capable of firing smaller projectiles. The above Accelerator for the 30-06 shoots a 55-grain, 22-caliber bullet at about 4,000 fps MV.

SEAR

A bar or metal piece which translates the activation of the trigger into the dropping of the firing pin. The sear is disengaged by the trigger pull and then the hammer or plunger is allowed to fall, thus firing the rifle.

SECTIONAL DENSITY

This is a ratio. It is the relationship between a bullet's weight in pounds divided by the square of the bullet's diameter in inches. The result is a number in decimal form. The higher the number, the greater the sectional density of the bullet. For example, a bullet of .226 sectional density compares poorly with a bullet of .286 sectional density, the latter handling the ravages of the atmosphere better, provided both bullets have similar profiles.

SIGHT RADIUS

The distance between front sight and rear sight on a rifle wearing metallic sights. Open sights and aperture sights pertain.

SPITZER BULLET

A pointed bullet as opposed to a round- or flat-nosed bullet.

SPRUE

The channel in the bullet mold through which the molten lead is poured to form a projectile. Also the tiny projection of lead on the projectile left where the sprue plate cut the sprue away from the missile. This small projection is supposed to be loaded upward in the muzzleloader for round-ball-shooting rifles.

SQUIB LOAD

A subpower load, underload, usually with reduced powder charge.

SWAGING

Bullets, including round ball, made by forcing lead into a die which sizes the projectile—as opposed to creating bullets with a mold and molten lead. Round balls so created have no sprue. The round balls currently produced by Hornady and Speer are of the swaged type and are exceedingly uniform.

STADIA WIRES

Within the scope sight, two horizontal crosswires used to gauge the distance to the target by knowing the size of the target. A determination of distance is assumed according to how much space is optically taken up by the object between the scope's two horizontal crosswires.

TAKEDOWN

Rifles which may be broken down, as by dividing the rifle into two parts, generally separated at the action, are of the takedown, or take-down, variety. The takedown rifle is very portable.

TIME OF FLIGHT

Reference to the elapsed time for a bullet to travel a specific distance.

TRAJECTORY

The arc described by the bullet from muzzle to destination. This arc is a parabola, a specific curve. The path the bullet takes is its trajectory. In sighting-in, the idea is to take best advantage of the bullet's trajectory potential.

TRANSDUCER

Effectively, an electrical means of calculating the pressure generated in the breech of the rifle. A specific quartz crystal is used. These crystals emit an electrical response to pressure. Pressure on the crystal results in more response for more pressure. A device transfers the chamber pressure to the crystal and a readout is translated into psi, pounds-per-square-inch pressure.

VELOCITY

In rifle shooting, the speed of the projectile, measured in feet per second (fps). Derived from a chronograph.

VENT

The channel within the nipple of the percussion rifle which allows the fire from the percussion cap to find its way toward the main charge in the breech. Similar to the touchhole in the flintlock rifle, which allows the flame from the FFFFg pan powder to dart into the main charge in the breech.

WINDAGE

Horizontal movement of sights, as opposed to elevation. Also the space between the projectile and the bore in the muzzle-loader, which space is taken up by the patch.

ZERO

That point at which the rifle is sighted-in to deliver its group. A rifle "zeroed" for 200 yards prints on the bull's-eye at 200 yards.

Directory of Manufacturers and Suppliers

MODERN RIFLEMEN have a wealth of firearms and accoutrements at their beck and call. Everything from the frontstuffing muzzle-loader to the most refined target rifle for Olympic competition is available, along with a wide range of gear to go with the guns. This abridged listing will help the reader in locating rifles, ammo, and incidentals which enhance rifle shooting. Most of these importers and manufacturers have excellent catalogs available for prospective customers.

ACCURATE ARMS COMPANY
Route 1, Box 167
McEwen, TN 37101

A line of reloader powders which adds to the range of loads for the rifleman-handloader, including a good powder for squib loads.

ALLEN FIREARMS
2879 All Trades Rd.
Santa Fe, NM 85701

Importers of muzzle-loading rifles, including the Santa Fe Hawken. Also replicas of the old lever-action rifles.

ARMSPORT, INC.
3590 NW 49th St.
Miami, FL 33142

Importer of various rifles, including double-barreled models. Also luggage-type gun cases and more.

BARNES BULLETS
POB 215
American Fork, UT 84003

Makers of special bullets for reloaders, including many heavyweight projectiles in various calibers. For example, there is a 195-grain, 7mm bullet for the 7mm Magnum and 7mm Weatherby.

B.E.L.L., Ltd.
800 W. Maple Ln.
Bensenville, IL 60106

Cartridge cases especially for the gone-but-not-forgotten rounds of yesteryear, as well as foreign cartridge cases which are very difficult to locate.

BEEMAN, INC.
47 Paul Dr.
San Rafael, CA 94903

Famous for air rifles of many kinds.

BAUSKA RIFLE BARREL CO., INC.
Box 511
Kalispell, MT 59901

Imports the unique Brno rifle. Also makes special custom barrels, octagonal as well as round, and offers rechamberings from one caliber to another. Barrel liners for shot-out rifles also available.

BISHOP STOCKS
POB 7
Warsaw, MO 65355

Custom stocks are the specialty here; however, Bishop also makes a custom rifle to the specifications of the shooter. Many styles and many calibers are offered.

DAISY MFG. CO.
POB 220
Rogers, AR   72756

Makers of the famous air-rifle BB gun.

BROWNING ARMS CO.
Route One
Morgan, UT   84050

Long line of rifles, including bolts, pumps, semiautos and lever-actions. Also replica rifles, examples being the Model 1895 and the Model 1886 lever-actions. Gun safes.

BUFFALO BULLET CO.
7352 Whittier Ave.
Whittier, CA   90602

Special conical projectiles for muzzle-loaders.

BUSHNELL OPTICAL CO.
Division of B&L
2828 E. Foothill Blvd.
Pasadena, CA   91107

Full line of optics for riflemen, including binoculars, spotting scopes, and rifle scopes.

C. SHARPS ARMS
POB 885
Big Timber, MT   59011

Replica Sharps rifles, including Old Reliable in 45-120-550.

CHARTER ARMS, INC.
430 Sniffens Ln.
Stratford, CT   06497

Maker of the Explorer 22-rimfire survival rifle.

CROSMAN GUNS
Routes 5 & 20
East Bloomfield, NY   14443

Various air rifles, including pneumatic and spring-piston, as well as CO_2 types.

DGS, INC.
1764 S. Wilson
Casper, WY   82601

Magnabed compound for bedding rifles.

DIXIE GUN WORKS
Gunpowder Ln.
Union City, TN   38261

Full line of muzzle-loaders and accoutrements. Big catalog.

DYNAMIT NOBEL OF AMERICA
105 Stonehurst Ct.
Northvale, NJ   07647

RWS air rifles, including match grade, as well as full line of ammunition, many foreign calibers, and Brenneke shotgun slugs.

FEDERAL CARTRIDGE COMPANY
2700 Foshay Tower
Minneapolis, MN   55402

Ammunition from 22 rimfire through big bore, including the Premium line with Nosler Partition bullets.

FORSTER PRODUCTS
82 E. Lanark Ave.
Lanark, IL   61046

Tap-O-Cap for homemade percussion caps, full line of reloading devices, and black-powder kit.

FRONTIER CARTRIDGE COMPANY
Hornady Manufacturing
POB 1848
Grand Island, NB   68801

Ammunition loaded with Hornady bullets, including Interlock style.

HATFIELD RIFLE WORKS
2028 Frederick Ave.
St. Joseph, MO   64501

Makers of semicustom and full custom rifles designs based on the original Hatfield rifles of Hatfield clan fame. Many calibers.

HARRIS ENGINEERING
Barlow, KY   42024

The Harris bipod, professionally designed for rifle accuracy enhancement in the field.

HODGDON POWER CO.
POB 2932
Shawnee Mission, KS   66201

Powders for reloaders; handloading manual for these excellent powders.

HORNADY MANUFACTURING
POB 1848
Grand Island, NB   68802

Hornady bullets of many designs. Noted for Interlock big-game bullet. Reloading tools.

HERCULES, INC.
Hercules Plaza
Wilmington, DE   19894

Excellent line of powders for reloaders.

JONAD CORPORATION
908 Center Rd.
Hinckley, OH   44233

Superior lubricants and other chemicals for shooters.

KIMBER OF OREGON
9039 SE Jansen Rd.
Clackamas, OR   97105

Semicustom rifles, mainly smaller caliber, and newly designed actions for custom rifles.

LEUPOLD & STEVENS
POB 688
Beaverton, OR   97075

Leupold scopes, Nosler bullets, full line of both, including compact scopes and the famous Partition bullet.

LYMAN PRODUCTS
Route 147
Middlefield, CT   06455

Reloading equipment of all kinds, plus many molds for various bullet styles in cast projectiles.

THE MARLIN FIREARMS COMPANY
100 Kenna Dr.
North Haven, CT   06473

Noted rifles, such as the Model 336 lever-action and Model 39 lever-action, also the 1895 in 45-70 and many 22-rimfire bolt-action models and semiautos.

MOSSBERG (O.F. Mossberg & Sons)
7 Grasso St.
North Haven, CT   06473

A lever-action 30-30, many 22 rifles, Model 1500 Mountaineer lightweight bolt-action in calibers from 222 through 338.

MOWREY GUN WORKS
800 Blue Mound Rd.
Saginaw, TX   76131

Muzzle-loaders on the Ethan Allen design.

N&W PRODUCTS
RR 1, Box 38
Philipsburg, PA   16866

Special cleaning/loading rods for muzzle-loader and modern.

NAVY ARMS CO.
689 Bergen Blvd.
Ridgefield, NJ   07657

Full line of muzzle-loaders, especially fine replicas of conical shooters; all accoutrements as well.

N.E. Industrial, Inc.
2516 Wyoming St.
El Paso, TX   79903

Many molds in a myriad of designs for cast bullets of various calibers. Also specialty molds for hard-to-get bullet sizes.

NORMA-PRECISION
POB 1327
Dayton, OH   45401

Norma rifle powders for reloaders and other quality products.

OEHLER RESEARCH
POB 9135
Austin, TX   78746

Chronographs.

OMARK INDUSTRIES
POB 856
Lewiston, ID   83501

Speer bullets and round balls, RCBS reloading equipment from dies to scales, special dies for wildcat calibers, rifle maintenance chemicals, gun cases, rods, and more.

OX-YOKE ORIGINALS
130 Griffin Rd.
West Suffield, CT   06093

Cleaning patches, lubes, jags, and more for rifle maintenance, muzzle-loader and modern.

OZARK MOUNTAIN ARMS
141 Byrne St.
Ashdown, AR   71822

Noted for fine replica of Hawken rifle; also Muskrat rifles and other muzzle-loaders in semicustom and custom manufacture.

PACHMAYER GUN WORKS
1220 S. Grand Ave.
Los Angeles, CA   90015

Fine rifle accessories and a new text, Extended Ballistics for the Advanced Rifleman *with data on factory ammo.*

REDFIELD
5800 Jewell Ave.
Denver, CO   80224

Complete line of rifle scopes in various sizes and designs, as well as spotting scopes for shooters.

REMINGTON ARMS COMPANY
POB 1939
Bridgeport, CT   06601

Rich line of rifles from 22 rimfire to 458 in various models, including easy-handling bolt-action lightweights.

RUGER (Sturm, Ruger & Co.)
30 Lacey Pl.
Southport, CT   06490

Known for its rifle designs from 22 rimfire up, semiautos and bolt-actions, including the Model 77 in many big-game chamberings.

SAVAGE INDUSTRIES, INC.
Springvale Rd.
Westfield, MA   01085

Famous for its Model 99 as well as a full line of rifles in various calibers.

SIERRA BULLETS
POB 3104
Santa Fe Springs, CA   90670

Known for its long line of accurate bullets. Big-game designs as well as target style.

THOMPSON/CENTER
POB 2426
Rochester, NH   03867

Popular muzzle-loaders in calibers 32 through 54. Also single-shot rifle with interchangeable barrels and scope sights with lighted reticle.

ULTRA LIGHT ARMS CO.
POB 1270
Granville, WV   26534

Ultra Light Arms produces an extremely light rifle of high accuracy in various calibers, with synthetic stock and special bolt-action, manufactured in the plant, with half-minute accuracy common in many samples.

UNCLE MIKE'S (Michaels of Oregon)
POB 13010
Portland, OR   97213

Scabbards, slings, swivels, ammo pouches, and a large assortment of tools for the rifleman.

U.S. REPEATING ARMS CO.
POB 30-300
New Haven, CT   06511

Winchester rifles from 22 rimfire to 458 Winchester, including the ever-famous Model 94 in a new modernized version.

WEATHERBY
2781 E. Firestone Blvd.
South Gate, CA   90280

The well-known line of bolt-action rifles in Weatherby calibers from 22 centerfire to the super-power 460 Weatherby cartridge. Scopes, too, and ammo.

WINCHESTER GROUP—Olin Industries
120 Long Ridge Rd.
Stamford, CT   06904

Ammunition of quality from this long-known company; everything from 22 rimfire up and in a great variation of loads.

WINCHESTER-SUTLER
Siler Rt. # Box 393-E
Winchester, VA   22601

Readyloads for muzzle-loader shooters, plus cleaning chemicals and other shooter products.

About the Author

Sam Fadala is an experienced outdoorsman and the author of eleven books on hunting, shooting, and the outdoors. Currently a technical editor for *Handloader* and *Rifle* magazines, as well as hunting editor for *Muzzleloader* magazine, he is a frequent contributor to *Gun World, Guns, Outdoor Life, Sports Afield,* and other periodicals. He lives in Casper, Wyoming, with his wife, Nancy, and their four children.